RAINCOAST BOOKS
www.raincoast.com

NG IN

MPANY'S

APITAL

Dear Reviewer / Producer,

*It is our pleasure to send you
the enclosed title(s).*

*Reviewers may reprint cover illustrations
to accompany the review with the following credit:*

COURTESY OF RAINCOAST BOOKS

Please send two copies of the review to:

Danielle Johnson
Publicity Department
9050 Shaughnessy St
Vancouver, BC
V6P 6E5
www.raincoast.com

*If you require any further information
or press materials, please call:*

Monica Bisal (604.323.7141)
Selina Rajani (604.323.7133)
David Leonard (416.934.9903)
or Danielle Johnson (604.323.7163)
in the Publicity Department.

INVESTING IN YOUR COMPANY'S HUMAN CAPITAL

---◄○►---

Strategies to Avoid Spending
Too Little—or Too Much

Jack J. Phillips, Ph.D.

AMACOM
American Management Association
New York • Atlanta • Brussels • Chicago • Mexico City • San Francisco
Shanghai • Tokyo • Toronto • Washington, D.C.

Library of Congress Cataloging-in-Publication Data

Phillips, Jack J., 1945–
        Investing in your company's human capital : strategies to avoid spending too little—or too much / Jack J. Phillips.
            p.   cm.
        Includes index.
        ISBN 0-8144-0853-2 (hardcover)
        1. Human capital.   I. Title.
    HD4904.7.P48   2005
    658.3'124—dc22

                                                                2005004099

Printing number

10   9   8   7   6   5   4   3   2   1

Contents

Acknowledgments

Much of the information, examples, scenarios, and case studies in this book come from our clients. We have been fortunate to work with a delightful group of individuals in some of the world's most successful organizations. In most cases, we learn more from our clients than they learn from us. To our special clients, we salute their contribution to this book. We owe them a huge debt of gratitude!

We have attempted to add to the significant work of Jac Fitz-enz. Jac has been a friend and a colleague for twenty-five years. During this time, he has served as a mentor—even serving on my Ph.D. dissertation committee some twenty years ago. I greatly admire Jac's work; he is truly *the* pioneer in human capital measurement. He developed the first HR benchmarking project and built on that experience at the Saratoga Institute to become the undisputed leader and pioneer in human capital measurement and monitoring. I will always appreciate his personal support and his great work for the human capital community.

Several individuals helped to shape this project. Thanks go to Katherine Sanner for transcribing the original manuscript; she approaches these challenges in a delightful and eager way. Francine Hawkins-Oliveira did a superb job of assisting with manuscript preparation and initial editing. As usual, our editorial manager, Joyce Alff, has done a wonderful job of making sure the manuscript meets the needs of the publisher. We appreciate the excellent support from Adrienne Hickey, editorial director at AMACOM Books, along with the confidence she has placed in us to develop this manuscript.

Finally, my highest appreciation goes to Patti—my partner, my friend, my colleague, my wife. Patti inspires me to always be my best and encourages me to take on these types of projects. She provided the finishing touches to make this an excellent publication. I will forever appreciate her support, friendship, love, and understanding.

The Fascination of Management

Over the past sixty-five years, since Chester Barnard wrote what many consider the first book on the role of the executive, there has developed a vast body of work on how to structure organizations and manage the people who populate them.[1] New models hit the market every year. Some attract significant attention while others pass with little notice.

In contrast, consider the field of accounting. There is not nearly as much ink spent on the entire field of finance as there is on just one management topic—leadership. Why is there such a plethora of work on the leadership and management of people? The reason is simple. Things like accounting systems are passive. Even sophisticated financial instruments are fixed. Bonds, derivatives, options, and all the rest don't change. They have a fixed price and maturity. The only time they move is when a human being makes a decision regarding them. The reason that management of people, as opposed to financial instruments, attracts so much attention is that people are variable, unique, and to some degree, at least for managers, a mystery.

INVESTING IN AN UNKNOWABLE

Anyone who has ever had the dubious task of managing a large number of people, say, three or more, will testify to the vagaries of the task. Just when one believes he or she can predict employee or managerial behavior something unexplainable, illogical, and even eerie can happen. Although human psychology has been thoroughly charted from many angles, it cannot account for or predict with a high degree of confidence the behavior of people in various situations. People vary from things in that people are affected by external forces. People are active. People make choices. People's needs, values, and attitudes change thereby driving unforeseeable behaviors.

This unpredictability makes investing in people a high-risk adventure. As Jack Phillips demonstrates, there are different value systems regarding the utility of employees. These tend to lead organizations to under- or over-invest in their human capital. The interesting point is that any value system can be effective. Still, the question remains for the executive who must make the investment decision, "Which approach is right for my organization now?" Phillips provides a thorough and basic explanation of human investment options from which an executive can make a better decision.

WHERE TO START?

Among many examples of how different companies invest, from a learning standpoint, the most telling are Dell and Nike. In both cases, these companies made a strategic decision early on as to what type of organizations they would be. Beyond low or high priced, they structured themselves in a unique way to deliver what they were best equipped to provide. Although both fall into the broad manufacturing category, they don't actually make something. In Dell's case they are an assembler with a just-in-time parts delivery modus operandi. Nike is a design and marketing company. All their products are manufactured by others. Based on these clear visions of themselves, they have been able to craft a human capital investment philosophy that has proven effective over the long term. Stating who we are, provides an answer to where and how we should invest.

STRUCTURING FOR INVESTMENT

In the forty plus years of my organization experience, I have found one flaw that affects the utility of human capital investment. The universal defect is called misalignment. Logically, there should be a clear, unbroken line of communication and resource allocation between the vision and brand commitment of the enterprise, its strategic initiatives and goals, functional objectives, individual targets, and resource management. I doubt there is an organization that is so tightly structured with the possible exception of the military. Even there, among the discipline and rigidity, there is a wiggle of room and waste. And that comes from idiosyncratic human behavior.

The value of an aligned enterprise is that the wiggle room is minimized. People, in all their glory and frailties, will always find a way around even a direct order. But alignment helps to direct uncalled-for innovation. If a company decides that customer service is the principal initiative, then investment decisions to strengthen service are obvious. This would include human capital programs to reduce unwanted turnover of talent, training in customer service, incentives to provide extraordinary service, and so forth.

BACKWARDS INVESTING

As far back as I can remember, many decisions to invest in human capital have been based on current fads and isolated problems. Rather than parallel organizational alignment, investments are often made because there is a people problem of some unexplained source. Wage and salary increases are an example. One large financial institution was suffering from intolerable turnover of key people. It called in a consultancy who delivered a plan to raise pay across the board along with a large invoice for their wisdom. A year after accepting this solution in search of a problem, the bank found itself with both unacceptable turnover and profit levels.

In other cases the commitment of funds is based on what the competition is thought to be doing. Even if a competitor is spending heavily on recruitment, compensation, or employee development that does not necessarily mean we should do it. This is the downside of benchmarking. Trying to emulate General Electric, Wal-Mart, IBM, or others is often a fool's errand, since we do not bear any resemblance to them. Staying true to our vision is the lesson.

AMERICA'S CULTURAL DEFECT

This country was founded by people who were revolutionaries. It didn't take any great deal of intelligence to decide that bowing to and supporting an absentee monarchy was an unfulfilling destiny. Less than one hundred years after the revolution, Americans flooded west in search of land and still more freedom. The results that we carry in our national DNA are what I call the gunslinger gene. If there's a problem, we out a metaphorical gun and shoot at the irritant without understanding it. In short, we don't cater to analyzin' pardner. As Nike says, "Just do it!" We admire action over contemplation. While other nations love to philosophize, we love to act. In many cases this works well, but in some high-risk situations we need to commit to a better understanding of the issue.

Before we make human capital investments we need to recognize that we do not operate in a closed system. The point in question is not isolated. It is affected by and affects productivity, service, quality, processes, systems, technology, finances, brand, and external forces. The complexity of such analysis is not appealing to many of us and the reward system often punishes us for taking time to do it right the first time. The quality movement of the 1980s greatly aided our manufacturing capability. Unfortunately, now that it is no longer in fashion and since it was aimed at process more than people, its lessons and values have eroded.

COMMITMENT AND HOW TO GET IT

For the human resource executive the ongoing problem has been to sell top management on human capital investments. The answer is extremely obvious: show return on investment. There are several books on the subject, including this one. At the end of the day, what does anyone want? They want their needs fulfilled. In the case of senior executives their needs revolve around the profitability, stability, and predictability of the enterprise. Human resource programs usually contribute to that, but seldom show how and how much.

The great truths of life are simple. One of the most basic is a derivative of the Golden Rule: Do unto others as you would have them do unto you. As applied to requests for investments in human capital, the point to be advanced is that this investment serves the needs of the organization and the executive better than another investment.

Let me offer a case to make this final point. There is a successful company in the food service industry that began to see a fall off in same store sales year to year. It was rightly diagnosed that the store manager needed more support in the way of employee relations in order to improve customer service. At first, the CEO agreed to a study of what employees needed from supervisors as a means of improving their service skills. Then, in a sudden change of heart he decided to bring in a couple of high-priced speakers to motivate the supervisors and to have successful store managers tell what they had done to retain customers. This is a classic entertainment ploy. But what can a store manager in the barrio of East Los Angeles learn from a Boston, Augusta, or Miami manager? In short, the cowboy gene took over and bought cheerleading over training—with predictable failure.

Investment decisions require analysis and alignment to reduce risk and yield optimal return on investment.

Jac Fitz-enz
Founder, Human Capital Source
Founder, Saratoga Institute
Author of *The ROI of Human Capital*

NOTE

1   Chester Barnard, *The Functions of the Executive* (Cambridge, Mass.: Harvard University Press, 1938).

INVESTING IN YOUR COMPANY'S HUMAN CAPITAL

Introduction

The Expanded Role of Human Capital

The press is exploding with coverage of human capital. The number of documents produced containing the term "human capital" increased from almost 700 in 1993 to over 8,000 in 2003. This growth coverage underscores the importance of human capital in the management of organizations. While the term human capital is commonplace in organizations, management's role in this important resource is often unclear. This lack of clarity lends to the mystery of human capital investment. Investment in this resource now commands much executive time and attention—requiring a concerted pursuit for the optimum investment level.

The concept of human capital is not new. It has been used by economists as far back as Adam Smith in the eighteenth century. Recently, economists who specialize in human capital theory have won Nobel Prizes; Gary Becker is perhaps the most well-known. Human capital theory explores the ways individuals and society derive economic benefits from investment in people. From an economist's point of view, human capital designates investments in improving competencies and skills[1]

The management community has a broader view of human capital. For example, *The Human Resources Glossary* by William R. Tracey, published by St. Lucie Press, defines human capital as the return an organization gains from the loyalty, creativity, effort, accomplishments, and productivity of its employees. It equates to, and may actually exceed, the productive capacity of machine capital and investment in research and development.

While there is no consistent definition among human resources professionals and executives, a consistent theme is that human capital represents the relationship between what organizations invest in employees and the emerging success. The *relationship* to success is the mystery. Imagine this scenario. The CEO of a $5 billion revenue company proposes to its board of directors that the company make an investment of $1.8 billion for the coming year. When describing the investment, the CEO is optimistic that the returns will follow, although he does not know how much of a return will be realized and cannot estimate it reliably. However, he is confident that the investment is needed and that it will pay off for the company. The executive explains that this investment, which represents almost 40 percent of its revenues, is based on benchmarked data that shows other firms are making similar investments. When the investment is made and the consequences develop, the CEO admits that the value of this investment may still be unknown; but, nevertheless, he asks for the money.

The investment in question is the investment in human capital. As extreme as it may seem, this scenario plays out in organizations each year as they invest in the workforce. Budget approvals are granted on faith, assuming that the requested investment will pay off.

There is far too much mystery about the connection between the investment in employees and the success that follows. This mystery causes some organizations to invest too much or too little—either of which can end in disaster. This book's first part sheds new light on how to determine the optimum investment in human capital. Each of its first five chapters presents a specific strategy to define the actual investment. Simply put, these strategies are:

1. Let others do it
2. Invest the minimum
3. Invest with the rest
4. Invest until it hurts
5. Invest when there is a payoff

These strategies explore the range of possibilities, enabling executives to examine all the options before deciding on a particular one.

STRUGGLES OF THE HUMAN RESOURCES FUNCTION

Despite the importance of human capital, the mysteries surrounding the investment in it and the lack of progress in measuring it accurately have led the human resources function to receive a fair amount of criticism in recent years. A decade ago, a major article in *Fortune* magazine essentially said the human resources function was irrelevant. Thomas Stewart, the respected *Fortune* editor who wrote the article, said the HR function should be eliminated and the essential transactions should be performed by other functions or outsourced altogether. As the author bluntly described the situation, "Chances are its leaders are unable to describe their contribution to value added except in trendy, unquantifiable, and wannabe terms . . . I am describing your human resource department and have a modest proposal: Why not blow it up?"[2] Stewart reached this conclusion, in part, because the HR staff had failed to show their value.

While some may argue that this is an extreme view, it served as a wake-up call for many HR managers who concluded that there must be a better way to show value in the organization—that is, to show the contribution of the human resource function. This book attempts to show how this is being accomplished.

As the critics ask for more measurement and accountability, the HR function has been under pressure, internally, to show value. Because the investment is quite large, many top executives ask the HR manager to show the contribution to avoid budget cuts. In some cases, managers must demonstrate contribution in order to increase the budget or fund specific projects. When those fundings occur, executives want to see the actual return. While executives are compassionate about people and the role of people in the organization, they are also driven by the need to generate profits, enhance resource allocation, build a successful, viable organization, and survive in the long term. The philosophy of caring for employees and striving for results appears to some to be counterintuitive. It is not. Caring and accountability work side by side, as demonstrated many times in this book.

The typical human resource reaction to this movement toward accountability has been unimpressive. The HR staff has resisted the call for additional accountability in many ways. Some argue that people are not widgets, that they cannot be counted in the same way as products. Some consider the issue of accountability inappropriate and maintain that we should not attempt to analyze the role of people with financial concepts. They argue that the issues are too "soft," and much of what is invested in human capital will have to be taken on faith; investments must be made based on intuition, logic, and what others have invested. Still other executives simply do not know how to address this issue. They are not as familiar with the organization as they should be, they lack the necessary knowledge in operations and finance, and they are not prepared for this type of challenge. Their backgrounds do not include assignments where measurement and accountability were critical to success. Some do not understand the measurement issue and what can and should be done.

There are signs that resistance is diminishing. A tremendous shift has occurred as human capital measurement and investment is taking on a new life. The following table illustrates this paradigm shift from the traditional view of human capital to the present view.

Human capital perspectives.

Traditional View	Present View
Human capital expenses are considered costs.	Human capital expenditures are viewed as a source of value.
The HR function is perceived as a support staff.	The HR function is perceived as a strategic partner.
HR is involved in setting the HR budget.	Top executives are increasingly involved in allocating HR budget.
Human capital metrics focus on cost and activities.	Human capital metrics focus on results.
Human capital metrics are created and maintained by HR alone.	Top executives are involved in the design and use of metrics.
There is little effort to understand the return on investment in human capital.	The use of ROI has become an important tool to understand the cause-and-effect relationships.
Human capital measurement focuses on the data at hand.	Human capital measurement focuses on the data needed.
Human capital measurement is based on what GE and IBM are measuring.	Human capital measurement is based on what is needed in the organization.
HR programs are initiated without a business need connected to them.	HR programs are linked to specific business needs before implementation.
Overall reporting on human capital programs and projects is input focused.	Overall reporting on human capital programs and projects is output focused.

These shifts are dramatic for the human resources function. They underscore how the HR department is moving from an activity-based process to a results-based process as additional data are being developed to show the importance of the human resources function and its connection with business results. In addition, as specific programs and projects are implemented, follow-up analyses show the success of these programs. This focus on the success of HR is illustrated in the second part of the book. It details the intuitive and empirical-based reasons for investing in human capital. Chapter 6 presents the logical and intuitive case. Chapter 7 makes the empirical case and highlights a myriad of studies that show the connection between investment in human capital and organizational performance. And chapter 8 presents data on the impact of specific human capital programs, using return on investment as a measure. This discussion logically follows the detailed descriptions of the strategies available in part one. However, it may be helpful to examine the three chapters of the second part before reading the various strategies.

The CFO's Perspective

When investments are described, the chief financial officer (CFO) takes notice. Traditionally, the CFO is involved in investment decisions such as predicting them up front, auditing the success afterwards, and reporting them to top executives, directors, and shareholders. However, the concept of human capital places the CFO in an awkward position. CFOs realize that companies spend much money in this area—the investment is heavy. Yet few finance executives understand it in any detail or know how the investment creates value for the business. A recent study conducted by *CFO Magazine* and Mercer Consulting showed that only 16 percent of companies surveyed say they have anything more than a moderate understanding of the return of human capital investments. This is a problem for most finance executives. It means that in most organizations, traditionally accepted finance and accounting practices cannot be used for their largest investment, human capital. Despite the CFO's emerging role as the chief resource allocator—helping direct the resources to the most productive investment—human capital remains a vast area of spending where the finance function offers little insight beyond guidance on what the company can afford to spend.[3]

Part three contains the latest update on the specific human capital measures and sheds light on this important issue. Its single, comprehensive chapter provides the top twelve categories of human capital measures that are now being monitored by best-practice global organizations. This part of the book presents enough detail so that executives can understand how these measures are developed and how they can be used.

The Last Major Source of Competitive Edge

Most executives realize the importance of human capital in some way. They understand the fact that the other sources of capital in the organization—finance, resources, technology, access to markets—are basically the same for most organizations. A firm does not necessarily have a unique access to the other types of capital. This means the success of most organizations rests on human capital, thus making it the last source of competitive advantage. Analysis of the most successful organizations will reveal the source of that success. It is the people and how the organization has attracted, maintained, motivated, and retained the knowledge, skills, and creative capability of those employees. There is no doubt that human capital is critical, but in today's environment, there must be a greater understanding of it in order to make the appropriate investment.

The fourth and final part of the book presents the executive's role in the process and details what executives should do and how they can influence the success of the investment in human capital and maximize the return on this investment. One chapter is devoted to creating and using a human capital scorecard. Another chapter focuses on the strategies and actions needed to improve support and commitment for human capital management.

BARRIERS FOR CHANGE

There are several important barriers for change. First is the failure to "walk the talk." In brochures, handbooks, manuals, and training programs, executives proudly proclaim employees as their greatest asset, but they do not necessarily walk the talk. They treat employees as expenditures and investments in employees as expenses in the organization, quickly trimming employee numbers to save costs and to drive revenue.

The second barrier is the ownership issue: Who actually owns human capital measurement, monitoring, and management? For many years, it has been the human resources function. Executives have turned to the HR staff to claim ownership for, and make improvements in, this important expenditure. However, for the human capital investment to be successful, it must be owned by the entire organization and managed by the senior executives. HR managers and senior executives must take a role in assuring that proper programs are in place, the appropriate measures are tracked, and improvement is generated. It also means that chief financial officers and operating executives all have important roles in this process to ensure that it functions properly. This is an important focus of this book.

The third major barrier to change is the failure to consider the dynamics of the human capital investment. A variety of programs and projects are often implemented with little or no concern about how they affect various parts of the organization. Sometimes, projects even work in conflict with each other. There has been too much focus on the activities, programs, and projects and not enough on the outcomes, integration, success, and ultimate accountability.

A fourth major barrier is the lack of appropriate measurements. Executives who are concerned about the human capital investment do not have a clear understanding of what can be measured, what should be measured, and what is being measured. More important, they fail to recognize the connection between those measures and the success of the organization; or if a particular program or project is implemented to improve a particular measure, how to develop accountability around that project or program.

This book explores these important barriers to change, outlines what can and should be done to monitor and measure the human capital function, and ensures that all executives are involved in some way.

Focus of the Book

With this background in mind, it is helpful to clarify the focus of this book. This unique book addresses four critical questions.

1. *How much should you invest in human capital?* This question is addressed in part one, which shows five specific strategies, ranging from "Let Others Do It" to "Invest as Long as There's a Payoff." Each strategy is discussed in detail, leaving the executive with a clear understanding of which strategy is best for the organization.
2. *What is the importance and value of the human capital function?* This is where the mystery often exists—what is the actual value? Part two of the book focuses on three issues. First, the value and importance of human capital is presented, based on logic, intuition, and anecdotal information. Often, this is what is discussed in the press. Another chapter focuses on the macrolevel studies that show the connection between investing in human capital and the actual payoff in profits and productivity. Finally, a third chapter examines specific microlevel measurements, where the value of human capital projects is measured at the ROI level.
3. *What are the current measures in the human capital area?* Part three contains a comprehensive chapter showing the twelve key measurement areas that best-practice organizations use to place a value on human capital. This is a compilation of many studies and shows what is currently being done.
4. *What is the executive's role in this process?* With two chapters, part four discusses this issue specifically. The first chapter focuses on creating the desired sets of measures, building the appropriate dashboard, scorecard, or other measurement scheme, and using it to drive improvement. The final chapter focuses on the executive's role in influencing, managing, and directing the human capital function.

Who Will Profit from Reading This Book?

Investing in Your Company's Human Capital is designed for five audiences. First, top executives, senior administrators, managing directors, agency heads, and others who serve in top leadership positions will find it to be an indispensable guide to navigate a complex and often confusing situation. These leaders must decide how much and when to invest in human capital.

Second, HR managers and HR executives who provide the leadership for human resource functions will find it a helpful resource. Although written for senior executives, the book supports the approach that most HR executives are already attempting to implement. Consequently, many HR executives will recommend this book to their top executives.

The third audience is the HR staff members who need to understand some of the key issues that are critical to top executives. They need to see the importance of their role in developing appropriate measures, generating solutions, enhancing processes, and delivering information for action. The HR staff is essential in the overall human capital measurement and monitoring processes.

The fourth audience is other managers in the organization, particularly those who must support the human capital direction of the organization. They often need convincing evidence that the organization is moving in the right direction and that the human capital investment level is being maximized in the organization.

Finally, consultants, researchers, and observers of human capital issues will find this book an important addition to the literature on human capital in organizations. They should find valuable insights into issues such as human capital measures, investment strategies, HR accountability, and return on investment (ROI).

NOTES

1   Stephen Bates, "Linking People Measures to Strategy," *Research Report R-1342-03-RR* (New York: The Conference Board, 2003).
2   Thomas A. Stewart, "Taking on the Last Bureaucracy," *Fortune*, January 15, 1996.
3   Don Durfree, *Human Capital Management: The CFO's Perspective* (Boston: CFO Publishing Corp., 2003).

PART ONE

How Much Should We Invest in Human Capital?

Five Strategies for Decision Making

CHAPTER 1

Let Others Do It

Some executives prefer to take a passive role when investing in employees, attempting to minimize or avoid the investment altogether. While highly dysfunctional, this approach has proven effective for some organizations, depending on their strategic focus. This chapter explores the strategy of letting others do the investing, the forces behind this strategy, and the consequences—both positive and negative—of implementing it.

THE BASIC STRATEGY

The strategy is simple—let other organizations provide the investment for human capital. The motivating forces behind this strategy are grounded in cost management—the organization is either looking to cut costs or to avoid costs related to employees. This focus on cost is often due to instability in an organization or industry or to an organization's need for expertise in a specific area; it is also often indicative of a company with a short-term focus or one that is just trying to survive.

This strategy is implemented using three different approaches. Some executives use one or more of these approaches, while others use all three. The first approach is to recruit fully competent and capable employees who will not need training to successfully function in the job. With this approach, little or no additional development is provided to enhance the employees' performance or to develop them for future jobs. The second is to use contract and temporary employees in place of permanent employees. This arrangement allows the organization to add and remove employees with little or no commitment to them, thus reducing the expense connected to employee acquisition and termination. The third approach is to use outsourcing to get the job done, often at lower cost. Taken to the extreme, employers can outsource most of the functions that would be performed by regular employees in the organization. Figure 1-1 presents an overview of this strategy.

Figure 1-1. The strategy and its rationale.

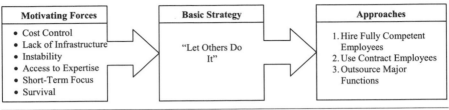

CASE STUDIES

Many organizations apply the "let others do it" strategy to avoid human capital cost. Consider, for example TechCo (not the actual name), a technology systems company that thrives in the market by recruiting capable staff from competing organizations. With this approach, TechCo recruiters eagerly lure systems engineers and specialists (trained and developed by their competitors), so they can hit the ground running. TechCo keeps track of the training programs of their competitors, particularly programs designed for new computer science and engineering graduates. Ideally, recruiters strike just as new graduates are completing a one-year training program. The new graduate, eager to take on "real" work, jumps to TechCo for a higher salary than he or she is being paid as a "trainee."

These new employees are expected to perform immediately when they are hired, are paid above-market wages, and are provided little additional development in their careers. There is an immediate impact on TechCo's bottom line due to their immediate level of performance. Although employees may not be committed for long periods of time, the company reaps rewards quickly because their investment in training, development, and employee socialization is virtually zero. Organizations such as this have a vulture-like reputation, preying on those companies that *do* invest in their employees.

KLA-Tencor Corporation uses this strategy. This $1.6 billion company with 5,500 employees is the leading producer of tools used to identify semiconductor defects during manufacturing. At KLA-Tencor, new employees hit the ground running (most of the time in sixty days or less from the time the company starts the hiring process). What does this mean for KLA-Tencor? Higher productivity, higher morale, and higher shareholder value[1]

The National Aeronautics and Space Administration (NASA) is an example of an organization that uses contract and temporary labor. During the past two decades, NASA has subcontracted much of their work. This approach reduces the full-time employee payroll, part of the U.S. government's move to reduce head count. Frequently, the work is handed off to employees of well-known contractors, with NASA paying a higher direct wage for the service. In a typical meeting at NASA, it is not unusual to find more contract employees in attendance than NASA employees, even though the purpose of the meeting might be to discuss an essential core issue. This practice has evolved over time and has proven to be the most effective approach for NASA to manage its overall employment costs.

Nike is a company that has taken outsourcing beyond that of most organizations. Nike essentially outsources all of their functions, maintaining only a very small corporate staff. Their basic philosophy is to minimize the number of employees and rely on outsource vendors and outsourced services to make the firm successful. Dell and Cisco Systems are two of many companies addressing the possibility that there are activities inside their firms that would best be carried out by someone else (outsourcing) or somewhere else (offshoring). Each company orchestrates a global supply chain for product delivery comprising many different companies and competencies—partnering, for example, with two electronic manufacturing services companies, Solectron Corp. (based in Milpitas, California) and Flextronics Corp. (headquartered in Singapore) for assembly, as well as FedEx and United Parcel Service for shipping.[2]

These examples underscore a trend of minimizing investment in employees or of avoiding the act of hiring employees altogether. There are many forces driving firms to pursue this strategy; however, two are critical. One is the cost of developing competent human capital and the other is the complex nature of HR development.

FORCES BEHIND THIS STRATEGY

Several factors motivate executives to pursue one or more of these approaches. The first and foremost issue is cost control or cost avoidance. Executives are concerned about (or are afraid of) the cost of employees. They know the cost of human capital is a major expenditure and they take a proactive approach to avoiding these costs.

Another factor is that to maintain a highly motivated, committed, and satisfied employee team, organizations are required to make a significant investment in employee systems and processes. Some executives cannot or will not build the infrastructure to support an effective employee group. For example, some executives will provide learning opportunities, yet will not invest in the support needed to transfer learning to the job, thus wasting resources.

A third motivating factor is the need to bring stability to the organization, particularly as expansion and decline occur in cyclical or seasonal industries. Letting others make the investment in human capital enables an organization to balance employment levels, address particular needs, and control costs at the same time.

A fourth factor is to use this strategy to tap into expertise that may be unavailable in the organization. It may not be feasible or practical to grow or develop the experience needed, so executives will take advantage of external expertise.

Still other executives pursue this strategy because they have a short-term focus instead of a long-term view. The company may not be as successful or as financially strong as it should be and executives try to maximize short-term successes.

Finally, in a related factor, some executives pursue this strategy for survival. They cannot afford to invest in human capital, at least not to the levels needed to build a successful team. They must rely on contract employees, outsourcing, or they hire only those who are fully competent. For an immediate period of time, this may be the only way to survive.

Collectively, these motivating forces drive executives to pursue one or more of the approaches outlined in this chapter. For some, it is the only strategic option available; for others it is the preferred strategy.

Cost of Competent Human Capital

Many of the organizations using this strategy realize that successful employee acquisition and maintenance is expensive. Table 1-1 shows the cost categories for acquiring and maintaining competent staff. Executives in some organiza-

Table 1-1. Total cost of developing and maintaining competent human capital.

- Recruiting
- Selection
- Indoctrination/Orientation
- Socialization
- Initial Training
- Continuous Development
- Career Management
- Competitive Pay and Benefits
- Reward Systems/Motivation
- Maintenance/Discipline
- Exit Costs

tions realize the magnitude of these expenses and have a desire to avoid part or all of them. Although the costs do not include the costs for office spaces and support expenses, they are still significant, often two to three times the annual pay.

Recruiting trained employees avoids the cost of indoctrination, orientation, socialization, initial training, development, and on-the-job training. Although the salary and benefits may be higher than that of less-skilled employees, other costs are avoided.

Executives hire contract employees in an attempt to avoid all of these costs, particularly the benefits and exit costs and some of the acquisition costs. Contract employees should be ready to work and make an immediate contribution. An example is in the U.S. Federal government. Contract employees are often not allowed to attend training courses offered to civil servants and military personnel. The total cost of a contract employee is usually less than what the organization is experiencing on a total cost basis.

Executives sometimes outsource major functions to lower their total cost of human capital. Most outsource providers offer needed services at lower cost. This often means that the pay and benefits structure may be less or the provider is using other ways to keep costs to a minimum.

The Nature of Human Resources Development

Organizations using this strategy realize that human resources development involves several different processes. Figure 1-2 shows the differences in training, education, and development in terms of the focus, cost, time for payback, and risk for payback of each. Within this context, it is easy to see that the low-risk, short-term payback approach focuses only on job-related skills and avoids the costs for education and development. Executives hiring competent employees avoid the costs of providing them with job-related skills as well as some of the costs of providing them with education and development.

Job-related training represents most of the traditional budget for developing human resources, providing an incentive to avoid this cost. When other

Figure 1-2. Human resources development issues.

	Focus	Costs per Employee	Time for Payback	Risk for Payback
Training	Job-Related Skills	Low	Short	Low
Education	Preparation for the Next Job	Moderate	Medium	Moderate
Development	Cultural Change and Continuous Learning	High	Long	High

education and development programs are scaled back or omitted, it is a plus. The result: organizations avoid a tremendous expense.

Recruiting Fully Competent Employees

This approach is controversial because it implies a negative view toward employee development. However, a few studies indicate that certain types of development can actually hurt organizational performance. One major study shows that training can actually decrease shareholder value, perhaps by training people into jobs that are not available, therefore, sending them to the competition.[3] Recruiting fully competent employees is basically an approach to control expenses and avoid delays. Employers investing heavily in education and development activities are often creating an opportunity to lose the individual, or they are investing in skills that may not be used. Either way, this investment represents a waste of resources for the organization.

Investing in job-related training is the low-risk option where a quick payback is ensured. MIT economics professor Lester Thurow touched on this problem in an article on building wealth.[4] He noted that rather than training employees, it is advantageous for companies to hire people who already possess the necessary skills. As Thurow indicates, when new knowledge makes old skills obsolete, firms want workers who already have that knowledge. They don't want to pay for retraining.

How does anyone rationally plan an educational investment? What skills would pay off? No one wants to waste investment funds on skills that will go unused. "You train, I'll hire" is the American way. This approach presents a dilemma for organizations, particularly from a public policy perspective. If organizations are not willing to train or develop employees, an underdeveloped or underprepared workforce may result. Companies who do train will be penalized through poaching, a practice traced back to fourteenth-century Germany. Poaching became a significant influence in modern-day corporate recruiting in the early 1990s, when conventional recruitment methods were deemed neither quick enough nor effective enough to find top talent.[5]

Sources

A challenge of the "let others do it" approach is to have adequate sources from which to select fully trained employees. Executives adopting this strategy often seek employees from successful organizations that:

- ❏ Enjoy a technological edge with high levels of investment in IT spending as a percent of revenue.

❑ Are leaders in the industry, usually in the top two or three organizations.

❑ Have achieved superior financial performance in terms of earnings before interest, taxes, depreciation, and amortization (EBITDA).

❑ Enjoy a reputation for innovation within the industry, particularly in the area where employees are being targeted for recruitment.

❑ Have significant growth in the industry in terms of revenue and productivity.

❑ Invest heavily in human capital, with a reputation for developing people.

Any or all of these criteria represent ideal targets for recruiting. The difficulty lies in enticing employees to leave these successful organizations.

Tactics

Tactics for implementing this approach are straightforward and involve several key challenges. One approach is to use innovative and successful recruiting processes, often going beyond the traditional processes of attracting employees. KLA-Tencor's approach places emphasis on netting the passive seeker by way of the Web.[6] Their methods of using the company's Web site to attract job seekers are critical to their success. For example, competitors visiting KLA-Tencor's Web site will see job opportunities scrolling in a banner window on the screen. The company attempts to brand itself as the employer of choice with stimulating and challenging opportunities and invites potential employees to share the excitement. This allows the company to attract and bring competent employees on board in minimum time.

KLA-Tencor is launching new products offered by its Web-solutions vendors that will improve efficiencies in HR's hiring practices, allowing the company to shave off valuable time during the offer-to-acceptance cycle for a new hire. The company has developed and is testing a job-profiling process that streamlines the hiring process and can also be used to assess employee development after hiring. Beyond just determining whether the employee has the necessary skills to do the job at the time of hire, the job-profiling process can also be used in workforce planning, performance assessment, compensation decisions, and leadership-development opportunities.

To attract and acquire passive job seekers, organizations need to pay higher-than-average salaries and benefits. Compensation may be higher than the organization's target for recruiting. Employees recruited through this approach must see immediate opportunities to entice them to leave their current position. They are often positioned as key employees in the organization and are given as much responsibility as they can absorb so they can make a contribution quickly and help others in the organization.

The challenge for a company is to build a reputation for high pay and achieve an image of the organization being a good place to work. This helps to attract and retain employees.

Disadvantages

This approach has disadvantages that make it undesirable for some employers. It is a short-term strategy for many organizations as they avoid the cost of initial development and training. Long-term employees may not be willing to stay with the organization; thus the stability of a tenured, long-term workforce is in jeopardy.

There are potential pitfalls to poaching. In most cases, poaching involves individuals who are not looking to change jobs. To entice them, a premium usually must be paid for their talent. Employers are likely to pay more for these candidates than they would for people recruited through other methods.

Another pitfall is that new talent is lured only by the promise of greater financial gain and does not give enough consideration to other employment needs. If people move only for the paycheck, chances are they will soon grow dissatisfied and regret accepting the position. This suggests a potential loss in effectiveness, and a disappointment for the new employer.[7]

Higher than desired turnover may result because of the organization's unwillingness to develop skills and invest in employees' careers. Continuous employee development is an important retention factor in today's organizations—even if it is in skills that they do not use immediately. Recent studies reveal a positive correlation between investing in new skills and retention. Thus, employees may desire to work for an organization that invests in them routinely.

Finally, with this approach, it may be difficult to develop a team-based organization necessary for success at some firms. Hiring fully competent, ready-to-compete employees may create mavericks and loners who pride themselves on their knowledge and skills but not as much on their ability to work as a supportive, helpful team member. Thus, the team-based approach that is often needed to provide seamless service to customers—internally and externally—may not exist.

Advantages

As we have noted, a principle advantage of this approach is the low cost of developing fully competent employees. Figure 1-3 shows the payoff of this

Figure 1-3. Comparison of the payoff for hiring fully competent employees rather than employees who must be trained on the job.

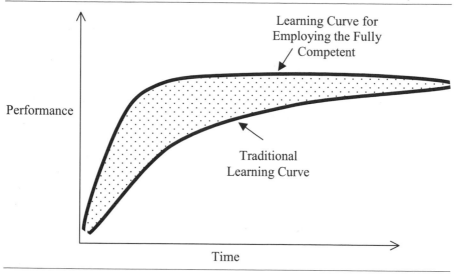

process. The lower line shows the traditional learning curve of an employee trained and developed in the organization. The upper line shows the learning curve for the individual recruited through a quick acquisition process where they are fully competent to perform the task. The shaded part of the curve shows the payoff in the first six to twelve months. Even if the recruit does not become a long-tenure employee, there is still a significant short-term payoff to the firm. This approach also avoids the disruptions and lag times in traditional education and development roles. For example, firms using the opposite strategy may employ MBA graduates direct from the university and then require their participation in a one- or two-year development program to prepare them for their assignments. Not only does this represent a tremendous expense, but there is also disruption and delay in the process of on-boarding talent.

EMPLOYING TEMPORARY AND CONTRACT WORKERS

Because of the high cost of attracting and retaining employees, particularly in cyclical industries, some firms resort to employing contract workers. This practice is based on the belief that the ups and downs of the employment cycle can create an unnecessary expense to acquire and remove employees. Table 1-2 shows all the cost categories related to turnover. In recent years, the departing costs have become significant, as employers spend large amounts on

Table 1-2. Turnover cost categories.

Orientation/Training Costs	Departure/Exit Costs
Pre-employment training	Exit interview costs
Development	Administration time
Delivery	Management time
Materials	Benefits termination/continuation
Facilities	Pay continuation/severance
Travel (if applicable)	Unemployment tax
Overhead (administration)	Legal expenses (if applicable)
	Outplacement (if applicable)
Orientation program	
Development	**Replacement Costs**
Delivery	
Materials	Recruitment/advertising
Facilities	Recruitment expenses
Travel (if applicable)	Recruitment fees
Overhead (administration)	Sign-up bonuses
	Selection interviews
Initial training	Testing/pre-employment examinations
Development	Travel expenses
Delivery	Moving expenses
Materials	Administrative time (not covered above)
Facilities	Management time (not covered above)
Time off the job	
Travel (if applicable)	**Consequences of Turnover**
Overhead (administration)	
Formal on-the-job training	Work disruption
Development	Lost productivity (or replacement costs)
Job aids	Quality problems
Delivery	Customer dissatisfaction
Management time	Management time
Overhead (administration)	Loss of expertise/knowledge

severance packages and services to enable employees to find other jobs. Coupled with the high cost of attracting and developing employees, these costs lead some organizations to conclude that a highly capable contract employee is the best option.

An organization's volatility is often a primary impetus for its decision to employ temporary and contract workers. When an organization's performance is in question, shareholders, customers, suppliers, and employees share the risk. Employees also recognize that volatility in the business means variability in their jobs and pay, as shown in figure 1-4.

Many organizations manage performance fluctuations by reducing the number of employees, often through a "last-in, first-out" process, which is frequently used by unionized organizations. This leaves the most senior employees, but not necessarily the most productive employees, on the payroll.[8]

Figure 1-4. Risk and its consequences.

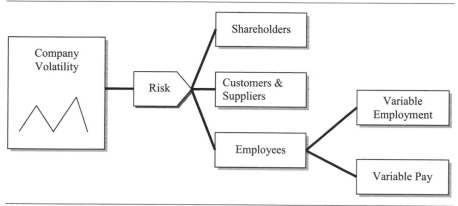

Source: Adapted from Nalbantian, et al., *Plan to Your Strengths* (New York: McGraw-Hill, 2004).

To avoid lowering employee morale by placing pay and jobs at risk and to prevent a loss of productivity, temporary and contract workers are hired.

Temporary employment is not limited to lower-level clerical, technical, or professional employees. Executives find opportunities in the temporary help arena. The largest poultry producer in the western United States found itself in need of technical expertise. Foster Farms, a 10,000-employee, privately held company headquartered in Livingston, California, had been plagued with technical problems while attempting for four years to convert its supply chain into an integrated $28 million SAP/ERP platform. Specialists contracted to implement the system charged the company $800,000 a month; as the problems mounted month after month, so did the bills. Instead of hiring a consultant or initiating a search for a technically skilled permanent CIO, Foster Farms chose a different model. It sought an experienced corporate leader with strong technical expertise and a flair for steering troubled companies back on course, a chief willing to come in-house, but only for as long as it took to get the job done. What Foster Farms wanted was a temporary executive. The company hired a seasoned CIO executive who had served at the corporate level for more than twenty years at companies such as True Value Hardware and The Stride Rite Corporation.[9]

A temporary person with the appropriate skills starts out with a clean slate and can be more efficient than those workers with a history at the company. When a company is in urgent need for skills, the person who steps in should be someone from outside rather than a reassigned in-house employee. Otherwise, jealousy and infighting can thwart any progress. Another practical reason for bringing in a person from the outside is that often the skills required for a rapid transformational change simply do not exist within the organization.

Tactics

Several tactics are important for success with this approach. First, it is important for the organization to secure great sources and work with them on a routine basis so that the best possible contract employees can be obtained. This relationship needs to be developed and nurtured. There are many sources for contract employees. For administrative and clerical employees, a variety of temporary services can provide quality employees, often at reasonable rates, to staff certain functions. In some professional areas such as accounting, engineering, and IT, professional agencies are available that specialize in a particular profession. Other agencies are also industry specific. For example, Lockheed-Martin, a leader in the aerospace industry, hires contract service employees for a variety of jobs through professional firms. These firms usually follow major government contracts from one company to another and offer contract services. Another alternative is to utilize leasing companies, which provide temporary employment. These companies become the employer and lease the employees to the organization. This concept is usually implemented in smaller companies that attempt to avoid the administrative and legal costs associated with maintaining employees.

Second, organizations should make contract employees as much a part of the team as possible. This helps create a cohesive unit as the contract employees interact with the permanent staff. Leaving contract employees out of key meetings, isolating them from permanent staff, and treating them differently will usually destroy the opportunity for teamwork.

A third consideration for success with temporary employees is to have them establish a clear set of goals at the beginning of their assignment. Without concrete deliverables, such as increasing performance by a specific percentage in a set period, temps can find themselves spending valuable time struggling to gain support for their ideas rather than just working to implement them. Still, experts say that even with industry expertise, fresh eyes, and clear goals, the early days of a temporary assignment can prove trying. Success is contingent on blending immediately, and contract employees must be perceptive enough to sense potential interpersonal trouble spots and deal with them quickly and smoothly.

Finally, organizations must show the cost versus the benefits of contract employees. Some employees (and managers) question the use of contract and temporary employees. They may think there is a sinister motive to eliminate jobs. Executives should show that hiring temporary staff enables the organization to maintain a stable, permanent group of employees, providing stability to the workforce and saving the company money.

Disadvantages

This approach has several disadvantages. It is an approach chosen by some organizations while they are trying to develop a more stable workforce to ensure short-term financial success. However, relying heavily on contract employees can generate morale problems, as the permanent employees feel that the best way to receive more compensation is to separate from the organization and be employed as a contract worker.

To better appreciate the kinds of problems that result when companies focus on temporary employment, consider the story of a healthcare provider referred to here as HealthCo.[10] HealthCo was struggling to reduce its costs as were other companies in the healthcare industry; insurance and government payouts were reducing reimbursements. The only way HealthCo could maintain profitability was to maintain their level of spending in some areas and cut spending in others. One of the cost-reduction options explored was to reduce its employee outlays—a major segment of its total cost structure—by focusing on the way it staffed its facilities, especially with regard to the use of part-time employees, to the amount of overtime worked, and to the managerial head count. After some deliberation, HealthCo decided to reduce overtime, to reduce the number of managers in its facilities, and to replace many full-time employees with temporary, part-time workers who cost less per hour in base wages and received fewer or no benefits.

The decision to rely on temporary, part-time employees appeared to give HealthCo both greater flexibility and lower costs. The schedules of temporary workers could be shifted with rising and falling patient censuses, and the pay and benefits of the temporary employees would be measurably less than those of their full-time counterparts.

Unfortunately, the company understood only half the equation. While it recognized its reduction in wage costs, HealthCo had data representing the contribution its staffing decisions had had on the organization. With the help of Mercer Consulting, it found that excessive use of temporary, part-time employees had actually hurt HealthCo's overall productivity.

The use of temporary and contract workers often generates an "us and them" mentality that diminishes team spirit. Contract employees are sometimes excluded from certain projects and issues, inhibiting the collaboration often needed. Organizational loyalty is seldom displayed by contract workers when compared to their permanent counterparts. Contract workers realize they can be replaced at any time; subsequently, there is no solid connection to the organization.

Finally, the accountability and commitment needed in the workforce may not be there with contract employees. Contract workers may feel that they do not have to perform—and certainly may not perform at the level necessary for top-notch organizations.

Advantages

Cost containment and stability are the huge payoffs of using temporary and contract workers. The primary advantage is cost control, enabling organizations to lower recruiting and departure costs of employees. In some cases, the total compensation costs may be reduced because contract employees often have a smaller benefits package. Another advantage is that contract employees allow organizations to manage the ups and downs caused by the cyclical nature of an industry, the economic variations, or the seasonal fluctuations. This provides stability for the permanent workforce, with contract workers coming and going as needed. Another advantage is the skill and expertise of some contract employees. Contract employees may be able to complete tasks or assignments that regular employees cannot accomplish. Finally, using contract workers can help circumvent some of the costs of benefits and compliance. Regulations aimed at providing benefit structures for employees who are terminated often apply to employees and not contract workers, although the lines are becoming blurred.

OUTSOURCING FUNCTIONS

Recognizing the high cost of maintaining employees, particularly on a long-term basis, some organizations have resorted to outsourcing to keep their employee head count to a minimum. This approach essentially creates a small number of employees and a tremendous network of subcontractors providing services that regular employees provide in other firms or that regular employees previously performed. Outsourcing usually costs less and sometimes brings in much needed expertise and specialization.

Targets for Outsourcing

When a company wants to ferret out costs and promote innovative management, all parts of the enterprise are fair game. Targets for outsourcing should be carefully selected and usually involve three general areas. As shown in figure 1-5, the first area is the nonessential activities, which are the easiest to outsource with little risk. Ideal targets are functions such as security, maintenance, cafeteria services, and facilities management. These can often be contracted for a much lower cost than when maintained as permanent functions of the organization. This approach is a "no-brainer" for many organizations.

The next group represents the non-core but essential parts of the organization and includes functions such as information technology, payroll, learning and development, and a variety of administrative support functions. Although more expensive than nonessential functions, these services can usually be outsourced at lower costs as well. There are many success stories for this type of outsourcing. One of the most significant is the outsourcing of payroll. In the last two decades, huge payroll processing firms have been developed to provide these services more efficiently and effectively than can be operated in-house.

The last group represents core processes. Sometimes, outsourcing core strategies follows the basic strategy of the organization. For example, consider Dell Computer. Dell manufactures nothing; it purchases parts from an array of suppliers, assembles them into computers, and sells them direct to consumers. To do this, it is wired into its suppliers and customers to the extent that it does not order a part until the equipment into which the part will be integrated is already sold.[11] Dell's basic strategy is *not* to be in the business of making parts. Outsourcing can go even beyond this, however, to almost every part of the business. This is true with Nike, where the company makes nothing and has outsourced even the marketing function. Thus, the company keeps both its head count and its employee human capital investment low.

Beyond the question of what is core, many companies are simply asking themselves which of their processes are location-independent and which locations would be best for those processes. HSBC, for instance, carries out credit card and loan processing from India; Allstate Corporation and Prudential Property & Casualty Insurance Company have application designers and call-

Figure 1-5. Outsourcing areas.

Functions	Difficulty	Costs	Risk
Nonessential	Easy	Low	Low
Essential, non-core	Moderate	Moderate	Moderate
Core	Difficult	High	High

center personnel working out of Ireland. Lost your luggage? Delta Airlines' India-based call-center staff will help you find it.

When companies decide on their outsourcing strategy, including the basis of core competencies and optimal location, the question of optimal governance of these processes arises. For some companies, it is attractive to contract with local service providers in India, Ireland, Malaysia, and elsewhere. British Petroleum, for example, has relationships in different parts of the world to take advantage of the competition among the service providers. The main advantages of this approach are flexibility and scale of operations. But this flexibility creates the need for investments in relationship management. (BP, for instance, has developed a set of Web-enabled tools for effective governance, including performance dashboards and stakeholder maps for managing relationships.)

Even the human resources function is subjected to outsourcing. The 1999 decision by BP to outsource HR administration to the startup Exult Inc. was a bold move that has triggered growth in the number of full-service human resources outsourcers (HROs). Others companies building positions as full-service HROs include companies well-known in IT outsourcing, such as Accenture, and established HR consultants, such as Hewitt Associates Inc. and Fidelity Investments. The "soup-to-nuts" HROs handle HR-process design and provide a full range of HR administrative services—payroll and benefits management, compensation, planning, recruiting, training of administrators, and management relocations. By offering integrated services, these HROs avoid the difficulties of coordinating and managing multiple vendors. Similar to IT outsourcers, the HROs have a level of expertise and a scale of operations that allow them to achieve efficiencies and service levels their customers cannot match.[12]

Tactics

Four important issues are essential for successful outsourcing. The first is to identify the appropriate targets for outsourcing, carefully analyzing the difficulty, cost, and risks, and consider the short-term as well as the long-term consequences. Selecting the wrong function or underestimating the cost, difficulty, and risks can be disastrous.

The second issue is to outsource for multiple reasons, not just to lower employee costs. Effective outsourcing can bring a variety of improvements, ranging from an increase in services to adding capability that does not currently exist in the organization. Outsourcing solely to avoid employment costs may not be viable in the long term.

Third, organizations should plan implementation carefully to enable a smooth transition. Planning the assignments, preparing the team, communicating regularly, and following through on action items will enable an effective implementation. Ineffective implementation can destroy the advantages of outsourcing. Many outsourcing projects fail because of implementation miscues.

Fourth, organizations should develop an appropriate measurement system to monitor the success of outsourcing with a long-view perspective. When the measures indicate a problem, corrective action can be taken. Measures should reflect the short and long term and include productivity, quality, time savings/efficiencies, costs, employee satisfaction, and customer satisfaction.

Disadvantages

This outsourcing approach comes with several disadvantages. While there may be lower costs in the short term, sometimes outsourcing results in problems in the long term. Service delivery, morale, bottlenecks, and inconveniences sometimes are generated through malfunctioning outsourcing arrangements. While the initial advantages look good on paper, the long-term realities can be disastrous. The services provided by the outsource supplier may not be at the same level as that achieved by in-house employees. The outsource supplier may not have the interest of the organization in mind at all times and may not be committed to provide the quality of service for which the organization is known. Finally, there is less control with outsourcing. Even though service-delivery agreements are in place, the employer may lack control over the outsourced supplier and be unable to take corrective action quickly.

Advantages

The principal advantage to outsourcing is cost savings. Employers using this strategy report reduction in the overall employment cost compared to what they would have incurred had they staffed the function themselves. Sometimes these firms have developed cumbersome bureaucracies that are difficult to manage. Not only are direct employee costs lowered, but the number of employees can often be reduced through an outsourcing arrangement, adding to the employee cost-saving advantage. Another important advantage is that there are fewer employee problems and issues to address. Employee concerns can demand a tremendous amount of time, even at executive levels. Providing the support and processes necessary to effectively address these concerns is beyond what some companies are willing to invest. Most of this can be completely avoided with the outsourcing arrangement. Some companies outsource to avoid restrictive work rules inherent in unionization. Outsourcing also can provide increased productivity or the same levels of productivity with fewer employees. Finally, outsourcing provides executives the focus they need to drive the critical parts of the operation. It allows them time to concentrate on more important issues and processes.

Summary

This chapter explored a human capital investment strategy that is often considered dysfunctional—"let others do it." While there may be a short-term benefit where survival is an issue, many firms are successfully using the approaches described here to keep their business viable even on a long-term basis. Hiring fully competent employees, using contract or temporary employees, or outsourcing major parts of the organization are the three basic approaches explored in this chapter. These three approaches represent serious alternatives to minimize human capital investment and ensure that it is not excessive or beyond what the organization can afford. The advantages and disadvantages of each were discussed, leaving possibilities for almost every firm.

Notes

1   Bruce N. Pfau and Ira T. Kay, *The Human Capital Edge: 21 People Management Practices Your Company Must Implement (or Avoid) to Maximize Shareholder Value* (New York: McGraw-Hill, 2002).

2   N. Venkat Venkatraman, "Offshoring Without Guilt," *MIT Sloan Management Review*, Spring 2004, pp. 14–16.

3   Bruce N. Pfau and Ira T. Kay, *The Human Capital Edge: 21 People Management Practices Your Company Must Implement (or Avoid) to Maximize Shareholder Value* (New York: McGraw-Hill, 2002).

4   L. Thurow, "Building Wealth: The New Rules for Individuals, Companies, and Nations," *Atlantic Monthly*, June 1999.

5   Penny Haw, "Poaching Employees from Rivals Has Its Pitfalls," *Business Day*, August 17, 2004, p. 26.

6   Bruce N. Pfau and Ira T. Kay, *The Human Capital Edge: 21 People Management Practices Your Company Must Implement (or Avoid) to Maximize Shareholder Value* (New York: McGraw-Hill, 2002).

7   Penny Haw, "Poaching Employees from Rivals Has Its Pitfalls," *Business Day*, August 17, 2004, p. 26.

8   Haig R Nalbantian, Richard A. Guzzo, David Kieffer, and Jay Doherty, *Play to Your Strengths: Managing Your Internal Labor Markets for Lasting Competitive Advantage* (New York: McGraw-Hill, 2004).

9   Gretchen Weber, "Temps at the Top," *Workforce Management*, August 2004, pp. 35–38.

10   Haig R. Nalbantian, Richard A. Guzzo, David Kieffer, and Jay Doherty. *Play to Your Strengths: Managing Your Internal Labor Markets for Lasting Competitive Advantage* (New York: McGraw-Hill, 2004).

11   Mark Hurd and Lars Nyberg, *The Value Factor: How Global Leaders Use Information for Growth and Competitive Advantage* (Princeton, N.J.: Bloomberg Press, 2004).

12   Edward E. Lawler III, "HR on Top," *Strategy + Business*, 2004, 35, pp. 20–25.

CHAPTER 2

Invest the Minimum

The previous chapter examined organizations that let others do the investing in human capital, this one looks at those that invest only the minimum in human capital. A few organizations adopt this strategy by choice; others do it out of economic necessity. Either way, this is a viable option for many organizations. This chapter explores the issues involved in selecting and using the strategy of minimum human capital investment and examines its challenges, consequences, and advantages. This strategy has several hidden land mines that can be detrimental to some organizations in the long term if not recognized.

THE BASIC STRATEGY

This strategy invests the very minimum in employees in every aspect of employee expenses: it sets salaries near the minimum-wage level or very low in the industry, provides benefits at a level just beyond what is legally required, invests in training only at the job skills level with almost no development and preparation for future jobs, and offers little in the way of employee-support services. Organizations adopting this philosophy operate in a culture that is sometimes reflective of the industry and the competitive forces in it. These organizations experience high turnover and usually adjust processes and systems to take into account the constant churning of employees.

This strategy should not be confused with efficient resource allocation. Obviously, efficiency is gained by keeping costs at a minimum. The strategy presented here is a deliberate effort to dispense only the minimum investment in human capital. This strategy is about facing the inevitable in some situations, or making a deliberate attempt to invest as little as possible in employees.

30

CASE STUDIES

The landscape is littered with examples of companies that make the minimum investment in their employees. While this strategy is common in many small businesses, it is also a deliberate choice in many large businesses. For example, Wal-Mart, the world's largest company, is noted for its low wages and a sparse benefits package. Wages are low enough to make *other* companies' workers go on strike. The employee relations' climate at Wal-Mart has been under scrutiny and examination for many years. Wal-Mart's violation of the Fair Labor Standards Act concerning overtime, discriminatory treatment of employees, and other related issues dominates the headlines. Wal-Mart has carved out a strategy to invest the very minimum in its employees but still try to make itself an attractive place to work. It is a model that has paid off quite well, as the company is very profitable and its growth is incomparable.

Wal-Mart casts their jobs in almost missionary terms—"to lower the world's cost of living"—and in this, they have succeeded spectacularly. One consultancy estimates that Wal-Mart saves consumers $20 billion a year. Its constant push for low prices, meanwhile, puts the heat on suppliers and competitors to offer better deals.

If a company achieves its lower prices by finding better and smarter ways of doing business, then yes, everybody wins. But if it cuts costs by cutting pay and benefits, then not everybody wins. Just as its "Everyday Low Prices" benefit shoppers who have never come near a Wal-Mart, there are mounting signs that its Everyday Low Pay (Wal-Mart's full-time hourly employees average $9.76 an hour) is hurting some workers who have never worked there. For example, unionized supermarkets in California, faced with studies showing a 13 to 16 percent drop in grocery prices after Wal-Mart enters a market, have been trying to slash labor costs to compete, and thus they triggered a protracted strike. Where you stand on Wal-Mart, then, seems to depend on where you sit. From the consumer's standpoint, Wal-Mart is good; from a wage-earner's standpoint—maybe not so good.[1]

Other organizations have not been as fortunate as Wal-Mart. A case in point clearly exemplifies the problems that can be created when there is minimal investment in human capital. Service Merchandise Company, founded in the early 1900s, provided a range of household products, personal items, and gifts. Service Merchandise's business model made it possible for customers to select items for purchase with little or no input from the sales staff and then their purchases were delivered on a conveyer belt as they left the store. Part of the Service Merchandise strategy was to invest the very minimum in employees by offering low wages and few benefits, resulting in an employee turnover rate exceeding 100 percent for full-time, permanent employees.

After years of dismal results with mounting debt, Service Merchandise changed the executive team. The goal of the new president was to change the business model to make the firm more responsive to the customer, provide products that attracted more interest, and provide a more efficient system to guide customer purchases.

As the company attempted to change its business model, they made a deliberate attempt to address the turnover problem. The actual cost of turnover was undervalued and underappreciated by the senior management team. A study was conducted to develop the annual cost of turnover for the permanent staff in an effort to get management attention. The results were staggering. When the study began, the human resources staff had estimated the annual cost of turnover to be in the $10–12 million range. When the study was completed, the total figure came in at $180 million! Neither the HR staff nor the management team had any idea of the extent to which turnover was devastating the business and influencing the business model as well as hurting customer satisfaction.

Unfortunately, Service Merchandise went into bankruptcy before they could completely change their business model. As one Wall Street analyst stated, "With another $100 million they could have survived long enough to make the transition."

This story highlights the tremendous cost of turnover that is almost always inherent in organizations investing the minimum in its human capital. The signs of under-investing are obvious: the company offers the lowest wages in its industry and a benefits package offering little beyond the legal requirements. There are literally no frills with this type of organization. Consequently, there is usually high turnover. Under-investing is inherent in some industries, particularly restaurants (for example, the fast food industry) and retail stores. Competition is fierce and prices are constrained to the point that executives are forced—at least in their thinking—to invest as little as possible in their people.

FORCES DRIVING THE STRATEGY

The primary forces driving this strategy can be put into three words—cost, cost, and cost! Some organizations work in such a low-cost, low-margin environment that a minimal human capital investment appears to be the only option. These low margin businesses, such as Wal-Mart, operate on volume to make significant profits. Competition forces this issue in many cases. Competing organizations in a particular business, such as the restaurant industry or retail store chains, might not be able to offer significant differences in pay and benefits. The range from the lowest to the highest is narrow in these industries and the benefits package may vary only slightly.

Minimum-wage employees are a fact of life in the business world. In the United States, 2.1 million employees earn wages at or below the federal minimum wage level. Table 2-1 presents a profile of these minimum-wage workers.

In some cases the minimum investment strategy is adopted out of the need to survive—the organization must invest as little as possible to survive, particularly in the short term. These organizations are often managed by executives who see little value in their employees and view them only as a necessary cost to deliver the service. They consider employees to be dispensable, easily recruited, and quickly discharged if they are not performing appropriately.

THE COST OF TURNOVER

Organizations investing only the minimum amount in human capital usually do not understand the true cost of turnover. They see the direct cost of recruiting, selection, and initial training, but do not take the time to understand

Table 2-1. Profile of minimum-wage workers in the United States.

Demographic Profile of Minimum-Wage Workers

- 72.9 million American workers are paid hourly rates. Of these, **2.1 million** earn wages at or below the federal minimum wage of $5.15/hour.
- Slightly more than half of workers earning minimum wage or less were **under age 25** and one-quarter were **between ages 16 and 19**.
- About **4 percent of women** paid hourly rates reported **wages at or below** the prevailing federal minimum, compared to 2 percent of men.
- Three percent of **white hourly workers** earned $5.15 or less, roughly the same proportion as blacks and Hispanics.
- **Never-married workers** were more likely to earn minimum wage or less than people who are married.
- **Part-time workers** were much more likely to be paid less than $5.15 an hour than their full-time counterparts.
- Almost two-thirds of all low-wage workers in 2003 were in **service occupations**, mostly food-service jobs.
- Among geographic regions, the **West had the lowest proportion** of hourly workers with earnings at or below minimum wage (about 2 percent), while the **South had the highest** (about 4 percent).

Source: Current Population Survey Bureau of Labor Statistics, 2003.

the other impacts. Both the direct and indirect cost of turnover must be taken into consideration.

The Impact

As illustrated in the Service Merchandise case study, the impact of turnover is both undervalued and underappreciated. Rarely is the total cost of turnover calculated in organizations investing minimally in their human capital. When the cost is estimated, it is often underestimated. More importantly, estimations of the total cost are not communicated throughout the organization, leaving the management team unaware of the potential costs. If turnover is a problem, the costs are always significant. In some cases, the actual impact can be devastating and can result in the organization's demise.

The Total Cost

The total cost of turnover involves both the direct and indirect costs. Figure 2-1 lists the costs in the sequence in which they occur. This figure suggests that there are many different costs, some of which are never known with certainty but can be estimated if enough attention is directed to the issue. When the total costs are calculated, it is often expressed as a percent of annual pay for a particular job group.

Table 2-2 shows the cost of turnover expressed as a percentage of annual pay for selected job groups. As this table shows, these costs, arranged in a hierarchy of jobs, are significant. The data for this table were obtained from a variety of research studies, journals, and academic publications where professors and consultants report the cost of turnover from their work. Also represented are data from publications for industries where turnover has become an issue and organizations in these industries have taken the time to calculate the fully loaded cost of turnover. The data also come from private databases of organizations working with this important issue as well as from professional organizations where turnover is an issue in the profession, such as nurses, truck drivers, or software designers. Collectively, these external studies provide a basis for understanding the total cost of this important issue and understanding the impact of turnover is the first step toward tackling it.

When the phrase *fully loaded cost* is used, it is important to consider what goes into those costs. The turnover costs in Table 2-2 contain the direct cost categories as well as those that are indirect. A complete list of cost categories is included in Table 2-3. This table contains a list of cost items that can be derived directly from cost statements and others that have to be estimated.

Figure 2-1. The turnover cost categories.

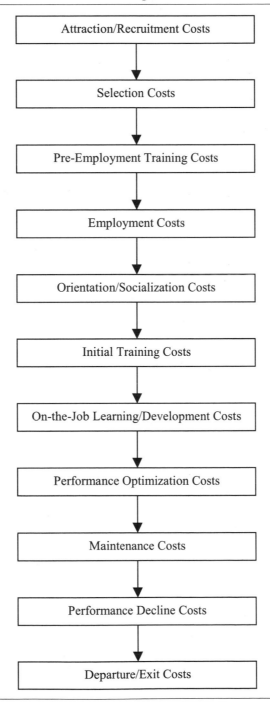

Table 2-2. Turnover costs for selected job groups.

Job Type/Category	Turnover Cost Ranges (Percentage of Annual Wage/Salary)*
Entry level—hourly, unskilled (fast food worker)	30–50
Service/production workers—hourly (courier)	40–70
Skilled hourly—(machinist)	75–100
Clerical/administrative (scheduler)	50–80
Professional (sales representative, nurse, accountant)	75–125
Technical (computer technician)	100–150
Engineers (chemical engineer)	200–300
Specialists (computer software designer)	200–400
Supervisors/team leaders (section supervisor)	100–150
Middle managers (department manager)	125–200

*Percentages are rounded to reflect the general range of costs from studies. Costs are fully loaded to include all of the costs of replacing an employee and bringing him/her to the level of productivity and efficiency of the former employee.

Table 2-3. Turnover cost categories.

Exit cost of previous employee	Lost productivity
Recruiting cost	Quality problems
Employee cost	Customer dissatisfaction
Orientation cost	Loss of expertise/knowledge
Training cost	Supervisor's time for turnover
Wages and salaries while training	Temporary replacement costs

Essentially, those on the left side of the table can easily be derived while those on the right side typically have to be estimated. When considered in total, excessive turnover is expensive and very disruptive.

Identifying and Supporting the Minimum

Wages

Setting a minimum investment strategy requires the same thought and rationale as that required for setting other investment levels. Obviously, if paying the legal minimum wage becomes the strategy, little thought goes into the process. However, most organizations attempt to pay above the legal minimum wage, while still limiting wages to a level they can afford. The wage must be high enough to attract reasonably qualified candidates for the job; otherwise, the job goes unfilled.

Benefits

When offering a benefits package, it is helpful to include as many of the low-cost items as possible so the package is complete. This often includes benefits such as accidental death and dismemberment and term life insurance, which can be inexpensive, but is important to many potential employees. Medical and retirement plans are sometimes made available for employees to purchase. The company may contribute little, if any, of the costs. Also, supplemental benefits plans with a wide variety of options can be offered at discounts to employees, resulting in no cost to the employer. When presented in total, the benefits package appears to be a costly investment in the employee. In reality, the investment is minimal.

Employee Support System

At a low investment level, with intense focus on cost control, it is difficult to provide resources to build an adequate employee support system. However, in an attempt to avoid turnover, there must be some basic levels of support, such as nonunion grievance procedures, employee assistance plans, and HR staff members who can provide assistance and basic counseling. With a support system, employees perceive a sincere investment in employee concerns on the part of the executives. Without a support network, employees perceive an organization that has no concern about the individuals who contribute to its success. Consequently, they may leave.

Tactics

The tactics involved in implementing this strategy are straightforward. Recruiting is the key challenge, particularly when offering low wages and benefits. Innovative recruiting efforts must be employed, highlighting the many positive attributes of the company. If the company has a positive image (such as Starbucks), recruiting can build on the image of the organization and actually be included as a part of the in-store policies and practices. The strengths of the organization must be highlighted in the recruiting efforts. If possible, security and stability must be emphasized. For a fast-growing chain such as Starbucks, stability and security are important issues that can be underscored. This is particularly helpful where jobs come and go in other organizations.

Employing the disabled is another potential tactic. Pizza Hut has employed thousands of individuals with disabilities over the last decade and a half, and turnover among them is dramatically less than turnover among other new hires. Pizza Hut saves millions of dollars from this low turnover. On top of that, it receives millions of dollars in Federal tax credits for hiring job candidates with disabilities. There are about 54 million Americans with disabilities. Most do not have jobs; most want jobs; most deserve them; most can do them. This opens up a big opportunity for organizations that can make only minimum investment in human capital.

Clothing retailer Eddie Bauer employs 6,200 hourly wage earners at 439 stores nationwide. Most employees are young—between twenty-five and forty years old, and like other retail cashiers and clerks throughout the country, make less than ten dollars an hour. They often occupy the vast economic category known as the working poor. At Eddie Bauer, these frontline employees make up the overwhelming majority of the company's 7,200-member workforce. They are the first and primary people customers come in contact with.[2]

The store recognizes the benefits of rewarding lower-wage employees with something extra in their paychecks. In an effort to energize its legions of hourly wage earners and maintain a committed workforce, the store launched a financial-reward program in 1998 that gives workers an additional 6.5 percent of their base pay if store goals are met. That amounts to $74.41 extra a month, or $18.61 per week, for a worker earning the minimum wage. An employee earning $10 an hour can pocket an extra $104 a month. That kind of financial incentive might make an employee think twice about leaving Eddie Bauer.

Such an incentive plan is one way of rewarding often-overlooked low-wage employees. Other large companies offer programs that help pay for child care, assist with education, or provide some other form of extra financial support. These programs not only help low-wage workers but also benefit the employer through increased loyalty and savings on hiring and retention. Maintaining a stable workforce is a business imperative. In the United States today, one in four workers earns $18,800 a year, or $360 a week. These people have jobs, but inadequate salaries and few if any benefits.

Clothing manufacturer Levi Strauss & Co. has a program that provides emergency financial assistance to all of its employees and retirees. The Red Tab Foundation, named for the familiar tag found on the rear pocket of the company's blue jeans, offers money to employees who need immediate help to pay for things like funeral costs, emergency car or home repairs, or shelter from a violent spouse. Executive director Ann Ure says the foundation is a public charity cofunded by contributions from Levi employees, executives, and board members. Unexpected financial need is a primary criterion for eligibility, so the majority of grant recipients are hourly wage earners and retirees living on fixed incomes. By its existence, the foundation gives Levi employees a sense that there is a financial safety net, Ure says. "Employees see it as a bridge between paychecks when an emergency occurs." From 300 to 900 Levi employees and retirees apply each year for grants, which average $1,000. Eighty percent of the requests are approved.[3]

Another important tactic for employers is to focus only on job-related skills, which provide workers with almost no preparation for future jobs or developmental opportunities for advancement. This is essential to maintain the minimum cost. With this approach, there are no elective training programs; skills are developed only when necessary. While some companies may not provide elective training and advancement, others, like Marriott International and Bank of America Corporation, which employ platoons of low-wage workers, are initiating benefits programs that include English-language instruction and free or subsidized child care. These programs differ widely in specific benefits, but each one addresses a low-wage employee's work/life situation. Leon Litchfield, one of the authors of a 2004 study entitled *Increasing the Visibility of the Invisible Workforce: Model Programs and Policies for Hourly and Lower Wage Employees* by the Boston College Center for Work and Family, says these programs are helping companies gain productivity and loyalty while saving on recruiting and new-hire costs.

DISADVANTAGES

Investing the minimum in human resources can result in negative consequences for organizations. First, a minimum human capital investment strategy should be considered only in the context of simple, lower-level jobs. Automation is desired if the jobs can be eliminated. If not, they must be broken down into simple steps.

Second, organizations using this strategy must be able to adjust to high turnover. With low wages and sparse benefits, employees will jump to another organization which offers just a slight increase in pay. Some organizations adjust quite well. Executives can ensure that hiring costs are minimal and initial training costs are extremely low. For example, McDonald's keeps the jobs simple and the training efficient, resulting in a low cost to build job capabilities. McDonald's executives expect high turnover and are willing to live with and adjust for it.

Third, this approach can have a long-term negative impact as the turn-over costs deteriorate the efficiency of the organization, the quality of service, and the ultimate impact on indirect costs. This is not a major issue in a fast-food chain where jobs can be broken down into small parts and administered efficiently. However, for a manufacturing organization or a large customer call center, it may be difficult to deal with the high turnover inherent with this strategy on a long-term basis. Also, high turnover and low pay often conjures up negative images of an organization taking advantage of employees. Mc-Donald's and Wal-Mart are two examples of low-paying organizations that are often criticized for their pay and benefits structure.

Advantages

Surprisingly, there are many advantages to this strategy. The first and most obvious is low direct costs. Executives taking this approach strive to be the low-cost provider of goods or services. In doing so, they must invest in human capital at minimum levels. Southwest Airlines strives to be the low-cost airline operator. Consequently, they have lower wage and benefit structures than many other airlines. However, the executives work hard to keep turnover low, by selecting the right people, creating a supportive culture, and establishing a motivational climate. These practices provide the stability in customer service and support needed to be profitable. They are the world's most profitable airline.

Another advantage is that this strategy usually applies to jobs, tasks, and processes. These job elements make recruiting, training, and compensation relatively easy.

Finally, this may be the best strategy for survival, particularly on a short-term basis. By the nature of the business, some organizations must operate with minimum commitment to employees in terms of investment levels.

Summary

This chapter provides a simple and basic strategy used by many organizations: invest in human capital at minimum levels. Sometimes this strategy is neces-sary due to the type of business, the challenge of low-margin survival, or the competitive nature of the industry. Organizations adopting this strategy will face challenges. The most significant challenges are in maintaining adequate levels of job satisfaction and low levels of turnover, as well as recruiting moti-vated and committed employees. The strategy to invest the minimum is challenging, but can be accomplished if the potentially negative consequences are addressed with the appropriate resources and focus.

NOTES

1   Jerry Useem, "Should We Admire Wal-Mart?," *Fortune*, March 8, 2004, pp. 118–120.
2   Thomas Nelson, "High Impact for Low-Wage Workers," *Workforce Management*, August 2004, pp. 47–50.
3   Ibid.

CHAPTER 3

Invest with the Rest

Some organizations prefer to invest in human capital at the same level that others invest. Using benchmarking data, these organizations determine specific measures from organizations often perceived to be best in practice and try to duplicate many of the investment levels in their organization. Benchmarking is a popular approach to understanding human capital issues, particularly human capital investment.

This chapter explains how to develop and implement a benchmarking project. With the proper focus and effort, executives can develop their own benchmarking study with rewarding results.

THE BASIC STRATEGY

Investing with the rest involves collecting data from a variety of comparable organizations, often those perceived as implementing best practices, to determine the extent to which these organizations invest in a variety of human capital functions, processes, and activities. Benchmarking data are used to drive improvement or changes, if necessary, to achieve or exceed the benchmark level. In essence, this strategy aligns the organization with the level of investment of the benchmarking organizations.

CASE STUDY

Motorola relies heavily on benchmarking data to set its human capital investment levels. Motorola participates in a variety of human capital benchmark projects to understand how they compare with others in the industry. This information is then used to drive improvement. The process is repeated to continuously improve processes toward the goal of developing or exceeding a best practice.

In addition to Motorola, many major organizations around the world use benchmarking. Benchmarking had its history in the United States with IBM in the 1960s and Xerox in the 1970s. Both organizations used benchmarking to bring dramatic improvements to their organizations. Since then, many well-known organizations, such as AT&T, Boeing, Caterpillar, DuPont, Eastman Kodak, Hewlett Packard, Johnson & Johnson, NCR, Procter & Gamble, and 3M, have used benchmarking extensively to improve processes. Benchmarking has become a standard tool for performance and process improvement in these organizations.

FORCES DRIVING THE STRATEGY

Benchmarking is, in general terms, the comparison of one organization's business or practices with those of other organizations. It should be an ongoing process of measuring products, services, and operating practices against competitors or those considered to be market leaders and is very much linked to a philosophy of continuous improvement. Benchmarking is often specifically aimed at comparing product quality so that improvements to one's own processes can be identified and implemented. In some cases, comparisons are made with organizations whose products may differ. Aspects of the organization's processes are compared to those of others to understand how they gain speed, efficiency, quality, or cost savings.[1]

Benchmarking has experienced phenomenal growth in the last decade. In some organizations, virtually every function has used benchmarking to evaluate activities, practices, structure, and results. Because of its popularity and effectiveness, many organizations use benchmarking to show the value and investment level for human capital. It is an excellent way to set standards for investment and processes. In many cases, the benchmarking process develops standards of excellence from "best practice" organizations.

In the area of human capital, benchmarking was pioneered by Dr. Jac Fitz-enz of the Saratoga Institute. In the early 1980s, Fitz-enz established the *Saratoga Report*, an exclusive benchmarking study for the human resources executive.

The cost of connecting to existing benchmarking projects is often very low, especially when considering data availability. Minimum, if any, analysis is required to secure the data. When a benchmarking project is initiated by an organization, the costs are insignificant when compared to detailed analyses that may be required for other strategies.

An important force driving the invest-with-the-rest strategy is that it is a safe approach. Benchmarking has been accepted as a standard management tool, often required and suggested by top executives. It is a low-risk strategy.

The decisions made as a result of benchmarking, when proven to be ineffective, can easily be blamed on the faulty sources or faulty processes, not the individuals who initiated or secured the data.

Finally, benchmarking is a strategy that can be used in conjunction with other approaches. Benchmarking, with its low-cost approach, can provide another view of the human capital function and the investment required for it.

HUMAN CAPITAL BENCHMARK MEASURES

With respect to benchmarking the human resources function and activities, it is important to identify the key HR drivers and performance indicators so that meaningful measures can be developed. By gathering internal client feedback about existing processes and practices, critical success factors within the HR function can be prioritized and the appropriate focus for benchmarking can be selected.[2]

For human capital investment, an important issue is deciding specifically what should be benchmarked and what data are available. Ideally, a complete profile of cost data should be monitored to understand the total investment in human capital. Table 3-1 shows the human capital benchmarks needed to determine the appropriate investment levels. The definition of a particular measure must be addressed and clarified in benchmarking along with the many options, combinations, and possibilities available.

The first measurement group represents the expenses of the traditional HR function. This is often referred to as the HR department costs included in the overall HR budget. This measure shows the efficiency of the HR staff to deliver services. Presenting these expenses as a percentage of operating costs, revenue, and on a per-employee basis provides an easy comparison to other organizations in the same industry.

From the human capital perspective, the second grouping is more important. This represents the total investment in human capital, which is the total HR department expenses plus salaries and benefits of all other employees. In essence, this group includes every function that exists in the chain of HR acquisition and maintenance. Attracting, selecting, developing, motivating, compensating, and maintaining employees are accounted for in this total cost. Because the traditional HR department expenses do not include salaries of other functions, this measure has the effect of showing the total cost. It should be reported as a percent of operating costs, or revenue, or on a per-employee basis to show realistic comparisons with other organizations. All of the direct employee-related costs are included in the human capital measure.

Human resources costs are sometimes associated with other functions

Table 3-1. Human capital investment benchmarks.

1. Human Resource Expenses (HR Department Costs/Budget)
   A. As a percent of operating costs
   B. As a percent of revenue
   C. Per employee

2. Total Investment in Human Capital (Total HR Expenses Plus All Salaries and Benefits of Non-HR Staff)
   A. As a percent of operating costs
   B. As a percent of revenue
   C. Per employee

3. HR Expenses by Function
   A. Recruiting and selection cost as a percent of total HR
   B. Recruiting and selection cost per new employee hired
   C. Training/learning/development costs as a percent of total HR
   D. Training/learning/development costs per employee
   E. Training/learning/development costs as a percent of compensation
   F. Compensation costs as a percent of total HR
   G. Compensation costs as a percent of operating expenses
   H. Compensation costs per employee
   I. Benefits costs as a percent of total HR
   J. Benefits costs as a percent of operating expense
   K. Benefits costs as a percent of compensation
   L. Benefits costs per employee
   M. Employee relations costs as a percent of total HR
   N. Employee relations costs per employee
   O. Compliance and fair employment costs as a percent of total HR
   P. Compliance and fair employment costs per employee

4. HR Expenses by Process/Programming
   A. Analysis and assessment costs as a percent of total HR
   B. Design and development costs as a percent of total HR
   C. Implementation and delivery costs as a percent of total HR
   D. Operations and maintenance costs as a percent of total HR
   E. Measurement and evaluation costs as a percent of total HR

5. Selected HR Costs
   A. Turnover cost per employee leaving
   B. Turnover cost as a percent of compensation
   C. Accident cost per incident
   D. Safety cost per employee
   E. Absenteeism cost per absence
   F. Absenteeism cost as a percent of average wage rate
   G. Health care cost per employee
   H. Health care cost as a percent of total benefits

that may not be normally captured in the HR budget. For example, finance and accounting may have transaction costs such as payroll; IT may be involved in the administrative issues of processing benefits claims or Web-based activities; security may be involved in some of the safety-related issues; property may be involved in providing facilities such as cafeterias and fitness centers. Identifying and capturing all the costs are important to show the total human capital investment and make realistic comparisons. It should be noted that the cost of maintaining office space and equipment for employees is not included. This cost is usually reported as tangible assets or operating expenses. Employee travel falls in the same category.

The third grouping is by function, which is important to compare the efficiency of the various parts of the HR process. Human Resources expenses are those normally found in the HR budget and the grouping is organized by traditional processes of:

- ❑ Recruiting and selection
- ❑ Training, learning, and development (including orientation and socialization)
- ❑ Compensation, which includes direct compensation, bonuses, and deferred compensation
- ❑ Benefits, which includes all benefits and the costs to the company as well as external providers
- ❑ Employee-relations costs, which includes labor relations for organized groups
- ❑ Compliance and fair employment, which covers legal issues including discrimination and sexual harassment complaints, along with a variety of other compliance-related issues

Group four is not normally reported but is becoming an important issue: showing the costs by various HR processes. As HR programs are launched or modified, it is helpful to understand the relative costs of the different steps to develop and implement them. Beginning with analysis and assessment, these categories include the typical program development phases and end with measurement and evaluation. Reporting these as a percentage of the total cost of HR provides insight into the relative investment in these processes in similar organizations. In recent years, there has been growth in costs as a percent of total HR in the initial analysis and assessment to ensure that a new program or project is needed and that it is aligned with the business. The same is true in measurement and evaluation because of the need to show the contribution of the HR program.

Group five shows some selected HR costs that need to be reported and, perhaps, compared with other organizations. They represent employee-related cost variables and are measures that can be quite expensive and must be managed. Proactively, these costs also represent values of important measures that can be improved with new or modified HR initiatives. These are invaluable data items when an organization attempts to calculate the return on investment (ROI) in human capital programs. Perhaps the most expensive measure in this group is the cost of involuntary employee turnover as described in chapters 1 and 2. Accident and safety costs are important for manufacturing and construction industries. Health-care costs are becoming increasingly critical for organizations providing funding for employees. Preventive programs are often put in place to eliminate these costs whenever possible.

BENCHMARKING ISSUES

Several issues that often inhibit the benchmarking process should be addressed before examining a custom-designed process for the organization. These issues underscore the weaknesses in current benchmarking reports.

The Elusive Best Practice

Inherently, the benchmarking process is designed to show what others accomplish or experience. The concept of the best practice is often an elusive goal because, in reality, many benchmarking projects involve participants that just happen to be in the same industry, the same setting, or are willing to participate in the study. They may or may not represent a best practice. Even deciding what is the best practice is elusive. How is "best practice" defined? What is the basis of determining best practice? Who decides what is or is not best practice? How credible are the data reflecting the best practices? These are important questions to consider when observing and using benchmark data.

Best practice is even more elusive when the concept of human capital cost or investment enters into the equation. Is a best practice the lowest investment? Not necessarily, because there is a perceived linkage between investing in human capital and subsequent organizational success: the larger the investment, the more successful the organization. In this case, the highest level of investment may be the appropriate choice to follow. But does a large investment in human capital imply best practice? Investment and cost must be explored from the perception of the outcomes and payoff. The investment in human capital should be examined in terms of its efficiency. For example, how has an organization been able to accomplish an impressive target at a cost lower than others? The concept of best practice must be clearly understood when benchmarking data are presented or when designing a custom process.

Benchmarking Sources

The sources for benchmarking involve two issues. The first challenge is to understand the sources that currently exist for benchmarking studies. Here, the principal organizations are needed for benchmarking studies involving credible data. Table 3-2 shows some of the benchmarking sources that attempt to offer HR data across most of the United States as well as provide some limited international data. Although no one source provides all the data listed in table 3-1, this list provides a cross-section of organizations developing some type of human capital data.

Table 3-3 shows the benchmarking data listed in the *Saratoga Report*. Some organizations may be interested only in select data. When this is the case, it is important to find a suitable source with which to partner to develop a custom-designed benchmarking study. This issue is described later.

Global/National Data

For large organizations operating outside the local or regional area, it becomes more difficult to make comparisons—not all areas are the same and there are huge geographic differences in the quality and quantity of the labor market from which an organization must choose. Also, when compared to others, some areas have more effective systems and facilities for developing capable, top-quality employees.

Table 3-2. Current benchmarking studies.

Benchmarking Sources

- Saratoga Institute/PWC
- American Productivity and Quality Center
- Society of Human Resource Management
- Conference Board
- Corporate Executive Board (Corporate Leadership Council)
- American Management Association
- Mercer
- Watson Wyatt
- Hewitt and Associates

Table 3-3. Saratoga Institute 2004 workforce diagnostic system™.

- Organization and Operations: Productivity and structure of the entire organization;
- HR Staff and Structure: Costs and structure of the human resources function;
- Compensation and Benefits: Costs and structure of compensation and benefits;
- Staffing and Hiring: Costs and efficiencies of the staffing function; and
- Retention and Separations: Employee retention and separations.

Collecting national data presents a two-fold dilemma. First, it is difficult to compare because of the geographic differences, unless the data are provided by region. (Consider, for example, the differences in human capital costs in New York City and Nashville, Tennessee.) The second issue is the limited sources available to provide credible data.

It is even more difficult to benchmark at the international level. A replication process is necessary for benchmarking in each country. When there are differences in the practices of the countries, making comparisons to organizations located in another country becomes fruitless. If a particular employee-benefit or HR program is implemented in one country, should it be included in other countries as well? These are dilemmas of operating globally, which make benchmarking data on a global basis unreliable. Still, attempts are made to benchmark the country through national surveys. A few of the organizations listed in table 3-2 provide international data from the participating units in those countries.

CREATING A CUSTOM BENCHMARKING PROJECT

Many of the issues described above leave organizations little choice but to develop their own customized benchmarking for human capital measurement. Although this appears unnecessary as well as expensive, it may be the only way to match the organization's interests and needs to those organizations pursuing the comparison. Incidentally, if more organizations developed their own benchmarking study, there would be more available data from the various partners. Figure 3-1 shows a seven-phase benchmarking process that can be used to develop a custom-designed benchmarking project. Each phase is briefly described next.

Determining What to Benchmark

The first step is to identify precisely what type of information is needed from benchmarking. This step deserves much attention because of the tendency to explore more areas than are feasible or necessary. Because of the time involved in securing the information, the problem with information availability, and the difficulty in finding a suitable partner, benchmarking initiatives must remain within prescribed boundaries. Attempts to collect data that are generally unavailable or difficult to obtain are usually unsuccessful. Also, a lengthy request can be overwhelming, making it difficult to obtain information from a benchmarking partner. The items included in table 3-1 detail the human capital investment issues. In addition to these, other non-cost-related measures may

Figure 3-1. Phases of the benchmarking process.

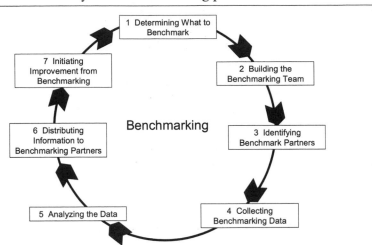

be sought. These include information such as absenteeism and turnover, time to fill jobs, hours of training per year, and absentee rates.

Building the Benchmarking Team

This phase is designed to ensure that an effective internal benchmarking team is in place. An effective team makes the difference between success and failure; it should be carefully selected and prepared to achieve the desired response. Ideally, the team should include the HR executive, several HR specialists representing the different HR functional areas, and a few non-HR managers and executives. Table 3-4 highlights some of the issues about the team, its processes, and its necessary support.

Table 3-4. Three important benchmarking team issues.

- Role of the Team Leader
  - Organize the team and define duties
  - Train and facilitate
  - Provide leadership
- Team Characteristics
  - Specific functional expertise
  - Interest in benchmarking
  - Reputation in the organization
  - Adequate interpersonal skills
- Team Support
  - Expenses/budget
  - Administrative support

Although an individual could perform the tasks for the project, the team approach is recommended based on the volume of work alone. However, using a team approach increases the ownership of the process and enhances the credibility of the final product. Also, the team approach helps to ensure that benchmarking results are applied within the organization.

Identifying Benchmark Partners

Identifying benchmark partners for the project is one of the most important parts of the process. Data can only be useful if collected from respected organizations. It is important to identify those organizations considered to have the best practices or to be the most admired for some predetermined set of criteria. The targets may be competitors or noncompetitors in the same industry. Organizations in the same geographic area may be important because of the concerns about local HR issues. Still, partnering with organizations sharing the same kind of structure (national, international, decentralized) may be desirable.

There are many reasons why the best organizations to benchmark against may be outside of the industry, and every attempt should be made to find partners who have an outstanding reputation in the area being benchmarked. It is important to think creatively. If the HR department views itself as a consulting function, then a good benchmarking partner might be a leading management consultancy offering HR skills.[3] On the other hand, if the HR function provides traditional support to the organization, it is feasible to benchmark against similar traditional HR functions in a variety of industries.

The task is to find the organization that potentially has the best practice or the desired practice based on criteria important to the benchmarking project. Finding these organizations can be a challenge. However, a variety of sources can help categorize organizations and identify needed data. Table 3-5 shows some of the sources available for locating potential benchmarking part-

Table 3-5. Finding the organization.

• Previous Award Winners	• Vendors
• State Governments	• Federal Government
• Academic Resources and Databases	• Business School Faculty
• Consultants	• Professional Societies
• Business Information Services	• Trade Associations
• Business Newspapers and Magazines	• Internal Sources
• Technical Journals	• Directories and References
	• Customers

ners. The challenge: Some of the best organizations do not publish data about their successes; they are sometimes reluctant to make professional presentations, they do not apply for human capital awards, and they may not participate in a variety of organizations where the information is readily available. Limitations notwithstanding, it *is* possible to identify candidates that can make great benchmarking partners.

Collecting Benchmarking Data

The first issue in this phase is to collect internal data. The data collection process, including the use of estimates, should be thoroughly tested within the organization to gain additional insight into the process. This provides a way to check the flow of data, quality of data collected, interpretation of data, and potential problem areas. If there are problems with internal information, other organizations will have problems delivering the data as well.

Next, the data are collected from the partners. Data collection arrangements should be negotiated in advance during requests from organizations agreeing to participate. Typically, a detailed questionnaire is mailed and a telephone interview is conducted to explain all of the questions, review the definitions, and address all concerns and issues. If feasible and appropriate, an on-site visit is conducted to capture high-quality data.

Analyzing the Data

After data are collected, they must be tabulated, organized, analyzed, and interpreted. Data are typically organized in a spreadsheet that lists the organizations and the various headings for capturing the data. Spreadsheet analysis is appropriate for tabulating much data that can be formatted for a presentation at a later date.

Distributing Information to Benchmarking Partners

If it is not perceived as adding value within the sponsoring organizations, developing and distributing a report for all benchmarking partners can easily be omitted. However, if the benchmarking partnership is to be a positive, long-term relationship, then information distribution must be handled with utmost care. Benchmarking partners require a report containing useful information that can be used internally to improve their processes. The quality of the report promised often creates the eagerness to become involved in the project. Table 3-6 shows the contents of a typical benchmarking report.

Table 3-6. Contents of the benchmarking report.

- An executive summary, which presents a brief conclusion from the survey data and provides a brief description of the overall process.
- A statement of the purposes of the project with details on the objectives.
- A listing of all participants.
- Summary of benchmarked items.
- Description of the methods for collecting and analyzing the data.
- An outline of the overall results and conclusions that shows what the data may mean to the organization.
- A description of the strengths within the group that attempts to determine best practices for each of the items benchmarked.
- A request for this procedure to be a continuous process with potential future plans.

Initiating Improvement from Benchmarking

The final, and probably the most critical, phase in the benchmarking process is implementing the improvements the process has shown as necessary. Until the improvements are implemented, there is no return on the often extensive effort that goes into the benchmarking process. When implemented, the return can be great.

Initiating improvement involves three important steps: calculating performance gaps, formulating action plans, and writing an internal report.

1. Calculating the performance gap is looking at the difference between the desired (benchmarked) value and the current value. The difference translates into a gap that needs to be closed by improving a specific process.

2. Formulating the action plan involves selecting the appropriate actions to resolve the problem or improve the process and then detailing a series of steps that must be implemented over a predetermined period of time to complete these actions.

3. The final part of the improvement is writing a report for the internal customers in the sponsoring organization—the individual(s) for whom the process is initiated. This report shows the gaps, actions, and success. Updates of this report provide a view of the continued success being made.

DISADVANTAGES

The benchmarking process is not without its share of problems, consequences, and issues. Benchmarking must be approached as a learning process, not necessarily a process to duplicate or replicate the accomplishments of others. Each organization is different. What is needed in one organization may not be the same as in another. Also, benchmarking is time consuming when a custom-designed benchmarking project is developed. It requires discipline to keep the project on schedule, within budget, and on track to drive continuous process improvement.

Determining what the best practices are is an elusive goal; benchmarking can create a misunderstanding that average data taken from a group willing to participate in a study represents the best practices. Gathering national and international data is a difficult issue that often limits benchmarking as a global tool. Finally, benchmarking is not a quick fix; it is a long-term improvement process. Table 3-7 shows some of the myths about benchmarking that cause the process to be misused or misunderstood.[4]

Advantages

Benchmarking has many advantages, satisfies a variety of needs, and is used for several important purposes. It is extremely helpful in the strategic planning of the HR function and for determining the desired investment level. Information and measures derived from the process can enable HR executives to help the organization meet its strategic objectives. It is also useful in identifying

Table 3-7. Benchmarking myths.

- The only way to benchmark is against direct product competitors.
- Benchmarks are only quantitative, financially based statistics.
- Benchmarking investigations are focused solely on operations showing a performance gap.
- Benchmarking needs to be done occasionally and can be accomplished quickly.
- There is a single company somewhere, most like my firm only much better, which is "*the* best practice."
- Staff organizations cannot be benchmarked.
- Benchmarking is a target-setting stretch exercise.
- Benchmarking can most effectively be accomplished through third-party consultants
- It is not obvious what should be benchmarked for each business unit.
- Processes do not need to be benchmarked.
- Internal benchmarking between departments and divisions has only minimal benefits.
- There is no benefit in qualitative benchmarking.
- Benchmarking is comparing an organization to the dominant industry firm and emulating the firm six months later.

Source: Updated and adapted from R. C. Kemp, *Benchmarking* (Milwaukee: ASTC Quality Press, 1989).

trends and critical issues for human capital management. Measures from benchmarking can become the standard of excellence for an activity, function, system, practice, program, or a specific initiative. It has become an important measurement and evaluation tool, as well as a routine management tool.[5] Benchmarking also allows the organization to compare certain product features and benefits with others. To be successful, several issues must be considered when developing a custom project. Table 3-8 shows the success factors for the benchmarking process. These issues must be addressed to ensure successful benchmarking implementation.[6]

Table 3-8. Success factors for the benchmarking process.

- A strong commitment to benchmarking from management.
- A clear HR understanding of present practices as a basis for comparison to best practices.
- A willingness to change HR practices based on benchmark findings.
- A realization that competition is constantly changing and there is a need to stay ahead of the trend.
- A willingness to share information with benchmark partners.
- The involvement of a small number of organizations that are recognized leaders in HR.
- Adherence to the benchmarking phases.
- A continuous benchmarking effort for long-term improvement.

SUMMARY

This chapter explored the strategy of investing with the rest. With this approach, executives use benchmarking to determine the desired level of investment in human capital and the mix of HR programs and activities to pursue or improve. Benchmarking has been used routinely for over two decades and is a mainstream management tool. In addition, it is used by many HR executives to set the human capital investment level. It can be used as the primary way to determine the human capital investment or it can supplement other strategies.

NOTES

1   Linda Holbeche, *Aligning Human Resources and Business Strategy* (Boston: Butterworth-Heinemann, 2001).

2   Linda Holbeche, *Aligning Human Resources and Business Strategy* (Boston: Butterworth-Heinemann, 2001).

3   D. E. Hussey, *Business Driven Human Resource Management* (New York: John Wiley & Sons, 1996).

4   R. C. Kemp, *Benchmarking: The Search for Industry Best Practices that Leads to Superior Performance* (Milwaukee: ASTC Quality Press, 1989).

5   Jac Fitz-enz, *Benchmarking Staff Performance* (San Francisco: Jossey-Bass, 1993).

6   J. J. Phillips, *Accountability in Human Resource Management* (Boston: Butterworth-Heinemann, 1996).

CHAPTER 4

Invest Until It Hurts

While some organizations invest at the same level of other organizations, many operate under the guise that more is better. They over-invest in human capital. The results of such an approach can be both disappointing and disastrous. A few executives do this intentionally; others do it unknowingly. Either way, this is a strategy that deserves serious attention.

THE BASIC STRATEGY

With this strategy, organizations invest in human capital beyond what is needed to meet the goals and mission of the organization. Executives implement almost every program or project they see, provide every employee benefit available, and teach every new idea that comes across the horizon. For most over-investing organizations, this strategy is not a deliberate pursuit; rather, it occurs unintentionally through a desire to do everything possible to ensure that human capital is well funded.

CASE STUDIES

An example of over-investing is an automotive company located in North America. This firm, with headquarters outside the United States, spent almost $4 million on a wellness and fitness center for its North American employees. The rationale for investing in this center was to increase the attraction and retention of employees. The executives wanted to maintain high job-satisfaction levels and thought that the wellness and fitness center would help accomplish these goals. In addition, they thought that a fitness center would be an excellent way to contain or lower healthcare costs. Some executives believed it would even reduce absenteeism and job-related accidents.

When examining these measures after the center opened, the status was far from what one would expect:

❑ Job-satisfaction levels were extremely high—beyond what was expected or perhaps could even be achieved in most organizations.

❑ Attraction was not an issue. Just a rumor that there might be additional jobs on the assembly line would create an overwhelming amount of applications in the HR department. (At one time, as many as 10,000 applications were received after an announcement that 200 jobs would be added in the plant.)

❑ Retention was not an issue. The company was experiencing less than 3 percent annual turnover—too low by some standards. Unless there is significant growth, a turnover level that low is unhealthy. Lower turnover probably could not be achieved, even if a variety of solutions were implemented. Low turnover was a product of satisfied employees, a superior benefits package, and wages that were double the average in the area. If attraction and retention improvement were the motive, the wellness and fitness center was a futile investment.

❑ Healthcare costs were below average for the manufacturing industry in the area. With the implementation of the wellness and fitness center, the costs were contained, but not reduced; the cost differential was very small—not enough to cover a fraction of the cost of maintaining the wellness and fitness center.

❑ The manufacturing facility enjoyed one of the best safety records in manufacturing. Because there is not (nor has there ever been) an accident problem, a reduction in accidents did not materialize since the center was developed.

❑ Absenteeism was not an issue and did not change significantly with the implementation of the wellness and fitness center.

Thus, from the return on investment (ROI) perspective, the wellness and fitness center failed to add value. This is a classic case of over-investing—adding a benefit or service that does not increase the value to the organization, yet adds significant costs.

The dot-coms littered the landscape with examples of over-investing, as company after company lavished their employees with benefits, perks, programs, and opportunities to buy their loyalty, motivate them to high levels of achievement, and retain them at all costs. One interesting organization investing heavily in human capital is SAS Institute, based in Cary, North Carolina. Jim Goodnight, the cofounder and CEO, has a reputation for showering his employees with perks. For example, employees work only thirty-five hours per week; sick days are unlimited, and can be used for tending to ailing family members. Company specialists can arrange expert help for aging parents. Benefits are extended to domestic partners. Employees at headquarters can take their preschool children to one of four daycare centers (two on-site, two off-site) for $300 per month (meals included). Each of the 24 buildings on this 250-acre campus has a break room on every floor stocked with refreshments and snacks. Employees can choose between two full-service cafeterias, and work off their meals in a 54,000-square-foot gym, with free personal trainers, an Olympic-sized swimming pool, aerobics classes, and a dance studio. A soccer field, tennis courts, and a putting green round out the sports amenities.

Is all of this necessary? Some would characterize this as going beyond what is needed to build a motivated, committed, and engaged workforce. Supporters suggest that this is the primary reason for their low turnover; however, according to internal executives, no analyses have been conducted to connect these perks to a specific retention amount.

SAS almost routinely appears in *Fortune* magazine as one of the 100 Best Companies to Work For. One publication characterized Goodnight as "extravagant."[1] In *Fortune's* analysis, they report, "This software maker is the closest thing to the worker's Utopia in America," highlighting the on-site childcare, health center with physicians and dentists, massage therapists, and a profit-sharing program as well.

In less than three decades, SAS has evolved into a world leader in intelligence software services, with 9,000 employees, offices in three countries, and revenues of over $1 billion. The company is very successful and enjoyed twenty-four consecutive years of double-digit earning growth until the technology crash in the early 2000s. Goodnight credits the success of the company to the gung-ho, dedicated workforce. Through a variety of perks and benefits, he attempts to make the employee's lives easier and believes they will give their all to work. As a private organization, SAS is not subject to the scrutiny of Wall Street analysts. If that were the case, the employee benefit structure might be different.

Is investing in human capital to this extent a good thing? Some will argue that you cannot over-invest in human capital and that the more you provide employees, the better. Others would argue that each time a new program, project, or benefit is added—particularly one that becomes a permanent fixture—operating costs are increased that will eventually place a burden on the company. At what point is there diminishing return on investing in human capital?

Rationale for the Strategy

Some advocates suggest that over-investing in employees is not an issue—the more you invest, the more successful the organization. Obviously, this is the position often taken by unions and other employee-advocate groups. However, others will note that over-investing occurs regularly and is unnecessarily burdening organizations with excessive operating costs. This approach puts pressure on others to follow suit, thus creating an artificial new benchmark.

Investing until it hurts is often not a deliberate strategy. Executives are unaware that the increase in spending is not adding value, as the case study on the automotive company illustrates. This company thought that the wellness center would enhance job satisfaction, without taking the time to analyze the current situation and project the impact of the investment.

In many cases, companies add benefits, services, and perks without anticipating the full impact of these investments. The two most vulnerable areas are retirement plans and healthcare benefits. In the 1970s, some companies began to switch from defined benefit plans to defined contribution plans, shifting the investment risk to the employees. Many organizations still provide these traditional defined benefit pension plans, which have proven to be extremely costly and difficult to change. Failure to make the switch has caused some firms not only to have excessive costs, but even to move into bankruptcy.

For the most part, executives do not anticipate the tremendous changes that lead to the burden of retirement. First there is the investment risk of the pension plan. When you maintain defined benefit plans, it becomes more costly for employers than anticipated, particularly in a recession. Second, employees are living much longer, thus retirement costs are increasing. Third, employers are often much more generous because they think short-term rather than long-term as they provide benefits and negotiate lucrative labor contracts.

Competition sometimes drives companies to adopt the strategy of over-investing. Some executives see others providing benefits or additional services so they think they should offer them as well. When a new benefit, program, or service is implemented in an organization, the publicity it generates causes other firms to jump on the bandwagon and implement it for their employees because they do not want to be outdone. For example, United, Northwest, American, and Delta Airlines provide lucrative benefit plans to remain competitive among the industry. Contrast this with newer airlines such as Southwest, Jet Blue, and AirTran, which do not have traditional pension plans. United Airlines faced pension payments of almost $600 million in 2004 and $4.1 billion by the end of 2008; Northwest and United Airlines have pension deficits close to $100,000 per employee; Southwest, Jet Blue, and AirTran have none.

Some executives over-invest because they have too much faith in the issue of investing in human capital. Executives conclude that every investment will eventually be returned in some way at some time. This describes the philosophy of overspending on human capital; employees are such a precious resource that they should be nurtured, supported, and maintained appropriately. IBM is a company that has always taken pride in human capital investment. For many years, they practiced the concept of full employment—refusing to lay off employees. IBM executives assumed that full employment meant that they would have loyal, stable, highly motivated employees. Unfortunately, that plan had to be abandoned as IBM faced a crisis in the 1990s.

This belief was also the motivation behind providing lucrative benefits for IBM's employees. For example, in 2002, IBM had to contribute almost $4 billion to make up the deficit in their pension plan. At the same time, they found that 75 percent of their competitors did not offer a pension plan and fewer still paid for retiree health care.[2]

As IBM attempted to change, its plan came under attack, particularly by employees. For example, IBM attempted to change the pension plans in 1995 and 1999. Some employees objected to this and ultimately sued. In 2003, employees won the first round in the case against the employer and IBM now calculates the case could cost as much at $6.5 billion if the plan's proposed remedy is accepted. This is a big number for a company with only $7.3 billion in cash on hand. Also, IBM is attempting to change its healthcare costs for retirees. In 1999, IBM capped the amount a retiree would pay at $7,500. Although IBM is certainly in no financial distress, its medical costs have been rising faster than revenue. In 2003, the company reported spending $335 million in retiree healthcare.

A final area that causes over-investing is talent chasing. In the 1990s, recruiting great talent for the organization became a critical issue. Literally, there was a war for talent, as organizations battled each other for highly skilled, highly specialized individuals. The war for talent spurred tremendous salaries, ever-increasing perks, signing bonuses, and other unheard of benefits. These perks and benefits were given not only to senior executives, but to middle- and lower-level professional employees as well. This placed a heavy burden on these employers, which, at the time, seemed reasonable—they could afford it. When economic times changed and they could no longer afford it, executives had to remove these perks. The result: a disgruntled workforce and increased turnover, a situation they were trying to avoid in the first place. This is a vicious cycle that can only be avoided by careful planning, with more focus on creating a workplace that is challenging, motivating, and offers exciting opportunities, instead of a place where employees are pampered and paid excessively. Part of the problem is that many executives believe that retention is directly related to pay, when it is not.

Whatever the reason, over-investing does exist and can be detrimental to the organization. A lucrative pay and benefit package is not so impressive. What's more impressive is the performance of a company like Southwest Airlines with its consistent profitability, low turnover, and wages and benefits less than other top airlines.

Signs of Over-Investing

There are several signs of over-investing that occur in organizations. The first and most obvious is the less-than-desired financial performance of the organization. Delta Airlines, for example, is one of many organizations teetering on the verge of bankruptcy. The CEO warns that unless the airline continues to receive concessions from its employees in pension liability and reduction in wages, the airline will face imminent bankruptcy. At one time, Delta was one of the most successful airlines. It is now in peril for many reasons. Stiff competition is one; the most difficult to embrace, however, is their huge pension cost. In 2003, the pension deficit was $5.7 billion. The deficit as a percentage of the company's market capitalization is 379.1 percent. In essence, Delta could go under because of the excessive spending on human capital, not airplane purchases or fuel costs.[3]

There are a few instances where companies are over-investing in training and development. For example, consider the comments of the CEO of Sears, Roebuck, and Company when announcing disappointing financial performance. In an interview with the *New York Times*, the CEO indicated that the company's poor performance was due, at least in part, to the excessive amount of training. He said that the amount of time employees spent in training left stores understaffed. Employees enjoy training, want to take any course that is offered, and store managers support the training. The result: There is not enough staff to serve the customers, causing customer dissatisfaction and ultimately loss in revenue. As in this case, when a company offers a variety of training opportunities, taken to an extreme, performance can deteriorate.

Some companies make a deliberate attempt to invest a certain number of hours or days in training. Consider, for example, the Saturn Corporation, once the shining star at General Motors. Saturn had a commitment that each employee in the plant would spend over one hundred hours each year in training. Manager bonuses were attached to this goal and trimmed significantly if those targets were not met. As expected, employees attended all types of training. Some employees complained that they were attending unnecessary training programs—often unrelated to their work—simply to make their training goals. What was designed to show a commitment to learning and development turned into expensive spending practices—and, in some cases, a major turn-off in the eyes of employees.

The signs of over-investing appear in an excessive number of programs. When Les Hayman took over SAP's human resources department, he discovered that it had more than 1,000 different programs in various stages of development. "We promptly culled them by two-thirds," he says. "Everyone in human resources was under tremendous stress, but a lot of it was wasted. They were doing things that had no impact on the business." Hayman surveyed the rest of the company and asked what they actually needed. "There were a lot of places where what we had built was really out of step. We had areas where the board had set a business strategy, but it wasn't translated into compensation planning at the level of the field organization. If you don't align the organization behind the strategy, it's a hope rather than a strategy."[4]

Hayman also revamped much of the curriculum at SAP University. "They were spending more time worrying about generic training courses, such as negotiation training and time management," he says. "You can hire outside people to do that." Instead, he and the institute's director devised new courses that focused on specific tasks that SAP managers handled in their jobs, such as giving performance reviews. Drawing from his own career experience as an autodidact—he taught himself computer programming, for example, by designing a computer game—Hayman also reduced the role of training in staff development. "You learn best by doing," he says. "So we build 10 percent of development around training, and another 20 percent around coaching. The other 70 percent comes from on-the-job training."

The cost of human capital usually appears in financial statements as part of the operating costs. Sometimes excessive operating costs are the result of over-investing in human resources. Companies within the same industry with excessive human capital costs have a distinct disadvantage in operating costs. For example,

❏ With their significant pension burden, IBM has a much higher operating cost than Microsoft, which does not have the traditionally defined benefit plan.

❏ Retail stores, such as Sears, with more lucrative healthcare and pension plans, have a difficult time competing directly with Wal-Mart, which has much lower healthcare and pension costs.

❑ Southwest Airlines has significantly lower operating costs when compared to some of its rivals, United, Delta, Northwest, and Continental.

Thus, the huge operating costs driven by excessive spending puts some organizations at a disadvantage.

High salaries are often an indication of over-investing—a sign that there is too much compensation for the industry. This trend develops when salaries are adjusted more than the competition and more than the economic reality dictates. The result is a higher compensation cost, perhaps higher than appropriate. The steel industry has been plagued by high labor costs for years, ultimately leading to the demise of many of the steel plants in the United States. While there are other contributing factors, the high labor costs are singled out as one of the more significant. Bethlehem Steel, which had high labor and benefit costs, was at a serious disadvantage in the cost of steel—sometimes as much as a $30 to $50/ton differential when compared to firms with lower human capital costs. In 2002, Bethlehem declared bankruptcy, wiping out retiree medical plans; their pension plan was taken over by the Pension Benefit Guaranty Corporation. At the same time, the employees' benefits were cut. Bethlehem's attempt to remain competitive in wages in the early years, ultimately led to their demise in later years.

In some cases, total benefits package can be the problem. Lucrative pension plans and healthcare cost arrangements have left many companies saddled with high costs and contracts that cannot easily be negotiated. For years, the U.S. auto industry complained about the high cost of its benefits package. Today, domestic car makers have some of the largest pension obligations and pools of retirees anywhere. General Motors has 514,120 participants in its hourly pension plan; 371,503 of whom are retired. Pension and healthcare costs for those retirees added up to $6.2 billion in 2003, or roughly $1,784 per vehicle according to Morgan Stanley. By contrast, the Japanese competition started manufacturing in the United States in the late 1980s at a far lower cost. Toyota's U.S. plan has only 9,557 participants and their pension cost is estimated at something less that $200 per vehicle. The impact on profits is dramatic. Excluding gains from its finance arm, GM earned $144 per vehicle in the United States in 2003. GM's margins are now .5 percent—among the worst in the industry. According to Morgan Stanley, without the burden of pension, retiree, and healthcare costs, the automaker's global margins would be 5.5 percent. That's not good news. In comparison, Asian car makers (like Honda Motor Corporation) earn 7.5 percent on their global sales.[5]

Either of the above examples can point toward over-investing. These situations often evolve slowly, catching the HR executive and other senior leaders unawares.

Over-investing occurs in other parts of an organization. Consider, for example, the IT area. In recent years, large companies have invested a great deal of money—and faith—in IT systems as a means of leading vital organizational or competitive change. More than half of the investment includes systems devoted to enterprise resource planning (ERP), supply chain management (SCM), customer relationship management (CRM), and e-commerce operations.

All too often, however, hopes are dashed, and the effort is deemed a failure. Various studies show that in 30 to 75 percent of cases, new systems do not live up to expectations, do not register a measurable financial impact, improve work processes, or bring about organizational change. In some cases, the result is catastrophic. Nike, for example, spent hundreds of millions of dollars on a system that forecasted sales inaccurately; Hershey Foods suffered through a Halloween season in which it failed to keep its candy in stock with major retailers; and FoxMeyer Drug filed for chapter 11 at least in part because of problems with its ERP implementation. These companies often purchase huge quantities of IT for reasons that have nothing to do with their business models or long-term strategies. All too often, a company sees that its rivals have purchased ERP or CRM applications and signed on to participate in a business-to-business (B2B) exchange, and it feels compelled to do the same. This follow-the-pack approach results in IT overspending. Morgan Stanley, for example, estimates that between 2000 and 2002, companies threw away $130 billion of the IT they purchased.[6]

Companies waste billions of dollars every year on new product enhancements that consumers do not want, cannot use, or will not pay for. The fact is that most new products, from automobiles to washing machines, are over-engineered. But corporate efforts to rein in excessive engineering costs frequently fail. CEOs and CFOs at manufacturing companies tell the same story: To achieve a margin on new products, engineers know they need to hit a target cost, but somehow they do not. Why not? Engineers argue they need to spend more to meet consumers' expectations.[7]

FORCES DRIVING THIS STRATEGY

Several forces come together to cause over-investing. Some of these are realistic challenges; others are mythical. Either way, they cause firms to routinely over-invest.

Union Demands

The automobile, airline, and steel industry cases are examples where the companies had to meet union demands to avoid a work stoppage. Thus, in their quest to have additional pay and benefits (and sometimes even more restrictive work practices), the unions have added to the economic decline. For the most part, these companies could not afford to have a work stoppage at any cost. Executives were meeting demands considered excessive to survive "today," even though they put their "tomorrows" in jeopardy. For many of those industries, tomorrow has come. This situation cannot be blamed entirely on the unions. Some critics blame the companies for giving in to the unions or creating the kind of adversarial relationship where a more acceptable agreement cannot be reached. Others blame the companies entirely for creating the problem.

Retention

During the 1990s, retention became the main battle cry for many organizations. The labor market was tight, skilled employees were scarce, and organizations would do almost anything to keep employees or attract new ones. This often led to investing in human capital well beyond what would be necessary or acceptable in many situations. It may be concluded that offering lucrative benefits, perks, and signing bonuses were necessary for business survival; however, many organizations and even industries were able to keep low turnover without having to resort to this strategy.

The problem may be a case of not understanding what really drives turnover and retention. To the surprise of many managers, the findings of research conducted by Mercer Consulting revealed that pay levels had the *weakest* impact on actual turnover; this was a striking contrast to what exit interviews usually suggest. As an illustration, the modeling in Fleet Financial Service determined that a 10 percent across-the-board increase in pay levels would reduce turnover by less than one percentage point. Thus, relying primarily on pay adjustments to stem turnover would have required a major commitment of resources with little payoff for the company. The real drivers of retention, according to the analysis, had little to do with pay and much to do with factors related to careers, such as promotions, pay *growth*, number of jobs, and breadth of experience.[8]

The Happy Employee Dilemma

For many years, executives have operated under the belief that more satisfied employees are more productive. By spending additional money on a variety of programs, services, and benefits, a company should increase the job satisfaction of its employees. If satisfaction increases, the resulting productivity compensates for the additional expense. Unfortunately for those who believe the happiness-equals-productivity equation, research indicates that job satisfaction does not correlate with productivity in most settings. Attempts to improve job satisfaction do not necessarily translate into corresponding improvement in team performance, measured in productivity and quality. The result: over-investing in human capital—beyond what is necessary to improve the performance of the organization.

Competitive Strategy

Some executives over-invest to remain competitive in the market. They must attract and maintain highly capable employees and are willing to pay the price for them. They sometimes offer stock options to all employees, which can cost the company much later. They want certain capabilities and use various perks to obtain and keep talent. The talent becomes an important part of competitive strategy. The intangible value is an important part of this over-investment—as much as maintaining the low turnover.

Some executives want to showcase the benefits package along with the awards received for investing in people. The goal is to be highlighted in magazines as a "Great Place to Work" and win awards for "best practice." This recognition is considered a part of competitive strategy and of developing the brand.

Quick Fixes

Some companies over-invest because they are searching for a quick fix. A serious problem exists that must be corrected; turnover is extremely high, absenteeism is destroying service delivery, or employee complaints are causing deterioration of quality and productivity. Believing money can solve the problem quickly, executives implement new projects, programs, or solutions. Unfortunately, these new services and benefits sometimes exceed what is needed and ultimately add a long-term, almost permanent layer of costs. Once implemented, they are difficult to remove.

Fad Chasing

Some executives have an appetite for new fads. They have never met one they did not like, so they adopt new fads at every turn, adding additional costs. The landscape is littered with programs such as Open Book Management, Seven

Habits of Highly Effective People, Empowerment, Fish, and dozens of leadership solutions. Once a fad is in place, it is hard to remove, adding layers of additional benefits and programs and going beyond what is necessary or economically viable. Executives are returning to basics: creating a great company, building a branded scorecard, or implementing Six Sigma.

The Analysis Dilemma

Some organizations over-invest because they are unwilling or unable to conduct the proper analysis to see that their investment pays off or that additional investment is needed. Analysis is a critical part of strategic management. Time and time again, if a corporate leader is successful, his or her vision is cited as the cause and lauded as the foundation of the leader's greatness. Vision, however, is only one component of the strategic management process. To develop an effective strategy, executives must determine where the organization is, agree on where they want to take it, and establish a plan to get there. Too many leaders seem to think that their vision alone should set this strategic development in motion. In the strategic management process, vision isn't the starting point—it's a byproduct of competent analysis.[9]

Sometimes, organizations suggest that there is no time for analysis— they must move quickly. Analysis does take time and consume resources; however, the consequences of no analysis can be expensive. If a variety of programs, processes, perks, and benefits are implemented without understanding the need and what particular issue they are addressing, the results can be more damaging than if nothing is implemented. When incorrect solutions or projects are implemented, the consequences can be devastating. Additional pay and benefit packages may do no more than create jealousy, anxiety, and dissension from those individuals who do not receive them or who have a different level of benefits.

Some executives do not understand analysis, what it means, and what it can do for them. When determining the particular issues being addressed, the resulting analysis can appear complex and confusing. However, some analyses are simple, straightforward, and can achieve excellent results. Sometimes analysis is a matter of taking the time to do it, keeping it simple, and taking action only when the analysis indicates additional levels of spending are needed.

Some executives are deeply suspicious of any analysis for something as subjective as human capital. They indicate that investment appears obvious, particularly after examining what other organizations are accomplishing. In reality, the obvious solution, program, or project may not be so obvious. Consider the issue of offering a longevity pay bonus, that is, paying people for achieving certain milestones. For example, a bonus is provided after completing five years of service, then for completing ten years, fifteen, twenty, and so on. While this may appear to be a rewarding bonus for those receiving it, it has almost no motivational impact and is often not considered part of the base pay. It is not an attractive recruiting technique because it does not take effect for five years. Attempting to remove this bonus can have a negative impact on morale. Unfortunately, when it is implemented, few executives take the time to analyze the situation, to see what value it creates, what problem it is addressing, and what is the ultimate payoff.

Still, in other situations, the HR staff does not know what kind of analysis to conduct in order to determine precisely if the new benefit, program, or services are needed and if there is a projected payoff. Those responsible for these analyses have not been trained to conduct them. The preparation for a typical HR manager does not include analysis techniques, and there is often a reluctance to bring in consultants to help with the analysis. Without knowing and understanding what to do, it often goes undone.

We Can Afford It

Some organizations over-invest because they can afford to do so. They are profitable, enjoy high margins and ample growth, and want to share the wealth with employees. While this may be a desired strategy, sometimes the mechanism used to share the wealth creates a long-term commitment; the wealth is passed on through benefits and pay structure which are considered permanent fixtures. If conditions change, removing or changing these mechanisms can cause serious problems. Consequently, they have a tendency to stay in place, like it or not. Sharing the wealth with employees through one-time bonuses, without a guarantee that they will continue, may be more appropriate and beneficial in the long term.

During the 1990s, many high-tech companies made tremendous amounts of money, significantly increased their stock value, and provided many opportunities to invest in human capital. A number of them over-invested because they felt they could afford to. When the economy turned, the company could not sustain some of the human capital expenditures, thus creating a bigger problem than they might have had without the excessive human capital spending.

DISADVANTAGES

The most important disadvantage of over-investment is the potential for less than optimal financial performance. By definition, over-investing is investing more than necessary to meet the objectives of the organization. The relationship between financial performance and investing in human capital has been documented in studies, but not enough attention has been paid to the issue of over-investing. A typical consequence is depicted in figure 4-1. As the figure shows, a certain level of investment yields additional financial results. Some of the studies described elsewhere in this book show that increased investment generates additional financial performance, but there is evidence of a point of diminishing return, where the added benefits peak, then drop as investment continues.

As indicated, the over-investing area reflects no increased financial performance for additional investments. There then is a point reached where the actual performance goes down. This is excessive investing and represents some of the extreme cases mentioned in the beginning of this chapter. Over-investing can eventually deteriorate performance in the organization, particularly in industries where the human capital expense is an extraordinarily high percentage of the total operating cost. The knowledge industry is a good example. A company over-invests in human capital and the impact on the bottom line is severe. In other industries, such as the chemical process industry, human capital investment is low and over-investing in human capital has less effect on the financial performance.

Sometimes over-investing can lead to less-than-optimum performance and too little turnover. Building on the concept that over-investing focuses on job satisfaction (and not necessarily on employee engagement or an organiza-

Figure 4-1. The relationship between over-investing in human capital and financial performance.

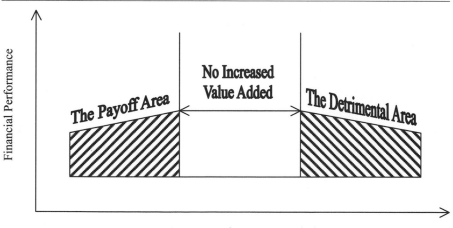

Investment in Human Capital

tion's commitment), there may not be any subsequent performance exchange for the investment. Turnover is one of those variables that can be either too low or too high. Excessive investment often leads to lower turnover because employees are tied to the organization. There is debate about how much turnover is too little. Most will agree that dipping below a certain level of turnover can be dangerous. If turnover is too low, the workforce becomes stagnant, generating few if any new ideas and limiting the level of talent in the organization.

Consider, for example, Birmingham Steel Company, recently acquired by Nucor. In one plant, the company paid twice the average wage in the community—a tremendous wage advantage. However, the working conditions were considered unfavorable. Although employees disliked their working conditions, they remained with the organization because of the salaries. They were not motivated to be high performers, but only to perform well enough to keep their jobs. The workers were typically young males who were able to satisfy their taste for expensive automobiles, as was evident in the parking lot. Inside, employees were demoralized and unmotivated, but would not leave. They were present physically, but checked out mentally. Over-investing can create this type of situation and result in inadequate turnover.

Another concern about the consequences of over-investing is the impact on the shareholders. These days, shareholders understand more about human capital and want their companies to invest appropriately. If they see signs of over-investing, they want to know why. For example, what is the logic in developing a $4 million wellness and fitness center? The investor, observing any of the signs of over-investing described above may sound the alarm and question the investment. Therefore, to keep shareholders happy, there should be a more optimum level of investment.

ADVANTAGES

Obviously, over-investing is not a recommended strategy. However, from the employee's perspective, over-investing is a good thing. It provides more money and benefits to those who need it most, helping to drive up the average salary and benefits packages for all companies. Also, for those organizations that can afford it—and when it is not having an unfavorable impact on financial performance—it may send an important signal to others. It underscores the importance these organizations place on human capital and may bring additional attention and concern for those that are not investing enough.

This strategy may be useful as a quick fix for an organization in serious trouble. High turnover, excessive work stoppages, or increases in employee complaints all have a tendency to deteriorate the wealth of the organization. A short-term, over-investment is absolutely essential to overcoming these problems. Over-investing can be effective if administered wisely and when the long-term impact of added benefits and programs is considered.

SUMMARY

Regardless of which side of the debate a person is on, over-investing exists and must be examined closely. This chapter details the signs of over-investing, the causes, and telltale indicators that a company may be spending excessive amounts on their employees. It also shows the forces that have come into play in recent years that often cause companies to over-invest in their employees. The consequences can be critical. However, there are a few advantages that make this a workable strategy for some situations.

NOTES

1　　　Kevin Freiberg and Jackie Freiberg, *Guts! Companies That Blow the Doors of the Business-As-Usual* (New York: Doubleday, 2004).

2　　　Nanette Brynes, "The Benefits Trap," *Business Week*, July 19, 2004, pp. 64–67.

3　　　Ibid.

4　　　Patrick J. Kiger, "Les Hayman's Excellent Adventure," *Workforce Management*, August 2004, p. 43.

5　　　Nanette Brynes, "The Benefits Trap," *Business Week*, July 19, 2004, pp. 64–67.

6　　　Andrew McAfee, "Do You Have Too Much IT?" *MIT Sloan Management Review*, Spring 2004, p. 18.

7　　　Christian Koehler and Robert Weissbarth, "The Art of Underengineering," *Strategy Business*, Issue 34, p. 14.

8　　　Haig R. Nalbantian, Richard A. Guzzo, Dave Kieffer, and Jay Doherty, *Play to Your Strengths: Managing Your Internal Labor Markets for Lasting Competitive Advantage* (New York: McGraw-Hill, 2004).

9　　　John Humphreys, "The Vision Thing," *MIT Sloan Management Review*, Spring 2004, p. 96.

CHAPTER 5

Invest as Long as There Is a Payoff

Some organizations prefer to invest in human capital when there is evidence that it is providing benefits. They often compare monetary benefits with the costs of human capital programs. This strategy is becoming more popular following the increased interest in accountability, particularly the use of return on investment (ROI) as a business-evaluation tool. With this strategy, all HR programs are evaluated and a few key programs are evaluated at the ROI level—the monetary benefits compared to the cost of investment—the same way the ROI is calculated for an investment in buildings or equipment.

THE ROI STRATEGY

The ROI strategy focuses on implementing a comprehensive measurement and evaluation process for the human capital expenditures in an organization. This involves capturing up to seven types of data when a human capital program is implemented, as shown in table 5-1.[1]

Table 5-1. Types of data collected with the ROI strategy.

Human Capital Program Measures

- **Reaction** to and **satisfaction** with the program
- Improved **knowledge and skills** necessary to make the program successful
- The **application and implementation** of the program
- Specific **business impact** measures directly linked to the program
- **Return on investment** data comparing the monetary benefits of the program to the costs
- Total **costs** of the human capital program
- **Intangible data**—not converted to monetary value (when the conversion is too expensive or lacks credibility)

Using this philosophy, only a small number of programs are taken to ROI, whereas every program is evaluated with reaction and satisfaction data. Also, when business impact and ROI are developed for an HR program, one or more techniques are used to isolate the impact of the program on the business data.

Case Studies

Wachovia Bank is the fourth largest banking organization in the United States (*the* largest bank in the southeast United States), with $464 billion in assets, 14 million customers, and 3,100 branches in 15 states. Wachovia takes a comprehensive approach to evaluating human capital initiatives. Data is collected for each program implemented by HR. All learning and development programs are evaluated for employee reaction and satisfaction. Sixty percent of the programs are evaluated to determine if the appropriate skills and knowledge exist to make HR programs work. Thirty percent of the programs are evaluated on a follow-up basis to determine if employees are using the skills and knowledge and that the programs are implemented effectively. Ten percent of the programs are measured for their impact on business in such a way that improvements linked to the HR program are isolated from other influences. Finally, about five percent of the company's HR projects and programs are evaluated at the ROI level, where the actual monetary value of an HR program is compared to the cost of the program. Table 5-2 shows the breakdown in terms of percentages of programs evaluated at each level.

To accomplish this comprehensive process, Wachovia has developed an assessment, measurement, and evaluation team (referred to as the AME network) for the entire HR function. This decentralized thirty-person team implements the AME in each business unit. Although full-time Wachovia employees, team members are not usually full-time AME professionals. They are HR professionals who, by the nature of their work and interest in mea-

Table 5-2. Evaluation targets for Wachovia Bank.

Level of Evaluation	Percent of HR Programs Evaluated at this Level
Level 1—Reaction	100%
Level 2—Learning	60%
Level 3—Application	30%
Level 4—Business Results	10%
Level 5—ROI	5%

surement, have taken on these additional responsibilities. While the overall strategy is coordinated by the vice president for AME in the corporate head-quarters, the work is accomplished in the regions and divisions through these teams. Team members, in concert with other HR staff and various stakehold-ers, ensure that appropriate standards, templates, tools, and processes are in place to streamline the data collection, analysis, and reporting. Also, AME team members develop impact studies and communicate them to various tar-get audiences. This collective effort provides Wachovia executives with infor-mation about the value of human capital. Executives decide on which programs are appropriate for impact and ROI analysis in the future. The total cost of this process is about 5 percent of the total HR budget, which includes the corporate university at Wachovia. All the data are combined to develop a human capital scorecard for executives to monitor.

At Suncor Energy, ROI is being used to make the human capital busi-ness case. When implementing a human resource management system (HRMS), the vice president of HR calculated the usual costs of the technology and the savings it would produce. But reducing HR transaction costs through automation—though important—was not the most important reason to pur-chase the system. The business case wasn't just about doing HR better but about delivering business value.

Suncor, a mining, natural gas, and refining company with about 3,200 employees, is based in Calgary, Alberta, Canada. It is one of a small but grow-ing number of companies savvy enough to understand that the traditional factors considered in calculating ROI—cutting administrative costs and re-ducing HR staff-to-employee ratio, for instance—are limited. Improving the entire company's productivity is the priority. So, the vice president of HR set out to measure the business impact of buying an HRMS. Her conclusion matches a growing consensus among consultants and practitioners that exec-utives have already squeezed all the inefficiencies possible from transactions and have reduced HR staff as much as possible. Now, the measures of success will be increased productivity and added business value.[2]

IBM spent over $30 billion in 2001—around 35 percent of its reve-nue—on its 341,000 employees, with approximately $1 billion dedicated to learning. Given the sums involved, top management asked HR to determine whether this investment was aligned with the company's strategic goals and whether it delivered an adequate ROI. In order to answer these questions, HR launched a measurement initiative to prove that learning is delivered in a cost-effective manner, reinforces the importance of human capital as a key differ-entiator for IBM, and ensures that the learning investment supports IBM's business priority of attracting, motivating, and retaining the best talent.[3]

The program began with a small team made up of representatives from corporate HR and professionals from the business strategy and finance departments. Each of the members possessed knowledge of the subject matter and a high degree of business expertise. After the team created a measurement framework, they began a scaleable project to leverage the HR and strategic business teams at each business unit.

Although the team began the pilot project in only one unit, as soon as it became clear their framework could become part of the overall strategic management system, they quickly expanded it to include all units. Within just over one year, the HR measurement program became embedded in the company's strategic-planning process.

First Tennessee National has long believed that its employees are the key to its business strategy and customer focus. When the Nashville-based financial services firm selected a new vice president for its HR function, it was seeking to understand and explain how the focus on employees affects financial results. The CEO wanted to be able to go to Wall Street and discuss the value of this employees-first culture.

Today, the HR vice president works closely with the CFO to improve how the company's biggest investment—its people—affects future results. She sees investors and analysts increasingly making the connection. Many of the analysts and investors confirm that First Tennessee is on the right path.

The first step in the process was an exhaustive study in 2000 examining how First Tennessee's reward and recognition system lined up with its business strategy. The study integrated all of the data First Tennessee had available: seven years of employee data collected on the company's central HR/IS system; all marketing and customer research information, including market share; customer value and loyalty information; profitability data; and employee survey data. The study validated the links First Tennessee already believed existed between high-performing employees, customer loyalty and retention, and higher profitability. Now, First Tennessee is grappling with how to quantify a return on human capital investment beyond looking at the connection between salaries, variable compensation, and financial results.[4]

When to Use This Strategy

This strategy is implemented from three different perspectives: defensive, responsive, or proactive.

1. *Defensive.* Most organizations address the payoff versus investment issue from a defensive posture. Additional measurement and evalua-

tion data are needed to justify, maintain, or modify the HR budget. Sometimes these types of data are necessary to avoid budget cuts or obtain additional funding for human capital projects. Still, in other situations, top executives request results. Consequently, HR executives use this strategy to respond to those requests.

2. *Responsive*. Approximately one-third of the organizations using this strategy are doing so because they perceive measurement and evaluation as a routine responsibility, such as budgeting and project management. Human resources executives understand that they must show a contribution for major expenditures and align HR programs and projects with the business. Also, this effort is necessary to keep the HR staff engaged and motivated so they can see the contribution they are making to the organization.

3. *Proactive*. Approximately 20 percent of organizations pursuing this strategy do so from a proactive stance. These HR executives have a desire to be leaders in their profession. They want to be the "best practice," "benchmarked," "most admired" organization, and the "best place to work." They have a desire to keep stakeholders satisfied and build critical relationships with key executives. Also, they want to make human capital management more efficient and effective and build on accountability. The ROI strategy provides a vehicle to transform the human capital function.

FORCES DRIVING CHANGE

Although the trend toward additional accountability has been increasing over a decade, there are several reasons why this strategy is critical at this time. In the last few years, HR professionals have had to demonstrate the value their programs and departments add to the organization. They have also had to develop the skills to communicate with other managers, in the language of business, the HR contribution to the financial bottom line. In a world in which financial results are measured, a failure to measure human capital policy and practice dooms this function to second-class status, oversight, neglect, and potential failure. It has become apparent that HR specialists need to be able to evaluate in financial terms the costs and benefits of different HR strategies and individual HRM practices.[5]

The increasing cost of human capital is another driving force. As discussed throughout this book, investment in human capital is quite large and growing. As HR budgets continue to grow—often outpacing other parts of the organization—the costs alone require some executives to question the value of human capital. Consequently, these executives often request or suggest that the impact of HR be determined or forecasted. In some cases, ROI is required at budget review time. A production manager, for example, may propose investing in new technology and incorporate into the proposal projected increases in productivity and decreases in unit production cost. With this in mind, HR professionals must compete for scarce organizational resources in the same language as their colleagues and present credible information on the relative costs and benefits of HR interventions.[6]

The desire for organizations to be more effective and efficient has brought a host of change strategies such as Six-Sigma transformation, reengineering, and other improvement processes. Many of these processes are focused on measurement issues and, in turn, drive more interest in measurement, including measurements for human capital. In some organizations, a measurement culture is created, driving additional requirements for all types of measures.

A special research report from *CFO* magazine provided input on ROI from the perspective of the chief financial officer: It made an argument for trying to calculate the ROI. Taken as a whole, the report concluded, human capital is an unavoidable cost of business. When considered as a collection of smaller investments, though, there are clearly choices to be made. Which training programs are worth investing in? What employee segments should receive higher compensation? What components should the employee health care plan include? If managers can gain some sense of the return on these different options, then they can ensure that money is being put to the best use. This may not mean putting a dollar value on the different choices, but perhaps understanding their effect on key nonfinancial indicators, such as customer or employee retention.[7]

More HR executives are managing the human capital function as a business. These executives have operational experience and, in some cases, financial experience. They recognize that human capital should add value to the organization and, consequently, these executives are implementing a variety of measurement tools, even in the hard-to-measure areas. These measurement tools have gradually become more quantitative and less qualitative. ROI is now being applied in human capital just as it is in technology, quality, and product development. A decade ago it was almost unheard of to use ROI in the HR area. Now, business-minded HR executives are attempting to show value in ways that top executives want to see. Top executives who are asking for value—including ROI—are viewing HR differently than they have in the past and are no longer willing to accept HR programs, projects, and initiatives on faith. This is not to suggest that they do not have a commitment to HR, but now they see that measurement is possible—and ROI is feasible— and they want to see more value.

These forces are driving a significant use of the ROI methodology described in this chapter.

PROFILES OF ORGANIZATIONS USING THIS STRATEGY

What types of organizations are applying human capital measurement, including ROI? Typically, there are common threads among adapters. They are:

- ❏ Medium to large in size, where the HR budget becomes a critical issue.
- ❏ Developing a performance-improvement culture and even a measurement culture. This culture is spreading to the HR function.
- ❏ Experiencing a leadership change in the HR area. A new HR executive is often willing to bring additional accountability to HR, and usually does not have the attachment to, or ownership of, previous HR programs.
- ❏ Going through constant and significant change; their world is always in a flux and on the move. To keep up with this change, many executives are asking for value from the multitude of HR programs implemented.
- ❏ Facing demanding top executives (even a CEO) who expect results from all types of HR programs.
- ❏ Straddled with a relatively low investment in measurement and have a desire to increase that investment.
- ❏ Attempting to rectify the problems generated in the past; it could be one or more HR programs that were considered failures or, in some cases, disasters.
- ❏ Suffering from a low approval rating from executives where the HR function is often perceived less than satisfactory in its effectiveness.

Table 5-3 shows a small sample of the over 2,000 organizations using the ROI strategy to help determine the human capital investment level.

THE ROI METHODOLOGY

To develop a credible approach for calculating the ROI in human capital, several components must be developed and integrated. This strategy comprises five important elements:

1. An evaluation framework is needed to define the various levels of evaluation and types of data, as well as how data are captured.

2. A process model must be created to provide a step-by-step procedure for developing the ROI calculation. Part of this process is the isolation of the effects of the HR program from other factors in order to show its monetary payoff.

3. A set of operating standards with a conservative philosophy is required. These guiding principles keep the process on track to ensure successful replication. The operating standards also build credibility with key stakeholders in the organization.

4. Resources should be devoted to implementation to ensure that the ROI methodology becomes operational and routine in the organization. Implementation addresses issues such as responsibilities, policies, procedures, guidelines, goals, and internal skill building.

5. Successful applications are critical to show how ROI works with different types of human capital programs and projects.

Together, these five elements are necessary to develop a comprehensive evaluation system that contains a balanced set of measures, has credibility

Table 5-3. Private-sector organizations using the ROI process.

• Allstate Insurance	• Home Depot
• Apple Computer	• Household Finance
• AT&T	• IBM
• Bank of America	• Intel
• Blue Cross and Blue Shield	• Lockheed Martin
• Bristol-Myers Squibb	• Microsoft
• British Telecom	• Motorola
• Caremark	• NCR
• CIBC	• Nextel
• Comcast	• Olive Garden Restaurant
• Dell Computers	• PricewaterhouseCoopers
• Deloitte & Touche	• QUALCOMM
• DHL Worldwide Express	• SAP
• Eli Lilly	• Scotiabank
• Federal Express	• Shell Oil
• General Mills	• Verizon Communications
• Genentech	• Wachovia Bank
• Georgia Pacific	• Wells Fargo
• Hewlett Packard	

with the various stakeholders involved, and can be easily replicated. Because of the importance of, and interest in this ROI strategy, the remainder of this chapter is devoted to taking a closer look at these five essential pieces.

THE EVALUATION FRAMEWORK

Seven types of data used in the ROI strategy were described at the beginning of the chapter. Figure 5-1 shows the types of data arranged as a chain of impact that occurs when a human capital program drives business impact. Also, the connection to the types of data is indicated within the blocks. Although these data types can be considered separately, they are inevitably woven together in this chain of impact and their meanings are integrated.[8]

Figure 5-1. Business impact and ROI from an HR program.

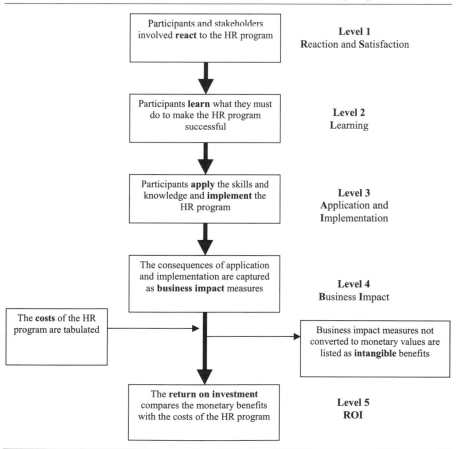

The levels of evaluation help explain the chain of impact. The higher the level, the more valuable the data for driving the business impact.

Usually the first type of data, reaction from HR stakeholders, is measured on almost all HR functions, programs, and projects with generic questionnaires and surveys. Although this level of evaluation is important as a customer-satisfaction measure from program participants and other stakeholders, a favorable reaction does not ensure that the participants know how to implement the HR program. A learning check is helpful to ensure that participants absorb new skills, knowledge, and know-how to make the HR program successful. However, a positive measure at this level is no guarantee that the program will be successfully implemented.

Measuring application and implementation is necessary to determine if participants implement the HR program successfully. The frequency and use of skills may be important measures at this level. In addition, this measure includes all the steps, actions, tasks, and procedures needed to implement the program. Although evaluation is important to gauge the success of the program's implementation, it still does not guarantee a positive business impact on the organization.

Measuring the business impact tracks the business results achieved directly by the HR program. Typical measures include output, quality, costs, time, employee satisfaction, and customer satisfaction. Although the HR program may produce a measurable business impact, there is still a concern that the costs for the program may be too high. Measuring costs involves monitoring or developing all of the costs related to the HR program. A fully loaded cost profile is recommended in which all direct and indirect costs are tabulated.

ROI is the ultimate level of evaluation, where the HR program's monetary benefits are compared with its costs. Although ROI can be expressed in several ways, it is usually presented as a percentage or benefit/cost ratio (BCR). In addition to tangible, monetary benefits, most HR programs will have intangible, nonmonetary benefits. Intangible benefits are defined as implementation and business benefits not converted to monetary value.

When the chain of impact occurs through each level, the HR program becomes successful. A positive reaction leads to learning and, as the implementation progresses, business impact and ROI are generated. If measurements are not taken at each level, it is difficult to conclude that the results achieved were actually produced by the program. Because of this, it is recommended that evaluation be conducted at all levels when pursuing an ROI evaluation.

The ROI Process Model

The chain of impact is detailed by the model in figure 5-2, the ROI methodology, which has been refined and modified over many applications.[9] As the figure illustrates, the process is comprehensive as data is developed at different times and gathered from different sources to develop the seven types of measures. Each part of the ROI process is outlined below.

Evaluation Planning

The first two steps of the ROI methodology focus on critical planning issues. The first step is to develop appropriate objectives for the HR programs and initiatives. These are often referred to as the ultimate objectives of the HR program. These range from developing objectives for satisfaction to developing an objective for the ROI. A specific program should have multiple levels of objectives.

With the objectives in hand, the next step is to develop two important planning documents. A data collection plan indicates the type of data that should be collected, the method for data collection, data sources, the timing of collection, and the various responsibilities for collection. The ROI analysis plan details how the HR program is isolated from other influences, how data are converted to monetary values, the appropriate cost categories, the expected intangible measures, and the anticipated target audience for communication.

Collecting Data

Data collected during the launch of the HR program (Levels 1 and 2) measures employee reaction, satisfaction, and learning to ensure that adjustments are made to keep the program on track. The reaction, satisfaction, and learning data are critical for providing immediate feedback so that early changes can be made. Post-program data are collected and compared with pre-program data and expectations (Levels 3 and 4). Both hard data and soft data, including work habits, work climate, and attitudes are collected. Data can be collected using a variety of methods, such as:

❑ Follow-up surveys and questionnaires to measure satisfaction and reaction from stakeholders, as well as to uncover specific application issues with HR programs

Figure 5-2. ROI process model.

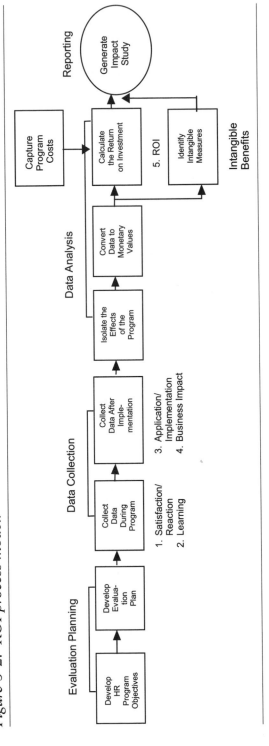

❑ On-the-job observation to capture application and use

❑ Tests and assessments to measure the extent of learning

❑ Interviews to measure reaction and determine the extent to which the program has been implemented

❑ Focus groups to determine the degree of application of the HR program in job situations

❑ Action plans to show progress with implementation on the job and the impact obtained

❑ Business-performance monitoring to show improvement in various performance records and operational data

The important challenge in data collection is selecting the method(s) appropriate for the setting and the specific HR program, within time and budget constraints.

Isolating the Effects of the HR Program

An often-overlooked issue in most evaluations is the process of isolating the effects of the HR program or project. This step is essential because many factors will influence performance data after a program is implemented. Specific strategies in this step will pinpoint the amount of improvement directly related to the program. The result is increased accuracy and credibility of the ROI calculation. The following strategies have been used to address this important issue:

❑ A pilot group of participants in the program is compared with another group (control group) not participating in the program in order to isolate program impact.

❑ Trend lines are used to project the values of business impact data, and projections are compared with the actual data after the program.

❑ Participants/stakeholders estimate the amount of improvement related to the program; supervisors and managers estimate the impact of the program on the output measures.

❑ External studies or previous research provides input about the impact of the program; independent experts estimate the impact of the program on the performance variable.

❑ Customers (internal or external) provide input about the extent to which the program has influenced their decisions to use a product or service.

Collectively, these strategies provide a variety of methods to tackle the critical issue of isolating the effects of an HR program.

Converting Data to Monetary Values

To calculate the return on investment (Level 5), business impact data must be converted to monetary values and compared with HR program costs. This requires a value to be placed on each unit of data connected with the program. The list below shows most of the key strategies available to convert data to monetary values. The specific strategy selected usually depends on the type of data and the situation:

- ❏ Output data, such as an additional product or service provided, are converted to profit contribution (or cost savings) and reported as a standard value.
- ❏ The cost of a quality measure, such as a customer complaint, is calculated and reported as a standard value.
- ❏ Employee time saved is converted to fully loaded compensation.
- ❏ Historical costs or value of a measure, such as preventing a lost-time accident, are used when available.
- ❏ Internal and external experts estimate a value of a measure, such as an employee complaint.
- ❏ External databases contain an approximate value or cost of a measure, such as employee turnover.
- ❏ The measure is linked to other measures for which the costs are easily developed (for example, employee satisfaction linked to employee turnover).
- ❏ Participants estimate the cost or value of the data item, such as work group conflict.
- ❏ Supervisors or managers estimate costs or values when they are capable of providing an estimate (for example, an unscheduled absence).
- ❏ The HR staff estimates the value of a data item, such as a sexual harassment complaint.

This step in the ROI methodology is critical and absolutely necessary for determining the monetary benefits from an HR program or solution. The process is challenging, particularly with soft data, but can be methodically accomplished using one or more of the above strategies.

Tabulating the Cost of the HR Program

The denominator of the ROI formula is the cost of the program. The following cost components should be included:

- ❑ Initial analysis and assessment, possibly prorated over the expected life of the program
- ❑ Purchase/acquisition cost, if applicable
- ❑ Development/design cost for the program (prorated if necessary)
- ❑ Participant/stakeholder time for the program using fully loaded compensation costs
- ❑ Materials and supplies for the program
- ❑ Application and implementation costs of the program
- ❑ Routine maintenance and monitoring costs
- ❑ Administration and overhead costs for the program, allocated in a convenient way
- ❑ Evaluating and reporting costs

The conservative approach is to include all these costs so that the total is fully loaded. All costs must be taken into account to ensure a stronger position from which to present the final findings.

Calculating ROI

The return on investment is calculated using benefits and costs. The benefit/cost ratio (BCR) is the monetary benefits of the HR program or intervention divided by the costs. In formula form, it is:

$$BCR = \frac{HR \text{ program monetary benefits}}{HR \text{ program costs}}$$

The return on investment uses the net benefits divided by costs. The net benefits are the program benefits minus the costs. In formula form, the ROI becomes:

$$ROI \ (\%) = \frac{Net \ HR \text{ program benefits}}{HR \text{ program costs}} \times 100$$

This is the same basic formula used in evaluating other investments where the ROI is traditionally reported as earnings divided by investment.

The BCR and the ROI present the same general information but with slightly different perspectives. The following example illustrates the use of these formulas. An absenteeism reduction program produced savings of $581,000, with a cost of $229,000. Therefore, the benefit/cost ratio is:

$$\text{BCR} = \frac{\$581,000}{\$229,000} = 2.54 \text{ (or 2.5:1)}$$

As this calculation shows, for every $1 invested, $2.50 in monetary benefits is returned. In this example, net benefits are $581,000 − $229,000 = $352,000. Thus, the ROI would be:

$$\text{ROI} = \frac{\$352,000}{\$229,000} \times 100 = 154\%$$

This means that for every $1 invested in the program, there is a return of $1.54 in net benefits, after the $1 is recovered. The benefits are usually expressed as annual benefits for short-term programs, representing the amount saved or gained for a complete year after the program has been implemented. Although the benefits may continue after the first year, the impact usually diminishes and is omitted from calculations in short-term situations. For long-term projects, the benefits are spread over several years. The timing of the benefits stream should be determined before the impact study begins, as part of the planning process.

Identifying Intangible Benefits

During data analysis, every attempt is made to convert all data to monetary values. For example, hard data—such as output, quality, cost, and time—are always converted to monetary values while soft data conversion is attempted. However, if the conversion process is too subjective or inaccurate and the resulting values lose credibility in the process, the data are listed as intangible benefits with the appropriate explanation. For some programs, intangible, nonmonetary benefits have highly perceived value, often commanding as much attention and influence as hard data. Intangible benefits may include items such as improved public image, increased job satisfaction, increased organizational commitment, reduced stress, and improved teamwork.

Reporting

A final operational step of the ROI methodology is to generate an impact study documenting the results achieved by the HR program and communicating them to various target audiences. The impact study presents the basic process used to generate the seven categories of data. The methodology, assumptions, key concepts, and guiding principles are all outlined before the actual results are presented. Next, the seven categories of data, beginning with reaction and satisfaction and moving through ROI and intangible measures, are presented in a rational, logical process, showing the building blocks to success for the study. Conclusions and recommendations are always a part of the study. This study becomes the historical document that presents the complete assessment of the program.

Since a variety of target audiences need information, different reports and formats are generated. All the stakeholders involved will need some communication about the success of the program, including executives who may not be interested in knowing the full details. A general interest report may be appropriate for stakeholders who are involved but not directly responsible for the project. A variety of reports and formats are used to disseminate the information, ranging from the complete impact study described above to a one-page summary for clients who understand the process. The key issue in this step of the ROI methodology is to analyze the target audiences detailed during the evaluation planning and develop the appropriate report to meet their specific needs.

OPERATING STANDARDS AND GUIDING PRINCIPLES

To ensure that each study is developed in the same way, consistent processes and operating standards for the measurement and evaluation process should be implemented. Table 5-4 presents the guiding principles used as operating standards when implementing the ROI methodology. These guiding principles will ensure that the proper conservative approach is taken and the impact study can be replicated and compared with others. More importantly, the principles build credibility with, and support from, clients and senior managers who review and scrutinize the results.

IMPLEMENTATION

The best tool, technique, or model will not be successful unless it is properly used and it becomes a routine part of the HR function. As with any change, it will be resisted by the HR staff and other stakeholders. Some of the resistance will be based on realistic barriers, while some will be based on misunderstandings that may be mythical. In both cases, specific steps must be taken to over-

Table 5-4. Operating standards for this strategy.

1. When an evaluation is planned for a higher level, the previous level does not have to be comprehensive.
2. When a higher-level evaluation is conducted, data must be collected at lower levels.
3. When collecting and analyzing data, use the most credible sources.
4. When analyzing data, choose the most conservative approach.
5. At least one method must be used to isolate the effects of the program.
6. If no improvement data are available for the performing group, it is assumed that little or no improvement has occurred.
7. Estimates of improvement should be adjusted for the potential error of the estimate.
8. Extreme data items and unsupported claims should not be used in ROI calculations.
9. The first year of benefits (annual) should be used in the ROI analysis of short-term programs.
10. Program costs should be fully loaded for ROI analysis.
11. Intangible measures are defined as measures that are purposely not converted to monetary values.
12. The results from the ROI methodology must be communicated to all key stakeholders.

come the resistance by carefully and methodically implementing the ROI methodology.

Implementation involves many issues, including assigning responsibilities, building the necessary skills, and developing the plans and goals around the process. It also involves preparing the environment, individuals, and support teams for this type of comprehensive analysis. The organizations experiencing the most success with the ROI methodology have devoted adequate resources for implementation and deliberately planned for transition from their current state to where they desire the organization to be in terms of accountability. Additional detail about this methodology is presented in chapter 8.

Disadvantages

The methodology described in this chapter is not suitable for every organization and certainly not for every program. It has some very important barriers to success. The ROI methodology will add additional costs and time to the HR budget, but not a significant amount—probably no more than 3 to 5 percent of the total direct HR budget. The additional investment in ROI should be offset by the results achieved from implementation. However, this barrier often stops many ROI implementations early in the process. Many HR staff members may not have the basic skills necessary to apply the ROI methodology within their scope of responsibilities. The typical HR program does not focus on results, but on qualitative feedback data. It is necessary to shift HR policy and practice from an activity-based approach to a results-based approach. Some HR staff members do not pursue ROI because they perceive the ROI methodology as an individual performance-evaluation process instead of a process-improvement tool.

ADVANTAGES

The ROI methodology has several important advantages. With it, the HR staff and the client will know the specific contribution of a program in a language the client understands. Measuring the ROI in an HR program is one of the most convincing ways to earn the respect and support of the senior management team—not only for a particular program but for the human capital function as well. The client who requests and authorizes an HR program or project will have a complete set of data to show the overall success of the process.

Because a variety of feedback data are collected during the program implementation, the comprehensive analysis provides data to drive changes in processes and make adjustments during implementation. Throughout the cycle of program design, development, and implementation, the entire team of stakeholders focuses on results. If a program is not effective, and the results are not materializing, the ROI methodology will prompt changes or modifications. On rare occasions, the program may have to be halted if it is not adding the appropriate value.

SUMMARY

This chapter provides an overview of the ROI strategy, underscoring the urgency and the challenge to develop a comprehensive measurement and evaluation process. Various forces create a critical need for increased accountability. An evaluation framework, the ROI process model, operating standards, implementation, and application are all necessary to develop a reliable, credible process that can be replicated from one HR project to another. This process is not without its concerns and barriers, but many of these can be overcome with simplified, economical methods and a disciplined approach.

NOTES

1   Jack J. Phillips and Patricia P. Phillips, *Proving the Value of HR: When and How to Measure ROI* (Alexandria, VA: Society for Human Resource Management, 2005).

2   Bill Roberts, "Count on Business Value," *HR Magazine*, August 2002, pp. 65–66.

3   Stephen Bates, *Linking People Measures to Strategy Research Report R-1342-03RR* (New York: The Conference Board, 2003).

4   Don Durfree, *Human Capital Management: The CFO's Perspective* (Boston: CFO Publishing Corp., 2003).

5   J. Pfeffer, *The Human Equation* (Boston: Harvard Business School Press, 1998).

6   Linda Holbeche, *HRM Strategy* (Oxford: Butterworth-Heinemann, 2001).

7   Don Durfree, *Human Capital Management: The CFO's Perspective* (Boston: CFO Publishing Corp., 2003).

8   Jack J. Phillips, Ron D. Stone, and Patricia P. Phillips, *The Human Resources Scorecard: Measuring the Return on Investment* (Woburn, MA: Butterworth-Heinemann, 2001).

9   Jack J. Phillips and Patricia P. Phillips, *Proving the Value of HR: When and How to Measure ROI* (Alexandria, VA: Society for Human Resource Management, 2005).

PART TWO

WHY DOES THIS MATTER?

The Importance and Value of Human Capital

CHAPTER 6

What We Know from Logic and Intuition

While all of the chapters in this section underscore the importance and value of human capital, this one examines the importance and value of human capital from a logical, intuitive basis, and introduces several arguments for why human capital is king or queen. It begins by looking at the role of people in organizations, and then explores issues such as how human capital is (or is not) accounted for. The role of human capital in highly successful organizations is examined in popular lists such as the Best Places to Work and the Most Admired Companies. In almost all cases, logical arguments point toward the importance of people to an organization, as people contribute most, if not all, of the organization's successes. The discussion emphasizes the value organizations place on their people and their reasons for doing so. The chapter ends with a concern for additional research—some managers and executives need more data to be convinced that human capital makes a difference.

CAN WE DO IT WITHOUT PEOPLE?

Some managers view the human aspect of organizations as an irritant, a burden, or perhaps a necessary evil. People cause most of the problems. It is the people who are dissatisfied, file grievances, lodge complaints, allege sexual harassment, get injured on the job, file workers compensation claims, go on strike, and create a host of other problems that not only take them out of service, but take precious time and resources to resolve. Some executives have estimated that employee problems account for as much as 20 percent of the total cost of human capital investment. If the people could be removed, the problems would go away; there would be no complaints, charges, gripes, grievances, accidents, or work stoppages. For some organizations, this would be Utopia and they strive to achieve this scenario.

THE TECHNOLOGY REVOLUTION

The advancement of equipment, machines, and technology has enabled many organizations to automate parts of the job and, in some cases, all of the job. As technology evolves, is it possible to have a completely automated workplace? Is it possible to remove the human factor, at least for the most part? Consider something that would almost be unheard of years ago: automated air travel. With the available technology, airplanes could basically take off, fly to their destination, and land completely automated. Much of the check-in, boarding, and logistics could be automated, as it is now to a certain extent. It may be possible for the entire process (from checking in to arriving at the desired destination) to be accomplished without any human interaction. To some, this seems like science fiction, but it could be a reality. Is this desired? Perhaps not. What happens if technology fails or there is a glitch in the automation? The dream becomes a nightmare. It may be impossible to remove the factor in the short term, but this is a goal for many.

AUTOMATE, AUTOMATE, AUTOMATE!

Regardless of one's position on job automation, there are some jobs that should be eliminated; automation should be an essential and significant part of the strategy of deciding how much to invest in employees. Four types of jobs are ideal candidates for automation. First, the jobs that are considered very monotonous and boring should be eliminated. These jobs are routine and require little thought and concentration. Many assembly line jobs fit into this category. If possible, these jobs should be automated; otherwise, the monotony leads to dissatisfaction, which leads to absenteeism, turnover, injuries, withdrawal, sometimes even sickness. Employees have become sick solely because of the rote work they do.

Second, jobs that are highly dangerous should be automated. This is a critical issue in heavy industry, manufacturing, and mining—using technology to remove the employee factor so that injuries and deaths can be prevented. This is not only the cost-effective thing to do, but the humane thing as well.

Third, transaction-based jobs should be automated. These jobs involve simple-step transactions that can be handled much more efficiently with technology. Consider the issue of booking an airline reservation—a very transaction-based process. A few years ago it was all done on the phone or face-to-face; now the majority of reservations are made on the Internet, thus eliminating many people who have to be involved in the process. Some airlines charge an additional fee when reservations are made via the phone, thus providing an incentive to reserve a seat via the Internet. The newer technology produces fewer errors, is quicker, and less costly for the organization.

Fourth, jobs that are difficult to recruit capable employees for should be automated, if possible. Many organizations are automating processes, steps, and even entire functions. Consider the local service station and the job of fueling your automobile. Gone are the days when three attendants ran out to your car, filled the tank, checked the oil, washed the windshield, put air in the tires, and took your money. Today, the individual consumer is familiar with the gas pump. By following a few simple directions, the consumer fills the tank, pays with a credit card, and goes through an automatic car wash. These "modern" conveniences have enabled companies to provide more efficient delivery of their gasoline. If an attendant had to pump the gas and take the money, the associated cost would have to be passed onto the consumer—some estimate as much as 5 to 10 cents per gallon. This automation has eliminated jobs that are hard to fill and those that have high turnover. At the same time, there is increased efficiency and convenience. The hours of store operation are no longer a consideration; you can fuel your car at any time, any day of the week.

GURUS AND MORE GURUS

It would be remiss to discuss the importance of human capital—from a logical and intuitive perspective—without mentioning the impact and influence of management gurus. They are the first to say that the organization cannot be successful without human beings. Dozens of gurus have been advocating that employers should invest more—not less—in their people. Two of the most notable have been Stephen Covey and Ken Blanchard. Covey is the best-selling author of *7 Habits of Highly Effective People* (1989), selected by *Chief Executive Magazine* as the most influential book of the twentieth century. He has devoted his career to teaching leaders and individuals the value of people in the organization. Blanchard is the author of over thirty books, including The *One Minute Manager, Gung Ho, Raving Fans,* and *Empowerment Takes More than a Minute.* His concept of return on people (ROP) is intended to flag the importance of the people side of the business.

Other gurus, such as Tom Peters, who wrote the best-selling book, *In Search of Excellence,* continues to stalk the speakers' circuit, telling businesses what they need to do and what they need to stop doing. Among his themes is the importance of people, unleashing their power, and getting out of their way in the organization. For half a century, Peter Drucker (considered the father of management) has advocated investing more in employees. At age ninety-four, he is still stressing the importance of people in an organization's success, particularly the importance of the knowledge worker. Much of the current interest in the value of human capital is based, in part, on Drucker's assumptions, which he developed well ahead of his peers.

PEOPLE *ARE* NECESSARY

With the previous discussion as a backdrop, several conclusions can be reached about the role of people in the workplace. First, minimizing the numbers is not necessarily a bad strategy. In the name of efficiency, employee welfare, and the desire to have motivating and challenging jobs, certain jobs need to be eliminated or minimized, as outlined above.

Second, human capital investment at some level is necessary. Even in a completely automated transaction, people are involved in making key decisions, solving problems, and ensuring that the processes work correctly. The investment still exists; it is just that it may be a smaller percentage of the operating expenses.

Third, in a highly automated workplace, people are still critical. Sometimes their skills are upgraded because of problems that arise when transactions fail, or when technology or equipment fails. They are also needed to coordinate and implement the new technology in the first place. In an ideal situation, as jobs are eliminated, skills are upgraded so that the workforce is maintained or, in some cases, even grows. A firm that has both job creation and significant automation is adding tremendous value to the economy, which is the challenge of many organizations.

STOCK MARKET MYSTERY

When considering the value and importance of human capital, executives need to look no further than the stock market. Investors place a tremendous value on human capital in organizations. For example, consider QUALCOMM—a San Diego, California-based organization—a leader in developing and delivering innovative digital wireless communication products and services, based on the company's CDMA digital technology. QUALCOMM is included in the S&P 500 Index and is a Fortune 500 company traded on the NASDAQ stock market. QUALCOMM is a very profitable company with revenues in 2003 of $4 billion, a gross margin of 64 percent, and a net income of $827 million.[1]

QUALCOMM reported total assets (tangible) on its balance sheet of $8,822,436,000; however, the market value is much higher. The stock price in mid-2004 was $70 per share, and the company had a market value of $57,242,850,000. In essence, tangible assets represented only 15.4 percent of the market value and included not only the current assets of cash, marketable securities, accounts receivable and inventories, but also property, plants, equipment, and even goodwill.

Thus, investors see something in QUALCOMM that has a value much greater than the assets listed on the balance sheet. This "hidden value," as it is sometimes called, is the intangible assets, which now represent major portions of the value of organizations, particularly those in knowledge industries, such as QUALCOMM. It is helpful to understand what comprises intangible assets; human capital is certainly a big part of it.

A Brief History of Interest in Intangible Assets

The concern for intangible assets and their values can be traced back many years, but this concern gained popularity in the late 1960s and early 1970s in the form of human resources accounting.[2] Although interest diminished in the early 1980s, human resources accounting (HRA) enjoyed renewed emphasis in the late 1980s and continued strong throughout the 1990s. Human resources accounting was originally defined as a process designed to identify, measure, and communicate information about human resources in order to facilitate effective management within an organization. It was an extension of accounting principles—matching costs, revenues, and organizational data to communicate relevant information in financial terms. With HRA, employees are viewed as assets or investments for the organization. Methods of measuring these assets are similar to those of other assets; however, the process includes the concept of accounting for the condition of human capabilities and their value.

In the 1980s, organizations began developing case studies describing their application of HRA principles. For example, UpJohn used HRA to measure and forecast the return on investment in people. Even professional baseball teams began to use the concept to place a value on their talent. Three important questions placed HRA under scrutiny: Are human beings assets? What costs should be capitalized? What methods are most appropriate for establishing a value for employees with the eventual allocation of such values to expense?[3]

In 1986, Karl Erik Sveiby, manager and owner of a Swedish-based publishing company, published *The Knowledge Company*, a book that explained how to manage these intangible assets.[4] It was one of the first books to focus on "intellectual capital" and inspired other critical research in Europe. In Asia, the idea developed as firms attempted to show the value of their intangible assets. Japan's Hiroyuki Itami published an analysis of the performance of Japanese companies.[5] The study concluded that much of the performance differences of the firms is the result of intangible assets. In 1991, Skandia AFS, an insurance firm in Sweden, organized the first known corporate Intellectual Capital Office, naming Leif Edvinsson its first vice president for Intellectual Capital.[6] Edvinsson's mission was to learn how others were managing intellectual capital and using it to generate profits.

In 1991, Thomas Stewart, a member of the editorial board at *Fortune* magazine, wrote an article on brainpower, which began to discuss the idea that intangible assets had much to do with profitability and success.[7] This was followed by a cover story on the subject.[8] Since then, dozens of books have been written and hundreds of articles in professional journals have dominated print space on this critical issue. The topic of intangible assets often dominates conference agendas with some conferences devoted exclusively to the subject. The need to understand, measure, and use it in a productive way has led to a proliferation of information sources, benchmarking possibilities, and consulting groups.

INCREASED INTEREST IN INTANGIBLE ASSETS

Major changes in the economy and organizations have created a tremendous interest in intangible assets. In the last century the economy's base has moved from agricultural to industrial to intellectual, as shown in figure 6-1.[9] The knowledge era is perhaps the most far-reaching and explosive of the economic eras.

During the agricultural era, the focus was on land and how to make it more productive. During the industrial age, which dominated much of the first half of the twentieth century, the focus was on how efficiency and profits could be generated through the use of machinery. In the knowledge economy, the focus is on the human mind and how knowledge is used to build a more productive and efficient economy.

DEFINITIONS AND CATEGORIES

When it comes to classifying intangible assets, there is no agreement on the specific categories; the assets are important and varied. A large technology company, such as QUALCOMM, has a market value far exceeding its actual book value, which reflects its tangible assets. Important intangible categories make up this huge difference in value.

Figure 6-1. The shifting economic eras.

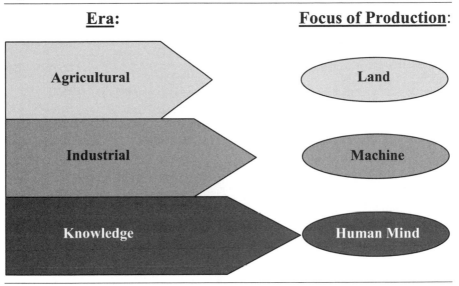

The first step to understanding the issue is to clearly define the difference between tangible and intangible assets. As presented in table 6-1, tangible assets are required for business operations and are readily visible, rigorously quantified, and represented as a line item on a balance sheet.[10] Intangible assets are key to enjoying a competitive advantage in the knowledge era and are invisible, difficult to quantify, and not tracked through traditional accounting practices. With this distinction, it is easier to understand the different categorizations.

Intellectual capital was early defined as the intangible assets that could be converted to profit. This concept has created a tremendous interest in understanding the impact of the knowledge contribution of successful organizations. Although there are more than a dozen ways to classify intangible assets, some categories are common between the groupings; three variations are presented here. A widely accepted grouping is contained in figure 6-2, where the enterprise is divided into tangible assets, intellectual capital, and financial capital.

In this arrangement, intellectual capital is divided into customer capital, human capital, and structural capital. Stewart, Edvinsson, Saint-Onge, and many others support this division. These categories will be discussed in this chapter with the phrase *intellectual capital* reflecting customer capital, human capital, and structural capital. Figure 6-3 shows the elements comprising intellectual capital offered by another researcher/practitioner in the field.[11] This

Table 6-1. Comparison of tangible and intangible assets.

Tangible Assets	Intangible Assets
Required for business operations	**Key to competitive advantage in the knowledge era**
• Readily visible	• Invisible
• Rigorously quantified	• Difficult to quantify
• Part of the balance sheet	• Not tracked through accounting practices
• Investment produces known returns	• Assessment based on assumptions
• Can be easily duplicated	• Cannot be bought or imitated
• Depreciates with use	• Appreciates with purposeful use
• Has finite application	• Multi-application without reducing value
• Best managed with "scarcity" mentality	• Best managed with "abundance" mentality
• Best leveraged through control	• Best leveraged through alignment
• Can be accumulated	• Dynamic: Short shelf-life when not in use

categorization includes research and development, intellectual assets, and knowledge, with knowledge being divided into tacit knowledge and codified knowledge.

Figure 6-4 offers a second grouping.[12] In this categorization, renewal capital reflects intellectual properties and marketable innovations. Relationship capital reflects networks and customers.

Still, another definition comes from Thomas Stewart[13] who suggests that human capital has three elements:

1. *Collective Skills*. These represent the talent of individuals, colleagues, and teams to build on the skills of each other.
2. *Communities of Practice*. Organizations are made up of communities and these communities of professional practice have become a recognized part of business life. The nature of knowledge will require companies to foster communities where there is a high level of candor and where corporate speak has no place.
3. *Social Capital*. What transforms workers into colleagues is social capital. It is the stock of active connections among people, the trust, mutual understanding, and shared values and behaviors that make cooperative action possible.

Whatever the definitions, human capital is a significant part of intellectual capital; intellectual capital is an important part of intangible assets. For

Figure 6-2. Categories and relationship of intellectual capital.

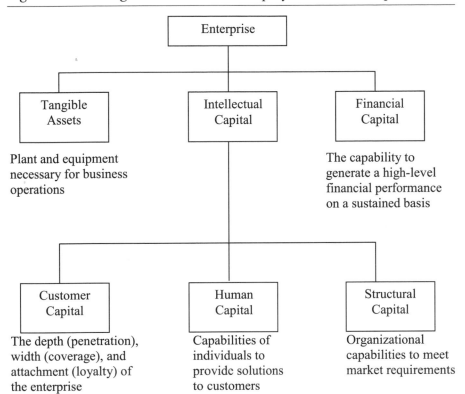

organizations—including knowledge-based organizations—intangible assets are often far greater than the tangible assets. The bottom line: We're in the knowledge era. Knowledge comes from people—not machines, financial resources, or natural resources.

ACCOUNTING DILEMMA

One of the problems of attempting to place a value on intangible assets stems from accounting standards. Both financial accounting (which appears in annual reports) and management accounting (which enables managers to take action) are inadequate for current organizations. Although there has been much discussion, the Generally Accepted Accounting Principles (GAAP) offered by the Financial Accounting Standards Board (FASB) are inadequate for placing a value on intangible assets and, in particular, the human capital issue. Even Alan Greenspan, chairman of the Federal Reserve Board, com-

Figure 6-3. Elements comprising intellectual capital.

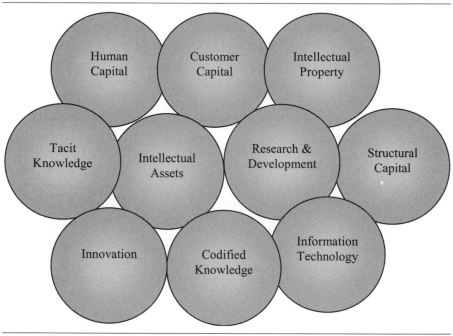

Figure 6-4. Categories of intellectual capital.

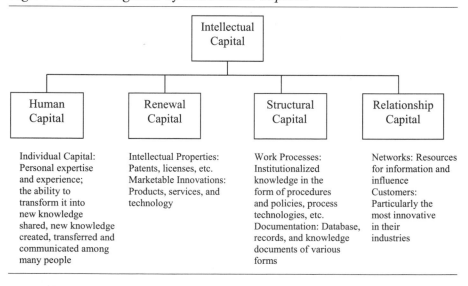

plained that accounting was not tracking investments of intellectual assets and that changes in technology have muddied the crucial distinction between capital assets and ordinary expenses. FASB indicates that accounting's fundamental purpose is to provide information that is useful in making rational investment, credit, and similar decisions. This is not happening. If the books were communicating stories that investors found useful, then a company's market value should correlate with the value accountants place on it. The QUALCOMM example illustrates the tremendous difference between market value and book value.

Professor Baruch Lev, who specializes in valuing trademarks and patents, conducted a series of in-depth comparisons of corporate asset values (book values) and share prices.[14] He concluded that the financial reporting methods used by nearly all corporations—the methods codified by the FASB and required of public companies by the Securities and Exchange Commission (SEC)—were giving "exactly the wrong impression" of the real comparative worth of corporations. In growth industrics, in particular, thc accounting numbers consistently overstated the value of physical assets (like buildings and machinery) and consistently underestimated other assets, especially the intangibles that were, in the early 1990s, just coming to be seen as critical sources of corporate competitiveness.

The debate will continue as the accounting profession tries to adjust to the new economy organizations. The issue of measuring the value of human capital is explored further in chapters 9 and 10.

SUPERSTAR PHENOMENA

As there are superstars in almost every area in life, so there are superstar organizations—those perceived as being extraordinarily successful, based on major accomplishments. One common denominator for the superstar organization is recognizing the people factor. Executives at superstar organizations give recognition to the people who have created the outstanding performance. Six examples highlight the importance of human capital in achieving superstar status.

QUALCOMM

Consider the success of QUALCOMM, described earlier. QUALCOMM has earned a distinguished reputation in technology innovation. It has more than 3,000 patents, most of which have been filed with key foreign jurisdictions around the world. In exchange for good ideas and hard work, the company provides an environment that fosters creativity and recognizes achievements. A continuous learning organization, the company is dedicated to promoting the growth of their employees and development of the surrounding community. As a global organization, QUALCOMM works with people around the world, helping create and transform technology to meet the needs of people at home and on the job. QUALCOMM has been recognized for this outstanding success. The American Association of Retired People (AARP) has labeled QUALCOMM as one of the best employers for workers over fifty years old. It is listed in the Black Collegians Top 100 Employers as well as *Business Week's* IT 100 and Global 1,000. In financial terms, QUALCOMM is on the list of Most Valuable Global Companies and is in *Fortune* magazine's list of the most admired companies. Also, it is consistently listed in *Fortune* magazine's 100 Best Companies to Work For. The success of the organization and the importance of people who make it happen go hand-in-hand in public statements, demonstrated activities, and supporting recognition.

General Electric

Jack Welch, former chairman and CEO of General Electric, achieved extraordinary results with uncanny consistency. He achieved growth year after year, helping to build his reputation as an outstanding business leader who could do no wrong. He was a role model for others to emulate; double-digit annual growth became the benchmark for all CEOs and corporations in America. Welch debunked many of the most common myths of management, for example, that the command-and-control model is the best way to run a large company. But his ultimate legacy is that he created a learning culture within a mammoth corporation that had an amazingly diverse business portfolio.

Welch defined a learning organization as an organization in which employees and managers soak up good ideas from everywhere. He felt that the organizations that would ultimately achieve a sustainable competitive advantage were those that continuously learned, and then translated that learning into action. "You need to believe that you are a learning institution," he once commented, "and to constantly challenge everything you have." In a learning organization, employees are given access to critical information and are expected to search out creative solutions to problems.[15]

Welch did not start as GE's chairman with the notion of creating the world's largest learning organization, nor did that accomplishment come easily or quickly. It took many years, lots of sweat and blood, and a series of courageous decisions in the intervening years. He *did*, however, send the right message almost from the very start: learning would be a top priority at General Electric.

The following steps represent what Welch did in his "business laboratory" (a favorite Welch term) at GE from 1981 to 2001. They are less a comprehensive blueprint than a general framework:

1. Make sure the company is financially sound before embarking on something as sweeping as developing a learning culture.
2. Set a definitive strategic direction and make sure that the vision is articulated throughout the organization.
3. Make sure that there is a stated set of values to guide the company.
4. Establish an environment of trust and openness.
5. Create a "boundary-less organization."
6. Make speed, flexibility, and innovation a reflex.
7. Make sure that everyone in your organization is encouraged to seek out the best ideas from anywhere.
8. Implement a best-practices program. Importing the best ideas should be a process, not simply a mindset.
9. Reward behaviors and actions that promote a learning culture.
10. Establish processes and an infrastructure for converting learning into results.
11. Use companywide initiatives to spread the gospel.[16]

By any measure, GE under Welch placed high value on human capital and its importance to success. Welch believed that behavior is driven by a fundamental core belief: the desire and the ability of an organization to continuously learn from any source, anywhere, and to rapidly convert this learning into action is its ultimate competitive advantage.

When he took over, GE's total market capitalization was $13 billion. In the spring of 2000, GE became the most valuable company in the world, worth an astounding $596 billion (before sliding substantially in the market downturn of 2001 and 2002). There is little doubt that Welch's learning culture played a prominent role in GE's transformation from an aging manufacturing bureaucracy to one of the world's largest, most valuable global multinationals.

Honda

For more than forty years, Honda has continued to grow and expand in America. Today, with a presence in all fifty states, their investment in sales, manufacturing, and research operations in the United States exceeds $5.9

billion. By 2004, Honda's direct employment in the United States rose to 24,000 associates with an annual payroll of $1.2 billion. Their plants, facilities, and authorized dealerships currently employ more than 120,000 Americans. The importance of employees to generate success is underscored when examining the role of employees at Honda's newest U.S. automotive plant located near Birmingham, Alabama. Employees—known as "associates"— are encouraged to solve problems in groups rather than fretting over them alone. The practice comes to life both on the assembly line and in big, open offices that lack the isolating cubicles common in so many U.S. companies.

Working for Honda, which put its first manufacturing facility in the United States twenty-five years ago, is not anything like toiling in one of the old steel mills or foundries that used to dominate Alabama's manufacturing base, employees say. Paint booths have replaced blast furnaces, and employment for life does not seem like a particularly bad idea, with assembly line wages starting at more than $15 an hour, not including benefits. Shifts rotate regularly so no one gets stuck on the graveyard shift forever.

The Alabama factory began making Odyssey minivans and engines in November 2001. In 2004, it added a second assembly line that makes the Pilot sport utility vehicle. In all, the $1 billion factory can manufacture 300,000 vehicles annually.

American and Japanese engineers write on big white boards to hash out problems, relying on hand-drawn sketches where needed. Their commitment to quality is amazing. The engineering tolerances are set, and they stick to them.

Commenting on the twenty-fifth anniversary, Masaaki Kato, the president and chief executive, said the company has succeeded by emphasizing respect for individual employees. "We look to associates not just for their physical skill, but for the ability and willingness to challenge with their ideas," Kato said in a speech to an automotive conference.[17]

Southwest Airlines

Creating a culture of accountability ensures that a superstar is developed. When employees at all levels understand their role and their connection to the success of the company, they will help it become a superstar. Take, for example, Southwest Airlines. With 35,000 employees, this airline is, no doubt, the most profitable airline in the world—it has never failed to make a profit. Even in tough years when other companies were losing billions, Southwest was making a profit. Among other factors, the most important consideration for success was the employees. Southwest employees understand their roles and what they must do to make the airline profitable—and they share in the profits. They understand that great customer service, efficient and profitable turnarounds, and controlling costs at every angle make the airlines more profitable. Because of this, some of the early Southwest employees have become millionaires with the wealth created through their stock plans. This success stems from the culture created—a culture that is focused on getting things done and meeting the challenges that many said could not be accomplished.[18]

The president and chief operating officer of Southwest Airlines, Colleen Barrett, helped Herb Kelleher found the company more than thirty years ago in Dallas, Texas, and has been the inspiration behind Southwest's amazing culture. In 1990, she formed Southwest's Culture Committee to preserve and promote the organization's core values, known collectively as "SPIRIT." From day one, Barrett perceived the essential role that culture would play in differentiating Southwest Airlines from its industry rivals.[19]

From 1997 to 2001, Southwest was in the top five of *Fortune's* list of the 100 best companies to work for in America. In 2002, it did not make the list because Barrett had the guts to remove the company from the competition, saving more than $100,000 of employee time that goes into applying for the honor.

Was it a good decision? If success is a measure, it was. In the wake of the 9/11 terrorist attacks, many U.S. airlines were forced to borrow cash, cancel aircraft orders, cut flights, lay off employees, and slash fares. Southwest's story was dramatically different. The airline's employees remained strong, dedicated, empathic, united, and highly spirited. The post-9/11 results speak for themselves. Southwest operated at 100 percent of capacity without a single layoff and fully met its obligations to its employees profit-sharing and savings plans, which totaled $197.5 million. It inaugurated new routes and its revenue-per-passenger-mile (RPM) share of the U.S. domestic market increased by approximately 25 percent. It reported 2002 revenues of more than $5.5 billion, with net income of $241 million and a growth margin of 30.5 percent, compared to 26.02 percent for the industry.

USAA

General Wilson Cooney, former president of the property and casualty insurance group, USAA, was monitoring the phones at its San Antonio, Texas, headquarters one day when he happened to catch a conversation between a service representative and an eighty-one-year-old customer. "I need some help, but I'm not sure what with," the customer began, and that seemed true enough as she rambled on. Eventually, she explained her confusion: "I lost my husband three weeks ago and I don't know what to do." She had seen some insurance papers around the house, but had no idea what to do about them.

After offering condolences, the service representative suggested that the customer gather the papers together. The customer warned it might take a while—and it did. In fact, the call lasted sixty-five minutes. By the time it ended, the service representative had resolved all the woman's problems with her auto, life, and estate policies.

"I just want to tell you this is the nicest thing that's happened to me in three weeks," the customer said. She sent the representative flowers. "Those are the kinds of things that go on every day," Bill Cooney said.[20]

For more than eighty years, USAA has focused on achieving the best customer service in its industry, and it has succeeded: 98 percent of its customer base is in the top 40 percent for customer satisfaction; 98 percent of its members renew their policies each year. The secret, according to Cooney, is in the interface between USAA's people and its customers. The company's skill at maximizing its employee assets is legendary.

The member-owned Fortune 500 company manages more than $71 billion in assets and is recognized as a leader in the financial services industry. In 1998, it earned $980 million on revenues of $7.7 billion. Phoenix Marketing International reported USAA received the highest client-satisfaction score from affluent investors with 83 percent. This compared to others such as TIAA-CREF (77 percent), A.G. Edwards (75 percent), and Vanguard (75 percent).

The company uses technology to furnish employees with up-to-the-minute information, makes the most of its employee assets, and consequently provides greater value to customers. At the same time, the company insists that employees be, as Cooney puts it, "passionate about serving people." Many of its 22,400 employees have special qualifications for empathizing with the dire circumstances that many of its customers find themselves in.

The leaders of USAA want to know what their employees are thinking and feeling. That kind of knowledge is useful when you want to instill in employees the attitudes that make for a service-first company. The company's investment in employees thus takes many forms. USAA knows that it is not enough to employ good people. To create value, employees must be properly trained, equipped, directed, and motivated. USAA provides a best-practice standard in this area. *Working Mother Magazine* has named USAA to its list of "100 Best Companies for Working Mothers" for six years in a row. Along with this, USAA has been recognized as a best place to work for commuters as well as being named best employer for the fourth time by *LATINA Style* magazine.

SAP

Failure to focus on people can be detrimental. Les Hayman, Chief Officer of Global Human Resources at software giant SAP, puts it more bluntly, "I remember a lot of great companies from the 1970s that have since disappeared because their focus was on products, not people."[21] Hayman assumed his new post after serving as Chief of SAP's Asia Pacific operations. In eight years, he built SAP's Asia Pacific business from a paltry $6 million in sales to an astonishing $800 million. Hayman credits his success to getting the most out of his staff's talent. "If you talk to technology companies, you always hear them say that what they really need is a killer application," Hayman says. "That's rubbish. That's really the by-product of what you do. You need a good strategy—not a brilliant one, but one you can execute. And you need a performance-driven culture and people who are emotionally engaged. If you have all those things, you'll create the right product."

As of March 31, 2004, SAP had over 30,000 full-time-equivalent employees. Software revenues in the United States increased 63 percent to 140 million (2003: 86 million). Employees are critical to an organization's success and the superstars are the showplace examples. Most executives not only declare that their people are the most important assets, but make statements like, "We could not have done it without the people."

Some will argue that the success of an organization can only be defined in terms of employees. Success cannot be generated in any way without successful people, not only at the top, but at all levels. People *are* the most important asset and no organization has been successful without them. A superstar company has to rest on the success of its people.

SOME CHARACTERISTICS OF SUPERSTARS

The Best Idea Will Fail Without Proper Talent and Execution

Talent management is fundamentally about ensuring that the right people are positioned in the right places and keeping them over the long haul. Business leaders clearly understand their talent pool. They work hard to identify the key players who have critical relationships with customers and suppliers, and then work even harder to nurture and keep those players.[22]

A number of business leaders have asserted that coming up with the best talent for their companies is the most important task they have to perform. Some, like Jack Welch and Honeywell International's Larry Bossidy, spend an inordinate amount of time searching for the best talent within their own employee pools, hoping to build leadership that way. Both Welch and Bossidy have frequently said that all the great strategies in the world will have little effect on a company unless the right people are chosen to execute those strategies.

Leaders understand this and put a premium on keeping the talent they need for growth. They do what is necessary to ensure that key people are secure and do not leave because of low morale, thus preventing a defection domino effect.

In recent years, there has been much interest in the subject of executing strategies. Leaders are beginning to make the connection between executing strategies and results. Execution does not happen without top-quality people in key jobs.[23] To understand the execution of strategies, three points should be kept in mind:

1. Execution is a discipline that is integral to strategy.
2. Execution is a major job with business leaders.
3. Execution must be a core element of an organization's culture.

At the heart of executing strategies lies three core processes: the people process, the strategy process, and the operations process. Every business and organization uses these processes in one form or another. The people process is most critical; people must be engaged and committed to action plans to ensure that execution occurs. Top quality employees are necessary to ensure that the execution drives the organization where it needs to be.

Human Capital as the Last Major Source of Competitive Advantage

Today's organizations have access to many of the key success factors. Financial resources are available to most organizations with a viable business model. Although financial capital can freeze during economic downtimes, one company no longer has an advantage over another to access the financial capital needed to run a business. In addition, a company can readily adapt technology to a given situation or business model. It is difficult to have a technology advantage in an information-technology society.

Businesses also have access to customers—even if there is a dominant player in the market. Newspapers are laced with stories of small organizations taking on larger ones and succeeding. Having entry and access to a customer database is not necessarily a competitive advantage. What makes the difference, clearly, is the human capital of the organization. With relatively equal access to all the other resources, it is logical to conclude that human resources are where a strategic advantage can be developed. However, having capable human resources is no guarantee of success. What is important is the way those assets are managed.

Human capital value does not develop quickly—it develops over time. Consider, for example, an organization like Southwest Airlines, which is the most profitable airline in the business. If Delta Airlines—struggling near bankruptcy—decided to change its business model to mirror that of Southwest's, could it be as profitable? Unfortunately, while the business model may be adjusted quickly, the human capital may not adapt appropriately. Delta would struggle for years trying to imitate Southwest. It would have to change its habits, culture, practices, and adopt a new set of value systems—a system that has made Southwest Airlines so successful. In its frustration, employee turnover may be rampant and inefficiencies may develop as values and practices are changed. It may take years for the transition, if it occurs at all. Thus, the way in which the human assets have been acquired, maintained, and managed provides a unique opportunity to provide a competitive advantage. A company that gets its system of people management right has an extraordinary competitive edge over its rivals. It will obtain better performance from what is often the largest asset and will not have to worry about its rivals copying its keys to success. In doing this, a company is playing to its strengths.[24]

Good and Great

Perhaps there is no work that shows the importance of human capital more than the research done by Jim Collins. Along with co-author Jerry Porras in the book *Built to Last* (1994), Collins explored the deep reasons behind long-term corporate success stories in the United States. (*Industry Week* magazine declared *Built to Last* the number one business book for 1995.) Drawing on a six-year project at the Stanford University Graduate School, Collins and Porras studied each exceptional and long-lasting company in direct comparison with one of its competitors. The authors asked fundamental questions, "What makes the truly exceptional companies different from other companies?"

Throughout their research, the importance of people was evident in every aspect. These companies practice what they preach when it comes to the role of employees in the organization. Table 6-2 represents most of the

Table 6-2. A part of the core ideologies in the visionary companies.

3M	• Innovation; "Thou shalt not kill a new product idea" • Absolute integrity • Respect for individual initiative and personal growth • Tolerance for honest mistakes • "Our real business is solving problems"
American Express	• Heroic customer service • Worldwide reliability of services • Encouragement of individual initiative
Boeing	• Being on the leading edge of aeronautics; being pioneers • Tackling huge challenges and risks • Product safety and quality • Integrity and ethical business
Citicorp	• Expansionism—of size, or services offered, of geographic presence • Autonomy and entrepreneurship (via decentralization) • Aggressiveness and self-confidence
Ford	• People as the source of our strength • Products as the "end result of our efforts" (we are *about* cars) • Profits as a necessary means and measure for our success
General Motors	• Interdependent balance between responsibility to customers, employees, society, and shareholders • Individual responsibility and opportunity • Honesty and integrity
Hewlett-Packard	• Respect and opportunity for HP people, including the opportunity to share in the success of the enterprise • Contribution and responsibility to the communities in which we operate • Profit and growth as a means to make all of the other values and objectives possible
IBM	• Give full consideration to the individual employee • Spend a lot of time making customers happy • Go the last mile to do things right; seek superiority in all we undertake
Johnson & Johnson	• "We have a hierarchy of responsibilities: Customers first, employees second, society at large third, and shareholders fourth." • Individual opportunity and reward based on merit
Marriott	• Friendly service and excellent value • People are #1—treat them well, expect a lot, and the rest will follow • Work hard, yet keep it fun • Continual self-improvement
Merck	• "We are in the business of preserving and improving human life. All of our actions must be measured by our success in achieving this goal." • Honesty and integrity • Corporate social responsibility • Science-based innovation, not imitation

Motorola	• Continuous self-renewal
	• Tapping the "latent creative power within us"
	• Continual improvement in all that the company does—in ideas, in quality, in customer satisfaction
	• Treat each employee with dignity, as an individual
Nordstrom	• Service to the customer above all else
	• Continuous improvement, never being satisfied
	• Excellence in reputation, being part of something special
Philip Morris	• Winning—being the best and beating others
	• Encouraging individual initiative
	• Opportunity to achieve based on merit, not gender, race, or class
	• Hard work and continuous self-improvement
Procter & Gamble	• Continuous self-improvement
	• Honesty and fairness
	• Respect and concern for the individual
Sony	• To experience the sheer joy that comes from the advancement, application, and innovation of technology that benefits the general public
	• Being a pioneer—not following others, but doing the impossible
	• Respecting and encouraging each individual's ability and creativity
Wal-Mart	• Be in partnership with employees
	• Work with passion, commitment, and enthusiasm
	• Run lean
	• Pursue ever-higher goals
Walt Disney	• No cynicism allowed
	• Fanatical attention to consistency and detail
	• Continuous progress via creativity, dreams, and imagination

Source: Adapted from James C. Collins and Jerry I. Porras *Built to Last* (New York, NY: Harper Business, 1994).

core ideologies of these visionary companies. The researchers did not merely paraphrase the company's most recent missions, visions, and values, but tried to find out from a variety of sources the historical consistency of their ideologies through multiple generations of key executives. These values, missions, and philosophies highlight the importance of people and their contributions as the basis for companies that are built to last.

Jim Collins' next book, *Good to Great* (2002), was an attempt to understand what makes companies move from being defined as "good" to being defined as "great." In this work, Collins explored how good companies, mediocre companies, and even bad companies achieve greatness. Using a benchmark, Collins and his research team identified a set of elite companies that made the leap to "great" and sustained those results for at least fifteen years. The good-to-great companies generated cumulative stock returns that beat the general stock market by an average of seven times in fifteen years—better than twice the results delivered by a composite index of the world's greatest companies, including Coca Cola, Intel, General Electric, and Merck. The synthesis of the research published in *Good to Great* underscores the attributes of the truly great companies. The important ingredients are the quality of, and focus on, employees throughout the organizations.

The beginning point for these good-to-great organizations is the quality of leadership. When compared to high-profile leaders with big personalities who make headlines and become celebrities, the good-to-great leaders (called "Level 5 Leaders") seem to have come from a different planet. They are self-effacing, quiet, reserved, even shy; these leaders are a blend of humility and professional goodwill.

The various levels of leaders focus on the importance of people in the company and importance of individual contributors. Contributing team members provide individual capabilities to the achievement of group objectives and work effectively with others in a group setting. Highly capable individuals make productive contributions through talent, knowledge, skills, and good work habits.

The next issue focuses on ensuring that the right people are in place before actions and executions are taken—making sure the right people are on the bus. A third issue is to confront the facts and is a philosophy of all the leaders and employees in the organization. They realize that all companies face challenges. It is only by facing the facts and checking with the reality of the situation that progress can be made. A fourth issue focuses on the competencies in core business with the conclusion that a company cannot be great unless they are the best in the world at their core business. The fifth issue emphasizes the importance of having a committed, disciplined group of employees. Disciplined people lead to disciplined thought, which leads to disciplined action to achieve the breakthrough necessary to become a great company. Finally, the great companies think differently about the role of technology. They never use technology as a primary means of igniting a transformation, yet paradoxically, they are the pioneers in the application of carefully selected technologies.

This research underscores the people aspect of these companies. When the entire body of research is examined, what comes through is not the innovative products, unique markets, the nature of the business, or some other technological or resource advantage. The real advantage of these great companies is the people that make them great and then sustain the greatness over a long period of time.

The Great Places to Work

Probably no activity about the importance of human capital is more visible than the list of organizations selected as the 100 Best Companies to Work For. This list is published each year in *Fortune* magazine and has become the bellwether for focusing on the importance of employees.[25] Although other publications have spin-offs, this is the premier list that organizations strive to make. The most important factor in selecting companies for this list is what the employees themselves have to say about their workplace. For the 2004 list, some 46,526 randomly selected employees from 304 candidate companies filled out an employee-produced survey (The Great Place to Work Trust Index, an instrument created by The Great Place to Work Institute, San Francisco). Nearly half of them also provided written comments about the workplaces. These candidate companies also filled out a questionnaire detailing people policies, practices, and philosophies. Each company is evaluated on both employee surveys and company questionnaires with employee opinions accounting for two-thirds of the total score. The annual list presents each company in rank, along with:

❑ Total employment, detailed by the percent of minorities and women
❑ Annual job growth (percent)
❑ Number of jobs created in the past year
❑ Number of applicants
❑ Voluntary turnover rate
❑ Number of hours of training per year
❑ Average annual pay, detailed by professional and hourly
❑ Revenues

These lists are alive with tales of how the employers focus on building a great place to work and building employee respect, dignity, and capability. These firms are successful in the market. The 2004 list includes such well-known and successful companies as American Express, Cisco Systems, FedEx, Genentech, IBM, Eli Lilly, Marriott International, MBNA, Merck, Microsoft, and Procter & Gamble. Inclusion in the list has become so sought after by organizations that they change many of their practices and philosophies in an attempt to make it.

This trend all began with the pioneering work of Robert Levering and his partner Milton Moskowitz. Those two, along with Michael Katz, co-authored the best selling book, *One Hundred Best Companies to Work for in*

America (1985). In the late 1980s, Levering began to provide prescriptions for employees in his publication *A Great Place to Work: What Makes Some Employers so Good and Most so Bad* (1988). Later, they partnered with *Fortune* magazine to create the annual list. As employers make this list, their accomplishment becomes part of the recruitment advertising and is even included in other advertising channels. Plaques are displayed on-location to acknowledge their inclusion on this list.

This is truly a list that employers want to be on. More important, it shows the importance of human capital and what value companies place on it. It shows how diversity, job growth, turnover, and training make a significant difference in the organization. For the most part, these organizations invest heavily—far exceeding those on any other list. Investment, in their mind, translates into payoff.

Most-Admired Companies

Another important list is *Fortune's* America's Most Admired Companies, a list that is unique because the ranking is determined by peer groups. To develop the list, the Hay Group started with the ten largest companies (by revenue) in sixty-four industries, including foreign firms with U.S. operations. Then, they asked 10,000 executives, directors, and security analysts to rate the companies in their own industries with eight criteria, using a scale of one to ten. The respondents selected the ten companies they admired most in any industry. From a human capital perspective, it is interesting that four of the eight key attributes focused directly on human capital: employee talent, quality of management, innovation, and social responsibility. The other four were indirectly related. The key point is that investors and business people admire companies who place important emphasis on the human capital aspects of their business.[26]

A NEED FOR MORE RESEARCH

While this chapter provides some convincing, anecdotal, and intuitive evidence of the success of human capital, it does not necessarily present proof. Logic holds that no organization would be successful without competent human capital. Yet, some executives need proof about the correlation between investing in human capital and subsequent performance. Additional research is needed on that elusive connection, and chapter 7 presents more detail at the macrolevel (across firms).

From an organizational perspective, there are important challenges that emerge from this chapter. There is a persistent need to clearly understand the value of human capital—not only from the logic perspective, but a research perspective, as well. It is important to work more closely with Wall Street analysts so that they understand, at least partially, the worth of human capital when placing a value on a business. Also, there is a need to work more closely with the finance and accounting standards board and the accounting profession to continue to make adjustments in how organizations value human capital.

Within companies, there is the need to show the value of particular projects. One of the most important and challenging issues, initially introduced in chapter 5, is to show the value of the return of the investment in human capital. Measuring the return on investment is being done; it is one of the most persuasive ways to show the value of investing in this important resource. Chapter 8 presents a summary of the overwhelming research at the microlevel for measuring the return on investment in individual human capital projects.

SUMMARY

This chapter explored the intuitive, anecdotal, and logical evidence of the importance of human capital. Based on all the evidence available, the chapter concludes, at least for the most part, that investing in human capital is a good thing. This should be convincing enough for most executives. The chapter outlined the importance of human capital from several perspectives: examining the necessity of human capital in the first place, building on success stories of the superstars, and discussing the various lists that highlight human capital. There is much evidence that presents a convincing case.

It might be helpful to conclude this chapter with this significant observation: In 2001, JPMorgan Chase, in its annual report, proclaimed the importance of human capital. "At 23 Wall Street stands a building that was once JPMorgan's headquarters. In it is a vault (it is a bank building, after all). No money is stored there—it is a breakout room for the bank's training center. There, in the knowledge and skills of its people as manifested in intellectual capital, is where the real wealth for JPMorgan Chase or any company can be found."[27] The next two chapters examine the research that supports the importance of investing in human capital.

NOTES

1   QUALCOMM Annual Report. Available from http://www.qualcomm.com; Internet. Accessed 2 September 2004.

2   Eric G. Flamholtz, *Human Resource Accounting,* 2nd ed. (San Francisco: Jossey-Bass Publishers, 1985).

3   Wayne Cascio, *Managing Human Resources: Productivity, Quality of Work Life, Profits,* 4th ed. (New York McGraw-Hill, Inc., 1995).

4   Karl Erik Sveiby, *The New Organizational Wealth* (San Francisco: Berrett-Koehler Publishers, Inc., 1997).

5   Patrick H. Sullivan, *Value Driven Intellectual Capital: How to Convert Intangible Corporate Assets into Market Value* (New York: John Wiley & Sons, 2000).

6   Thomas A. Stewart, *Intellectual Capital: The New Wealth of Organizations* (New York: Doubleday Publishing, 1997).

7   Thomas A. Stewart, "Intellectual Capital: Brainpower," *Fortune,* June 3, 1991, p. 44.

8   Thomas A. Stewart, "Your Company's Most Valuable Asset: Intellectual Capital," *Fortune,* October 3, 1994.

9   Hubert Saint-Onge, "Shaping Human Resource Management Within the Knowledge-Driven Enterprise," *Leading Knowledge Management and Learning,* ed. Dede Bonner (Alexandria, Va.: The American Society for Training and Development, 2000).

10   Ibid.

11   Patrick H. Sullivan, *Value Driven Intellectual Capital: How to Convert Intangible Corporate Assets into Market Value* (New York: John Wiley & Sons, 2000).

12   W. Miller, "Building the Ultimate Resource: Today's Competitive Edge Comes from Intellectual Capital," *Management Review,* January 1999, pp. 42–45.

13   Thomas A. Stewart, "Intellectual Capital: Brainpower," *Fortune,* June 3, 1991, p. 44.

14   A. Kleiner, "The World's Most Exciting Accountant," *Strategy + Business,* Issue 35, 2004, p.35.

15   Jeffrey A. Krames, *What the Best CEOs Know: 7 Exceptional Leaders and Their Lessons for Transforming Any Business* (New York: McGraw-Hill, 2003).

16   Ibid.

17   John Hines, "Honda's Culture in the South," *Birmingham News,* 2004, p. C-1.

18   Andy Serwer, "Southwest Airlines—The Hottest Thing in the Sky," *Fortune,* March 8, 2004, p. 86.

19   Kevin Freiberg and Jackie Freiberg, *Guts! Companies that Blow the Doors off Business-as-Usual* (New York: Currency Books, 2004).

20   Richard E.S. Boulton, Barry D. Libert, and Steve M. Samek, *Cracking the Value Code* (New York: Harper Collins Publishers, Inc., 2000).

21   P.J. Kiger, "Les Hayman's Excellent Adventure," *Workforce Management,* August 2004, pp. 41–44.

22   Amir Hartman, *Ruthless Execution: What Business Leaders Do When Their Companies Hit the Wall* (Upper Saddle River: FT Prentice Hall, 2004).

23   Larry Bossidy, Ran Charan, and Charles Burck, *Execution: The Discipline of Getting Things Done* (New York: Crown Business, 2002).

24   Haig R. Nalbantian, Richard A. Guzzo, Dave Kieffer, and Jay Doherty, *Play to Your Strengths: Managing Your Internal Labor Markets for Lasting Competitive Advantage* (New York: McGraw-Hill, 2004).

25   Levering, Robert, and Milton Moskowitz. "2004 Special Report: The 100 Best Companies to Work For." *Fortune,* Jan 12, 2004, p. 56.

26   Ann Harrington, "America's Most Admired Companies," *Fortune,* March 8, 2004, p. 80.

27   Thomas A. Stewart, *The Wealth of Knowledge: Intellectual Capital in the 21st Century Organization* (New York: Currency Books, 2001).

CHAPTER 7

What We Know from Macrolevel Research

The previous chapter focused on the value of human capital based on testimonials, anecdotal evidence, logic, intuition, and personal successes. This chapter takes the empirical approach and presents data that show the linkage between investing in human capital across organizations and subsequent payoffs. For years, the need to collect more evidence to show these payoffs has been an important issue confronting executives and managers.

The issue is not *if* a company should invest, but *at what level*. Most executives are convinced that some level of investment must be made, but where is the minimum level or where can the payoff be maximized? Researchers have been wrestling with this dilemma for many years.

Research on the value of human capital can be grouped into two broad categories: macro- and micro-analysis. The macrolevel focuses on studies that examine relationships between variables across organizations, although sometimes the analysis can be developed at the organizational level. The micro-analysis examines the impact of a particular human capital program or project. Both are important approaches. This chapter explores the macrolevel approach; the next chapter shows the microlevel approach.

For decades, HR executives have attempted to show the value of their overall investment to understand the relationship between what is spent and the ultimate contribution of human resources. Macro vs. micro is an excellent way to address the human capital investment. After all, decisions must be made at both levels. At the macrolevel, organizations try to understand the value of the entire human capital investment and the relationship between investing and subsequent success on a long-term basis. At the microlevel, executives are often interested in funding decisions for particular human capital projects or programs or they may be evaluating a project or program to see if it is adding the value they had expected. The remainder of the chapter examines a variety of studies to show the connection between human capital and profits, productivity, share price, and other key measures. Each major group of studies is presented separately.

INDEX OF HR EFFECTIVENESS

Early Approaches

A few organizations have attempted to develop a single composite index of effectiveness for the HR function. The indices have been useful for comparing one organization to another and for establishing internal control and goal setting. However, most of these indices were not developed to be linked with organizational effectiveness. Thus, efforts to make this connection have been minimal.

One of the first examples of such an index was developed and used by the General Electric Company in the 1950s.[1] This Employee Relations Index (ERI) was based on eight indicators that were selected following a detailed study of different aspects of employee behavior, among them were absenteeism, initial dispensary visits, terminations, grievances, and work stoppages. The indicators were combined by means of a multiple regression formula with the variables above receiving different weights. Constants were added depending on the level of the variable in a plant and for the particular plant or group in question. According to its users, the ERI was intended to help managers evaluate policies and practices, trace trends in employee relations, find trouble spots, perform human relations duties more effectively, and control personnel costs. Index values were compared with plant profitability (the ratio of net income before taxes to capital investment). Although the plants with the higher ERIs were usually the more profitable ones, the relationship was not statistically significant.

Another example of an ERI was developed in the late 1970s.[2] According to its developer, the ERI provides a means to measure the status of employee relations and compare one department with another or one plant with another, provided similar variables are used. The index consists of weighted factors for measures of absenteeism, turnover, safety, grievances, complaints, motor vehicle accidents, and so on. Apparently, no attempts were made to relate the index to any organizational effectiveness measures such as profitability or growth.

JR LaPointe developed the Human Resource Performance Index (HRPX), which uses the massive data banks that human resources systems make available.[3] According to the author, the HRPX has been successfully used to evaluate HR functions such as selection, compensation, development, and retention. For example, in selection, the HRPX measures the effectiveness of college-recruiting activities in terms of success of recruits within the company and their retention rates. Recruiting success is measured by the annualized-compensation growth. No attempt was made to validate this index against organizational effectiveness.

A few organizations have developed a Human Resources Index (HRI) to compare progress over time and with other organizations. Pioneering work in cross-organizational exchange of attitudinal data has been done by the Mayflower group, which consists of over thirty companies, including Xerox, General Electric, IBM, and Prudential Insurance.[4] According to its developer, the HRI is proven to be effective in many organizations for measuring attitudes, overall satisfaction, and commitment to organizational goals as well as for pinpointing trouble spots and issues requiring concentrated efforts. In addition, it provides a meaningful, work-related basis for opening up two-way communications and initiating organizational development. The index contains sixty-four positive statements about the organization for which the employee is asked to indicate a level of agreement. The areas explored range from reward systems to quality of management. One concern about this index is its validity, which is based on content validity. The author concludes that no equivalent instrument with previous validated factors is known to exist. Therefore, it was not possible to determine the index's predictive validity by correlating it with a criterion measure. Content validity was determined on the basis of two expert judgments and each factor of the HRI was judged to be highly valid by a panel of survey design experts and personnel managers.

An index is appealing because it is simple to compute and easy to understand. However, an index often lacks a theoretical rationale for selecting component variables. Moreover, a single index is not likely to be adequate for defining and measuring the effectiveness of most of the tasks performed by the HR department. These problems are addressed in the following study.

Phillips/Saratoga Institute Study

In an attempt to provide more statistically significant research to the development of a human resource effectiveness index, a major study was conducted involving seventy-one organizations across several industry segments. The data were taken from the HR performance measures collected by the Saratoga Institute in its measurement project with the Society for Human Resource Management.[5] The study attempted to examine correlations among several measures in the Saratoga data with organizational effectiveness, including profits and productivity. Figure 7-1 shows the HR measures used in the study and the expected relationship with the output measures selected. The output measure included an overall productivity measure (*revenue* divided by employees) and a profitability measure (operating *income* divided by employment costs). Two other, less significant measures were tracked: *assets* divided by employee costs and *operating income* divided by stockholder's equity (operating return on equity, or O.R.O.E.). The financial data were taken directly from the organization's financial performance in the annual reports. The HR performance measures listed are self-explanatory.

Table 7-1 shows the significant correlation that exists from the measures of human resource performance and organizational effectiveness. The data in this table are for all industry groups. Specific detail on correlations of other

Figure 7-1. Expected relationships between firm performance and HR measures.

Measures of Organizational Effectiveness

HR Performance Measures	Revenue/Employees	Assets/Employee Cost	Operating Income/Employment Costs	Operating Income/Stockholder's Equity
HR Expenses/Total Operating Expenses	+	+	+	+
Compensation Expenses/Total Operating Expenses	-	-	-	-
Benefits Expenses/Total Operating Expenses	-	-	-	-
Training and Development Expenses/Employees	+	+	+	+
Absence Rate	-	-	-	-
Turnover Rate	-	-	-	-

+ = Positive Correlation
- = Negative (Inverse) Correlation

Table 7-1. Correlations between variables with the number of cases identified—data for all industries.

	Revenue	Assets	Income	O.R.O.E.	HRMEX	COMPEX	BENEX	T&DEX	Absence	Turnover
Revenue	1.000	30	68	19	68	71	71	23	48	55
Assets	.457	1.000	29	19	29	30	30	13	22	22
Income	.629*	.384	1.000	19	67	70	70	23	47	54
O.R.O.E.	.545*	.200	.654*	1.000	18	19	19	10	14	13
HRMEX	.374*	.202	.656*	.741*	1.000	68	68	20	45	53
COMPEX	−.619*	−.359	−.714*	−.259	−.422*	1.000	71	23	48	55
BENEX	−.527*	−.390	−.590*	−.228	−.433*	−.757*	1.000	23	48	55
T&DEX	.564*	.006	.465	.819*	.569*	−.323	−.435	1.000	19	22
Absence	−.217	−.102	−.367*	−.750*	−.333	.232	.160	−.391	1.000	43
Turnover	−.489*	−.089	−.635*	−.713*	−.376*	.505*	.372*	−.543*	.390*	1.000

Note: Number of cases shown upper right area of table.
*p<.01, one tailed.

segments in this study can be obtained directly from the author. Revenue divided by the number of employees (productivity) correlates with investment in human resources (as measured by the total HR investment divided by operating expenses). Revenue also has a significant, negative correlation with compensation and benefit expenses. This calls into question the idea that higher salaries drive increased performance. There is a significant positive correlation between revenue and training and development expenses and a significant negative correlation between turnover and revenue. No significant correlations were developed with assets divided by employee cost with any of the HR performance measures. This is apparently the result of missing data for that category. Income divided by employee cost correlates significantly with HR investment, compensation expenses, benefits expenses, absence, and turnover.

With the data from all industries, the correlations were in the expected direction, with significant correlations developed in every segment. The two measures of organizational effectiveness with the most significant correlations are revenue productivity and income. Overall, these correlations show some support for the expected relationships in the study.

The data for the six HR variables were standardized by industry segments and weighted based on the weighting scheme recommended by participants in the study. The data were converted to all positive values because four of the six variables were expected to have a negative relationship with organizational effectiveness (See figure 7-1). Also, the data values were added to develop the index. One problem with this analysis is that index values were calculated when data values were present for all six independent variables. The variable with the most missing data—training and development expenses— was dropped as an index component in an effort to increase the number of complete data sets. Weights were adjusted to fit the five variables and a new index was developed. Correlation coefficients were computed between index values and measures of organizational effectiveness.

Table 7-2 shows the results. In the data for all industries, significant correlations appear between index values and revenue, income, and operating revenue. This table also shows four industry groups and their significant correlations. Although these results are encouraging, the conclusions were somewhat hampered by the small sample sizes and the missing data items.

Four conclusions are derived from this study. First, the concept of a human resources performance index and the specific index in this study received favorable reaction from the HR executives. Second, significant correlations were developed between HR performance measures and productivity and income. The strongest relationships were found to exist between income

Table 7-2. Correlations with index values.

Index Values for:	Revenue	Assets	Income	O.R.O.E.
All Industries	.633* (41)	.523 (19)	.873* (40)	.663* (12)
Health Care	.497 (10)	—	.795* (10)	—
Chemicals and Drugs	.940 (4)	—	.986* (4)	—
Banking and Insurance	.868* (12)	.675 (11)	.854* (11)	.312 (6)
Combined Manufacturing	.444 (15)	.030 (4)	.912* (15)	.947 (4)

Note: Number of cases shown in parentheses.
*p. <.01, one tailed.

and human resource expenses, compensation expenses, and benefit expenses. Third, this is the first major study to show empirical support for the relationship between the investment in the HR function and organizational effectiveness. Increases in the investment in HR, through additional staff, programs, and resources, should improve the productivity and income of the organization. This important shift is a fundamental premise of this study. Fourth, support exists for the relationship between index values, which represent the combination of HR performance measures, and organizational effectiveness. Overall, these four conclusions make this study an important contribution to understanding the value of human capital.

PROFIT-CENTER APPROACH

According to some executives, the ultimate approach to evaluation is the profit-center concept, which shifts from the traditional view of the HR department as an expense center where costs are accumulated, to a view of HR as an investment, which can achieve a bottom-line contribution and, in some cases, actually operate with a profit. The profit-center arrangement involves managing and using the HR function as a revenue-generating center where the different parts of the organization are charged for the services and programs offered by the department. All of the HR department costs become offsetting expenses.

Competitive rates are established for services provided to users. In some cases, outside organizations may be competing with the internal HR services. Typical examples of programs or services "sold" to user organizations are training and development programs, recruiting, benefits administration, safety and health programs, administration of compensation programs, and the implementation of union-avoidance programs. The underlying premise of this approach is that user organizations, such as production, sales, and accounting, are charged for the services of the HR department and have the option of using external services in lieu of those offered by the HR department. A true HR profit center must allow the option to use other services in all HR programs and projects. In effect, the HR department makes a profit, breaks even, or experiences a loss. Assuming the services are priced on a competitive basis, the profit represents the return on the investment in the resources allocated to the HR function. Adoption of this approach requires the HR department to become client focused and quality conscious, when delivering services and programs. Some organizations have expanded this concept to include selling HR services to outside organizations, thus generating additional income for the organization.

The profit-center approach to evaluation is in its embryonic stage of development, but it is generating considerable interest. It represents a departure from the traditional view of HR management practices and may never be fully implemented in most organizations. To date, no true HR profit center has been developed for the entire HR function. However, it has been described as a trend in the human capital field and represents the movement of the HR department from an expense center to a customer-oriented function that is integrated with the business and generating income.

THE GALLUP STUDIES

Over the course of the last twenty-five years, Gallup researchers have qualitatively and quantitatively assessed the most salient employee perceptions of management practices.[6] In addition to designing customized surveys for nearly every organization with which Gallup works, their researchers have sought to define a core set of statements that measure important perceptions across a wide spectrum of organizations.

In developing measures of employee perceptions, researchers have focused on the consistently important human resources issues on which managers can develop specific action plans. These thirteen core items (twelve statements about the work environment and one question about overall satisfaction) evolved from a number of qualitative and quantitative studies:

1. Overall Satisfaction—On a five-point scale, where 5 is *extremely satisfied* and 1 is *extremely dissatisfied*, how satisfied are you with (name of company) as a place to work?
2. I know what is expected of me at work.
3. I have the materials and equipment I need to do my work right.
4. At work, I have the opportunity to do what I do best every day.

5. In the last seven days, I have received recognition or praise for doing good work.
6. My supervisor, or someone at work, seems to care about me as a person.
7. There is someone at work who encourages my development.
8. At work, my opinions seem to count.
9. The mission/purpose of my company makes me feel my job is important.
10. My associates (fellow employees) are committed to doing quality work.
11. I have a best friend at work.
12. In the last six months, someone at work has talked to me about my progress.
13. This last year, I have had opportunities at work to learn and grow.

Meta-Analysis

A meta-analysis is a statistical integration of data accumulated across many different studies. This analysis provides uniquely powerful information because it controls for measurement and sampling errors that distort the results of individual studies. A meta-analysis eliminates biases and provides an estimate of validity or relationship between two or more variables.

A total of twenty-eight studies conducted as proprietary research for various organizations are included in Gallup's database. In each study, one or more of the core items were used, and data were aggregated at the business-unit level and correlated with four aggregate performance measures: customer satisfaction/loyalty, profitability, productivity, and employee turnover.

Correlations were calculated, estimating the relationship of measures of employee perceptions to each of these four general business outcomes. Correlations were calculated across business units within each company, and these correlation coefficients were entered into a database for each of the thirteen items. Of the studies in this meta-analysis, customer satisfaction measures were available for eighteen studies, profitability measures were available for fourteen studies, and productivity measures were available for fifteen studies (turnover relationships are not recorded). The overall study involved 105,680 individual employee responses to surveys and 2,528 business units, an average of 42 employees per business unit and 90 business units per company.

Results

The following is a summary of the meta-analysis for each of the thirteen core items with regard to customer satisfaction/loyalty, profitability, and productivity. Items with the highest true validities of *customer satisfaction* that appear to generalize across companies include:

- ❏ I have a best friend at work.
- ❏ At work, I have the opportunity to do what I do best every day.
- ❏ I know what is expected of me at work.
- ❏ My supervisor, or someone at work, seems to care about me as a person.

Items that appear to generalize across companies and have the highest validities with the *profitability* criteria are:

- ❏ Overall satisfaction.
- ❏ My associates (fellow employees) are committed to doing quality work.
- ❏ At work, I have the opportunity to do what I do best every day.
- ❏ My supervisor, or someone at work, seems to care about me as a person.

Those items that have the highest validity estimates with *productivity* criteria were:

- ❏ I know what is expected of me at work.
- ❏ At work, my opinions seem to count.
- ❏ The mission/purpose of my company makes me feel my job is important.
- ❏ Overall satisfaction.

Implications

Through this research examining the linkages between key elements of a healthy business, the Gallup organization has developed a model that describes the path between the individual contribution of employees and the ultimate business outcome of any company, that is, an increase in overall company value. For publicly traded companies, this is, of course, best measured by increases in stock price and market valuation. A brief overview of each step along the path follows.

1. *Real profit increases drive stock increases.* Many variables influence the market value of a company, including external variables beyond a company's control. However, of the variables a company *can* control, increasing real profit is the most important driver of stock price.

2. *Sustainable growth drives real profit increases.* Real profit increases can only be driven by sustainable growth. Sustainable growth is quite different from "bought growth."

3. *Loyal customers drive sustainable growth.* The most critical driver of sustainable growth is an expanding base of loyal customers. In some industries it is also critical to have a growing base of loyal customers who are willing to pay a premium price.

4. *Engaged employees drive customer loyalty.* An engaged employee is one who can answer with a strong affirmative to all twelve of those questions. The meta-analysis at the business-unit level showed the linkage to productivity, customer satisfaction, and profitability.

5. *The right people in the right roles with the right managers drive employee engagement.* At the entry point of the path, the first steps must be performed almost perfectly or the remaining linkages to customer satisfaction, revenue growth, and profit will not occur. First, you must identify the employee's individual strengths. In step two, you must position that individual to perform a role that capitalizes on these strengths. Failure to meet these two requirements cannot be corrected by either the employee's motivation or by expert coaching.

These studies have created a foundation for implementing human resources practices around the twelve items in the study. The Gallup studies and the business performance model have had a tremendous influence on many organizations.

THE SERVICE-PROFIT CHAIN

The link between investment in human capital and profitability is most apparent in service organizations. The new economics of service are perhaps most evident in U.S. companies where a radical shift has occurred in the way they manage and measure success. Customers and employees are key. The impact of employee satisfaction, loyalty, and productivity is linked to customer satisfaction and growth of customer loyalty.[7] The service-profit chain clarifies the links between the following:

- ❑ Customer loyalty drives profitability and growth.
- ❑ Customer satisfaction drives customer loyalty.
- ❑ Value drives customer satisfaction.
- ❑ Employee productivity drives value.
- ❑ Employee loyalty drives productivity.
- ❑ Employee satisfaction drives loyalty.
- ❑ Internal quality drives employee satisfaction.
- ❑ Leadership underlies the chain's success. Leaders of successful service companies emphasize, by their words and actions, the importance of each employee and customer.

Xerox polls customers annually regarding product and service satisfaction and they find that providing excellent service is significantly more likely to lead to repeat business than giving good service. Xerox aims to create "apostles" who are so delighted with the service they have received they tell others and convert skeptics. They also want to avoid unhappy customers who speak out against a poorly delivered service. MCI studied seven telephone customer service centers and found clear relationships between employee satisfaction, customer satisfaction, and customer intentions to continue to use MCI services. Factors relating to job satisfaction included the job itself, training, pay, advancement fairness, treatment with respect and dignity, teamwork, and company interest in employee well-being. All these factors are areas for strategic HR intervention and a shared responsibility between HR and key managers. Taco Bell, a subsidiary of Yum! Brands, Inc., has integrated measurement data about profit by unit, market manager, zone, and so on with the results of customer exit interviews. They found that those stores that were the top performers on customer service also outperformed the others on all measures. Consequently, managers' compensation in company-owned stores is now closely linked to both customer satisfaction and profits. HR processes are at the heart of every element of the service-profit chain to profitability.[8]

Sears Research

Perhaps one of the most well-known examples of a business turnaround using the service-profit chain is that of Sears Roebuck and Company.[9] In 1992, following a period of steady and serious business losses, Sears implemented a turnaround plan that involved the support of employees who were willing to make the business successful and from the residual loyalty of customers to the Sears brand, despite low levels of customer satisfaction. The company's service strategy was revamped, store operations were reengineered, and there was a heavy emphasis on training, incentives, and the elimination of unnecessary administrative staff.

Sears executives saw the need to engage managers' and employees' hearts and minds in developing the company's future. This emphasized the point that for Sears to succeed financially, the stores had to be a compelling place to work (that is, employees would be highly motivated) and to shop (that the best merchandise alone would not ensure the company's success). This became known as the three C's: to be a compelling place to work, a compelling place to shop, and a compelling place to invest.

Task forces were established to explore issues relating to financial performance, innovation, values, customers, and employees. The innovation task force did external benchmarking. The values task force collected the views of all 80,000 employees to identify the six core values they felt strongly about. These included honesty, trust, and respect for the individual. The customer task force studied customer surveys going back several years and found that, broadly speaking, customers wanted Sears to succeed. The employee task force conducted a survey and found that employees were generally proud to work for Sears.

The data gathered by all the task forces were used to establish goals, including building customer loyalty and providing excellent customer service by hiring and holding on to the best employees. Specific objectives were developed to achieve these goals.

Measurement was an integral part of the plan. The task force data provided preliminary measures within each of the three elements of the vision. So, under *A Compelling Place to Work* were measures relating to personal growth and development, empowered teams, and so on. Under *A Compelling Place to Shop* were measures relating to customer needs being met and customer satisfaction. Under *A Compelling Place to Invest* were financial measures linked to revenue growth, sales per square foot, inventory turnover, and so on. The team wanted to see if there were any links between the three areas of measurement. During 1995, metrics of every kind were gathered and causal pathway modeling applied to establish cause and effect.

As a result of this analysis, clear links were established between employee attitudes and customer service and revenue. Having isolated the "soft" issues that make a difference to the "hard" business results, Sears saw that a 5-point improvement in employee attitudes would drive a 1.3-point improvement in customer satisfaction that, in turn, led to a 0.5 percent improvement in revenue growth. The model has proved sufficiently accurate for Sears that it can be used for predicting business performance based on employee attitudes.

Measures alone were not sufficient to achieve and maintain high performance. A major training and learning initiative was launched to change the perceptions and attitudes of the workforce, to help employees understand how the business worked, and to improve their own approach to customer service.[10]

Current Use

The updated service-profit chain is now labeled the Value Profit Chain. The core to sustaining outstanding performance is based on "value equations" for customers, employees, partners, and investors.[11]

The elements of the cycle are self-reinforcing. Employee value leads to the satisfaction, loyalty, and productivity that produce customer value, satisfaction, loyalty, trust, and commitment. Satisfied, loyal, trusting, and committed customers are the primary driver of company growth and profitability, important determinants of investor value. Finally, the fruits of growth and profitability are reinvested in value for partners (suppliers, communities, and others), employees, customers, and investors.

In the past few years, value-profit chain concepts have been used as an underlying driver of change to one degree or another in a wide range of organizations, including Harrah's Entertainment, Taco Bell, Omnicom, ACNielsen, Office Depot, Limited Brands, American Express, PNC, Continental Airlines, Sears, SYSCO, and Loomis, Fargo & Co. in the United States. In other countries, the list includes British Airways, BUPA (England), CEMEX (Mexico), Swedbank (Sweden), the Bank of Ireland, and Banco Comercial de Português.

HUSELID-BECKER STUDIES

Throughout the 1990s and continuing today, Mark Huselid and Brian Becker have engaged in a program of research that showed the connection between HR systems and a variety of strategic outcomes. This research was based on the importance of HR systems (rather than of individual HR practices) and on the premise that for HR to be a strategic asset, those HR systems had to have a demonstrated influence on the measures that matter to CEOs, namely organizational profitability and shareholder value. By using measures of shareholder value, this research was also unique in that it focused on the level of the organization as opposed to individual employees or work groups.[12] Surveys were conducted with over 3,000 respondents representing all major industry groups; response rates of 20 percent were achieved.

This research highlights the difficulties of estimating the effects of an

HR system on organizational performance. As the researchers concluded, it is difficult to isolate the independent effects of HR on the organization's financial performance, given the multiple influences on organizational performance at any point in time. The approach taken was to isolate the other factors that have an impact on organizational performance and then control statistically for the connection between the HR system and organizational performance. The researchers estimated the statistical relationship between the firm's HR system and performance for firms in the same size and asset class, in the same industry, with the same historical growth rate, investment in R&D, unionization rate, and risk profile. They found powerful support for a positive relationship between a high-performance work system (HPWS) and organizational financial performance. HPWS includes the professional competencies within the HR function as reflected in their effectiveness across different functional activities, as well as senior leadership styles that emphasize motivation and vision, rather than command and control.

The model used to estimate these results includes, as control variables, total employment, percentage of unionization, R&D expenses/sales, organizational-specific risk (beta), and five-year percentage sales growth. When in-market value or gross rate of return is the dependent variable, in-book value of the plant and equipment is an independent variable in the model. The researchers suggest that the best reflection of the strategic impact of HR is the effect on market-to-book value. If the average organization were to improve its HR system by 33 percent (one standard deviation), then shareholder value would increase by approximately 20 percent. In addition to this impact on shareholder value, it is also clear that HR systems have beneficial effects on accounting profits, employee productivity, and turnover rate.

Using a technique called cluster analysis, the organizations in the sample were compared, based on how they structured the forty characteristics of HPWS into an overall HR strategy. In effect, this type of analysis indicates whether the organizations in the sample can be categorized by the way in which they structure their HR architecture. The researchers discovered four such systems:

1. *High-Performance Work Systems.* Organizations in this group score well above average on both the HR system and implementation alignment dimensions.
2. *Compensation-Based Systems.* Organizations in this group score above average on the HR system index, but below average on implementation alignment. This group is referred to as compensation-

based because the only reason they score well on the HR system index is their very high ratings on the compensation dimensions.

3. *Alignment Systems*. These are an unusual set of organizations. They are slightly above average on implementation alignment, but they score among the lowest on the HR system. These organizations approach strategic HR from the top down, but do not finish the job. Senior managers say the right things, and HR is considered to be part of the strategic planning process, but managers have never made the investment in the infrastructure of a high-performance work system.

4. *Personnel Systems*. These organizations are characterized by scores that are well below average on both the HR system and the implementation alignment dimensions. These organizations approach their HR systems in a traditional way and appear to make no effort to exploit HR as a strategic asset.

Taking into account other organization and industry characteristics, an organization pursuing a high-performance strategy had a 65 percent higher market value (for a given book value) than an organization using either the personnel or alignment strategy. Organizations using only the compensation strategy had a 39 percent higher market value than similar organizations using the personnel strategy.

These studies are significant because they provide more evidence of the value of human capital. This is on-going research that continues not only to establish a relation between human capital and organizational performance, but also to illustrate what types of HR systems produce the most results.

WATSON-WYATT STUDIES

In 1999, Watson-Wyatt, a human capital consulting firm, received responses to a structured questionnaire for human resource executives in over four hundred U.S.- and Canada-based publicly traded companies. Each company had at least three years of shareholder returns and a minimum of $100 million in revenue or market share.[13] A wide range of questions was asked about how organizations administer HR practices, including compensation, talent development, communications, and staffing. The responses were matched to objective financial measures, including market share, three-and five-year total returns to shareholders, and Tobin's q ratio, which measures an organization's ability to create value beyond its physical assets. Publicly available data were used to access the financial information needed. A variety of statistical analyses were performed to investigate the relationship between human capital practices and objective financial measures.

The relationship was so clear that a significant improvement in thirty key HR practices was associated with a 30 percent increase in market value. Using regression equations and standard scoring conversion, total scores were created for an individual organization so the results could be expressed on a scale of 0 to 100. A score of 0 represented the poorest human capital management while 100 was ideal. A summary score was the organization's Human Capital Index (HCI). In 2000, the project was repeated for a group of 250 European countries; in 2001, the HCI research was conducted again, this time with more than 500 North American companies. In 2001, the HCI research found that improvements in fifty-three key practices were associated with an increase of 47 percent of market value.

Although the survey questionnaire contained more than 130 items, most of these were related to a few human capital areas identified in the previous research as human capital drivers, among them were rewards, communications, career development, culture, and staffing. Table 7-3 shows a sample of the questions on the questionnaire where participants responded on a five-point scale, ranging from *strongly disagree* to *strongly agree*.

The researchers combined questions and areas into several different categories, condensing the work into a variety of human capital management strategies. These strategies were so detailed they could account for a particular percent of the market value. Because of this, the human resource executive could trace the connection between specific practices and the corresponding

Table 7-3. Watson-Wyatt studies with the human capital index.

A. Among new job applicants, this company has an established reputation as a desirable place to work.

B. Professional new hires are usually already well-equipped to perform their duties and do not require much, if any, additional training.

C. Hourly/clerical new hires are usually already well-equipped to perform their duties and do not require much, if any, additional training.

D. It is usually fairly easy to find applicants who possess the skills this company most needs to remain competitive.

E. During the hiring process, job candidates are interviewed by a number of individuals, representing a cross-section of functional areas.

F. Recruiting efforts are specifically designed to support the company's business plan.

G. There is a formal recruiting strategy for filling critical skill positions (i.e., positions requiring special knowledge and competencies that are directly related to the company's ability).

Source: Bruce C. Pfau and Ira T. Kay, *The Human Capital Edge* (New York: McGraw-Hill, 2002).

shareholder value. Table 7-4 shows the twenty-one human capital management strategies from this major research project.

The HCI studies are significant because of the large database and significant correlations. Some of the companies included in the global research are American Express, BIC Corporation, Campbell Soup Company, Daimler-Chrysler, General Motors Company, IBM, Kraft Foods, Liberty Mutual Group, and Siemens AG.

DELOITTE & TOUCHE STUDIES

Another series of studies have been conducted by the consulting firm of Deloitte & Touche, one of the big four accounting and consulting firms. This study was originally developed by Arthur Andersen & Company. With the demise of Andersen, over 1,000 of their Canadian partners joined with Deloitte & Touche in 2002. The data continued under the development of De-

Table 7-4. Twenty-one people management practices from the human capital index studies.

---

1. Approach recruiting and retention as mission-critical.
2. Hire people who will hit the ground running.
3. It's not enough to be a great place to work. You have to be known as a great place to work.
4. Involve employees in the hiring process.
5. Focus on the basics: People are more alike than different.
6. Link pay to performance.
7. Demand that CEOs hold a significant stake in the company.
8. Offer significant stock-based incentives across the board.
9. Synchronize pay.
10. Don't treat benefits as fringe.
11. Understand that employee satisfaction is critical to any business goal.
12. Minimize status distinction.
13. Make work arrangements flexible.
14. Don't underestimate the crucial importance of single leadership.
15. Learn how to manage change.
16. Don't assume workers no longer care about job security.
17. Be cautious about developmental training.
18. Make communications open and candid.
19. Enable employees to share knowledge by capitalizing on technology.
20. Be careful in implementing 360° feedback.
21. Physician, heal thyself: The role of HR.

Source: Bruce N. Pfau and Ira T. Kay, *The Human Capital Edge* (New York: McGraw-Hill, 2002).

loitte and reflected some very interesting results. Data were collected from more than two hundred U.S. and Canadian organizations across a wide range of industries. Almost 80 percent of the participants represented public companies and two-thirds operated in more than one country. Forty-two percent of the organizations reported annual revenue greater than $1 billion and 20 percent employed more than 20,000 full-time employees.

Deloitte collected data on human capital practices regarding pay, performance measurement, training and development, communication, and leadership. This was compared to the financial and organizational performance measures, including the most recent market-to-book ratio, three- to five-year total return to shareholders, and voluntary and involuntary turnover. In addition, information about each company's market orientation was developed. Market orientation involved product innovation, customer intimacy, and operational excellence.

The results of these studies suggest that human capital practices may account for as much as 43 percent of the difference between one company's market-to-book value and another's. As powerful as this finding may be, it becomes even more commanding when specific human capital practices are examined in a framework of how they drive market value across different types of companies. For example, some human capital practices appear to drive market value universally; they are appropriate and actionable by all companies. Other high-value practices drive market value, but only for companies with a certain market orientation. Although the human capital ROI survey instrument included 114 separate items to assess a company's practices, Deloitte's analysis identified 17 of these that are most critical and drive superior performance. These are contained in table 7-5. The bottom ten items are considered universally applicable.

Figure 7-2 shows how much of the difference in market-to-book value is attributed to human practices. The human capital ROI study clearly demonstrates that while some practices will add value to any organization, other practices must be viewed from the perspective of the individual organization. There are no panaceas. Organizations must carefully consider who they are and how they do business before adopting any practice, no matter how successful it may be for other companies.

KNOWLEDGE ASSET MANAGEMENT STUDIES

Another interesting study attempted to compare the investment in human capital to the stock price. This research was conducted by Knowledge Asset Management (now Bassi Investments) and has been spearheaded by Laura Bassi,

Table 7-5. *Deloitte & Touche survey items.*

Setting starting salaries

1. The company accepts significant differences in base salaries for similar positions in order to recruit top talent.

Measuring employee performance

2. To what extent is employee performance measured on developing new skills?
3. To what extent is employee performance measured on meeting productivity standards?
4. To what extent is employee performance measured on ensuring quality?

Enhancing productivity

5. Workflows are designed to encourage cooperation and effectiveness across work groups.
6. Investments in training programs are one of the first things to be reduced when the company needs to manage expenses.
7. Employees have easy access to the mechanisms the company uses to communicate (e.g., intranet, e-mail, bulletin boards, meetings).

Managing talent

8. The company has identified critical jobs and potential replacements for these jobs.
9. Employees have multiple opportunities to develop their careers within the company.
10. The top performers within the company have been identified for retention, succession planning, and career development purposes.

Rewarding performance

11. To what extent are incentive pay plans for employees below executive level driven by individual performance?
12. To what extent are incentive pay plans for employees below executive level driven by overall company performance?
13. To what extent are incentive pay plans for executives driven by individual performance?
14. To what extent are incentive pay plans for executives driven by overall company performance?

Communicating strategically

15. Communication efforts provide employees with information about customer satisfaction.
16. Communication efforts provide employees with information about key competitors and recent trends in the industry.
17. Communication efforts provide employees with an understanding of company business strategy and financial performance.

Figure 7-2. Human capital practices represent as much as 43 percent of the difference between market-to-book value.

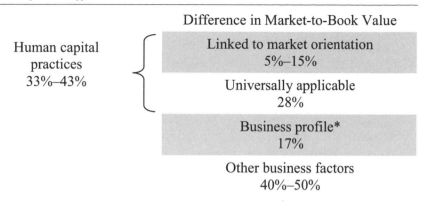

Difference in Market-to-Book Value

Human capital
practices
33%–43%

Linked to market orientation
5%–15%

Universally applicable
28%

Business profile*
17%

Other business factors
40%–50%

*Revenue, market orientation, organizational culture, and number of countries with business operations

Source: Deloitte & Touche.

former vice president of Research of the American Society for Training and Development (ASTD). Their findings suggest that over the past five years, portfolio firms that made unusually large investments in employee education and training outperformed the S&P 500 by a factor of two (113 percent versus 55 percent). This result holds in both bull and bear markets and across industries. This research was developed using a database from ASTD's benchmarking service and multivariate techniques to control for other potential confounding factors, including industry. Researchers conclude that this is not simply spurious correlation; extensive research indicates that it is predictive. Great efforts were taken to avoid the statistical sin of "over-prediction." Researchers also have developed a human capital capability scorecard, focusing directly on what organizations can do to increase the human capital investment and achieve outstanding results.

OTHER STUDIES

This chapter has presented a few of the key studies showing the connection between investing in human capital and organizational outcomes. While these studies are impressive, collectively they represent only the tip of the iceberg. There are literally hundreds of similar studies. One group of researchers listed over fifty studies that make the connection between human capital management and the performance of the firm.[14]

Much of this work was initiated in the 1990s. During that decade, demonstrating the positive link between human resource management and performance became *the* dominant research in the human capital field. Academics and practitioners alike have been interested in understanding the effects of specific HRM practices for many years. The economic boom in the 1990s sparked an intense need to better understand the value of human capital. This is good news for practitioners because of the tremendous number of studies generated.

While the studies outlined above have included many global organizations, the database is predominantly comprised of U.S. companies. Fortunately, many other countries have been studying the same issues and with consistent results. For example, consider table 7-6, which reflects the results of a major study in Canada.[15] This study recorded a statistically significant association between participation-based HR practices, employee behavior, and operating outcomes, and a less significant association for financial outcomes. Some studies have dramatic claims and impressive conclusions. For example, a startling British research report shows that the quality of HR initiatives has a significant impact on the level of patient care and subsequent mortality in hospitals.[16]

Although most of the studies in this chapter have reflected data across organizations, which is very important for macrolevel policy and practices for human capital, major studies are also conducted within the organizations themselves. Some will argue that this represents microlevel analysis, nonethe-

Table 7-6. Proportion of establishments reporting improvements in performance outcomes by human resource strategy, 1988–1993.

Performance Outcome	Human Resource Strategy	
	Traditional	Participative
Behavior Outcomes		
Resignations	42.0	55.0
Accidents	37.0	46.0
Grievances	33.0	40.0
Operating Outcomes		
Labor productivity	79.0	85.0
Unit costs	35.0	49.0
Product/service quality	95.0	94.0
Financial Outcomes		
Profits	47.0	52.0
Sales	63.0	66.0
Market share	66.0	71.0

Source: Adapted from Gordon Betcherman, et al., *The Canadian Workplace in Transition* (Kingston, Ontario: IRC Press, 1994).

less, it still reflects the overall view of the relationship of human resources in the organization—not the payoff of a specific program. Larger organizations tackle this issue themselves. Consider the quest of Les Hayman, chief officer of Global Human Resources for SAP, a large software company based in Germany. Hayman made his mark on the operating side of the business, having grown the Pacific region at SAP to dramatic success. He brings a pragmatic approach to the human resources function; that approach tells him that human capital will be taken seriously only if it is shown to relate directly to profits. While many are developing and using metrics for measuring the effectiveness of human resources, Hayman wants to go much further. He aims to take the mountains of data generated by SAP's software and crunch the numbers to calculate the impact of a variety of HR measures on the bottom line. He's funding a research and development effort by Boston Consulting and Accenture to determine its feasibility. His dream is an objective standard for human capital similar to the Generally Accepted Accounting Principles (GAAP). "I want people to compare Company A and B. The ultimate step is that you'd integrate it into the balance sheet."[17]

Multiply the efforts of Les Hayman by literally hundreds of other progressive human resource executives and consider the dominant research that continues in the human capital field. This means that there will be a continuous stream of additional research showing the value of human capital, leaving little doubt that human capital makes a difference in influencing many of the key measures of success in an organization. Investing in human capital—more specifically investing in more progressive, critical practices—will add value to the organization.

DISADVANTAGES

Several disadvantages are inherent in macrolevel analyses. First, a study is often very complex, difficult to conduct, and often requires skills that are beyond the capability of many human capital managers. Attempting to replicate a study at the organizational level may be impossible for most human capital functions. Second, the data usually does not show the cause-and-effect relationship. Did the investment in human capital drive the organization's success or did the success of the organization enable it to invest more in human capital? This is a question that is raised in many analyses and sometimes the answer is not very clear. Third, the macrolevel view may not be helpful to a human resources manager struggling to improve the budget for a program or project or trying to continue funding for a particular program that has been in place for some time. It also may not help a manager to understand the connection between making adjustments and changes in a program and the ultimate consequences. Thus, a microlevel analysis, covered in the next chapter, is needed to complement the macrolevel analysis.

Advantages

Macrolevel analyses provide the perspective across the entire investment in an organization or across the entire investment for an industry, community, or country. Because these studies provide insight into the contribution of human capital, they are helpful for planning overall policies and connecting strategies in a general way. This is important information for top executives and the senior HR staff. These studies show the connection between the specific practices, activities, and processes used by human capital professionals and the contribution to the organization. Finally, these studies help build respect for a part of the business that has suffered in terms of its attention, focus, and reputation.

Summary

Had enough? Do you need another research study? Probably not. The aim of this chapter was to present enough data to show that human capital makes a difference in organizational performance. Building on macrolevel studies across a variety of organizations, this chapter has methodically and systematically shown the connection between human capital investment and outcomes. More specifically, these studies show that certain human capital practices have more potential for driving business value than others. Some of the studies show which practices have made a difference.

These types of studies originated as part of the research agenda with professors, along with progressive executives who were willing to let their organizations serve as a laboratory. The research has evolved into mainstream analysis conducted by the larger and more prestigious consulting firms. The data are used to drive a variety of human resource practices. Collectively, there is a tremendous amount of data about the value of investing in human capital and the corresponding payoff. The next chapter examines the microlevel view—the payoff of investing in a specific HR program or practice.

Notes

1   W.V. Merrihue and R.A. Katzell, "ERI—'Yardstick of Employee Relations'," *Harvard Business Review*: 33(6), 1955, pp. 91–99.

2   "You Can Measure Your Employee Relations," *National Productivity Report*: 7(15), 1978, pp. 1–4.

3   JR LaPointe, "Human Resource Performance Indexes," *Personnel Journal,* 62 (1983): 545, 553.

4   F.E. Schuster, *The Schuster Report: The Proven Connection Between People and Profits* (New York: John Wiley, 1986).

5   Jack J. Phillips, *Accountability in Human Resource Management* (Woburn: Butterworth-Heinemann, 1996).

6   Marcus Buckingham and Curt Coffman, *First, Break All the Rules: What the World's Greatest Managers Do Differently* (New York: Simon & Schuster, 1999).

7   James L. Heskett, W. Earl Sasser, and Leonard A. Schlesinger, *The Service Profit Chain* (Boston: Harvard Business Review, 1997).

8   Linda Holbeche, *Aligning Human Resources and Business Strategy* (Woburn, MA: Butterworth-Heinemann, 2001).

9   Anthony J. Rucci, et al., "The Employee-Customer-Profit Chain at Sears," *Harvard Business Review*: Jan–Feb, 1998.

10   Linda Holbeche, *Aligning Human Resources and Business Strategy* (Woburn, MA: Butterworth-Heinemann, 2001).

11   James L. Heskett, W. Earl Sasser, and Leonard A. Schlesinger, *The Value Profit Chain: Treat Employees Like Customers and Customers Like Employees* (New York: The Free Press, 2003).

12   Brian E. Becker, Mark A. Huselid, and Dave Ulrich, *The HR Scorecard: Linking People, Strategy, and Performance* (Boston: Harvard Business School Press, 2001).

13   Bruce N. Pfau and Ira T. Kay, *The Human Capital Edge: 21 People Management Practices Your Company Must Implement (or Avoid) to Maximize Shareholder Value* (New York: McGraw-Hill, 2002).

14   David E. Bowen, "Understanding HRM-Firm Performance Linkages: The Role of the 'Strength' of the HRM System," *Academy of Management Review*, vol. 29, no. 2, 2004, pp. 203–221.

15   Gordon Betcherman, K. McMullen, N. Leckie, and C. Caron, *The Canadian Workplace in Transition* (Queen's University, Kingston, Ontario: IRC Press, 1994).

16   Zoë Robert, "IIR 'Can Lower NHS Death Rates'," *People Management*, October 11, 2001.

17   P.J. Kiger, "Les Hayman's Excellent Adventure," *Workforce Management*, August 2004, pp. 41–44.

CHAPTER 8

What We Know from ROI Analysis

Chapter 7 focused on the macrolevel view of the value of human capital, highlighting various studies and research efforts that examine the relationship between investing in human capital and subsequent outcomes. This chapter takes a microlevel view, showing how detailed impact studies are conducted on specific human capital projects, initiatives, and solutions. This view, which in the last decade has been presented in the form of ROI studies, provides decision makers with detailed information about the success (or lack of success) of specific initiatives. This microlevel analysis helps drive decisions to implement future human capital projects. These studies can also improve ongoing projects and help set priorities based on which ones are adding the most value. When combined with the macrolevel analysis, ROI impact studies provide overwhelming evidence of the importance and value of human capital.

This chapter shows how the ROI methodology described in chapter 5 has evolved into a widely used method, briefly describes the processes used and the standards employed, and discusses best practices. It also offers a brief summary of the many applications of this methodology for human capital. The chapter provides an overview of ROI's use as well as its success, barriers, and benefits.

ROI PROGRESS AND STATUS

Before examining the progress of ROI, a few global trends about measurement and evaluation should be examined. The following trends have been identified and are slowly evolving across private- and public-sector organizations and cultures in over forty countries.[1] Collectively, these trends have a significant impact on the way accountability is addressed. They include:

❑ Evaluation is an integral part of the design, development, delivery, and implementation of human capital programs and projects.

❑ A shift from a reactive approach to a more proactive approach is developing, with evaluation addressed early in the human capital cycle.

❑ Measurement and evaluation processes are systematic and methodical, often built into the implementation process.

❑ Technology significantly enhances measurement and evaluation and enables large amounts of data to be collected, processed, analyzed, and integrated across human capital programs and projects.

❑ Organizations without comprehensive measurement and evaluation have reduced or eliminated significant parts of their HR program budgets.

❑ Organizations with comprehensive measurement and evaluation have enhanced their HR department budgets.

❑ The use of ROI is emerging as an essential part of the measurement and evaluation mix.

❑ A comprehensive measurement and evaluation process, including ROI, can be implemented for about 3 to 5 percent of the direct HR department budget.

Progression of ROI Across Sectors

The ROI methodology described in this book had its beginnings in the 1970s when it was applied to the development of a return on investment for a cooperative education program at Lockheed-Martin.[2] Since then it has been updated, refined, and expanded in all types of situations, applications, and sectors. Figure 8-1 shows how the process has evolved within the various sectors. Applications began in the manufacturing sector, where the process was easily developed because it was a natural fit in the production environment. It migrated to the service sector, as many major service firms such as banks and telecommunications companies used the ROI process to show the value of various HR programs. Applications evolved into the healthcare arena as the industry sought ways to improve educational services, human resources, quality, risk management, and case management. Nonprofit applications began to emerge as these organizations looked for ways to reduce costs and generate efficiencies. Finally, applications in the public sector began to appear in a variety of government organizations. An outgrowth of public-sector applications spread to the use of the process in the educational field where it is now being applied. Public-sector implementation has intensified

Figure 8-1. Progression of ROI implementation.

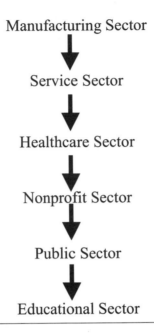

Movement Within the Sectors

Manufacturing Sector

Service Sector

Healthcare Sector

Nonprofit Sector

Public Sector

Educational Sector

in recent years. All types of organizations and settings now apply the ROI methodology.

ROI Networks

Perhaps one of the most visible signs of the acceptance of ROI methodology is the proliferation of ROI networks. Founded in 1996, the first ROI network was formed by a group of practitioners involved in implementing the ROI process. The purpose of the organization is to promote the science and practice of individual and organizational measurement and accountability. The network established three strategic goals:

1. To leverage the knowledge, skills, and experience of practitioners and sponsors.
2. To reinforce and support practitioner knowledge, skills, and experience.
3. To promote innovative ROI measurement and evaluation practices.

Through Web sites, list serves, newsletters, research grants, and conferences, the network routinely exchanged information about the ROI process.

In 2002, the network was acquired by the American Society for Training and Development (www.astd.org). In addition to this global ROI network, other networks have been developed for specific countries, regions, states, cities, or even companies. For example, Canada has a very active ROI network sponsored by the Canadian Society for Training and Development; Puerto Rico enjoys one of the most active and supportive ROI networks where practitioners meet monthly to discuss challenges, concerns, and issues on ROI and exchange information. In the United States, some specific states have ROI networks; the state of Mississippi has an active network in which individuals exchange information on a routine basis. Some cities and large organizations have ROI networks. For example, Comcast, the largest cable company in the United States, has an ROI network of almost forty HR staff members who meet and exchange information about progress status as well as barriers to implementation. Networking is an excellent way to continue to develop this capability and share tools, techniques, and technology.

Global Expansion

Measuring the return on investment is becoming a global issue. Organizations from all over the world are concerned about accountability and are exploring ways to measure the results of programs and solutions. Whether the economy is mature or developing, accountability is still a critical issue. Professional associations in various countries offer workshops, seminars, and conferences dedicated to the measurement issue. Some associations sponsor individual workshops on ROI. Formal ROI presentations have been made in over fifty countries with implementation organized and coordinated in at least thirty-five countries.

A few examples underscore the role of these organizations in implementing ROI in their respective countries. Skillnet, an organization partially funded by the Irish government, sponsors workshops on ROI for HR professionals, conducts ROI studies, and assists with ROI implementation. The organization is taking the lead in coordinating and introducing ROI to organizations in Ireland.

Japan Management Association (JMA), an association of medium to large business organizations in Japan, introduced the ROI process to its member organizations. JMA translated one of the major books on ROI, and sponsored workshops and other learning activities about the ROI process. Through a professional association, JMA is coordinating the implementation of the ROI methodology in Japan. Part of this implementation was the development of a special publication on the application of ROI in HR, featuring case studies from Texas Instruments, Verizon Communications, Apple Computers, Motorola, Cisco Systems, AT&T, and the U.S. Office of Personnel Management. The purpose of the publication was to show Japanese business and industry how other organizations are using the ROI process.

In New Zealand, Deloitte & Touche has implemented the ROI methodology in both public and private sectors. Driven by a partner in the local practice, many organizations are building on Deloitte's advice and information. In Chile, a consulting firm (Mas Consultores) has implemented the ROI process with the translation of an ROI book, an advertising promotion campaign throughout the country, a variety of workshops and executive briefings, and a detailed certification for specialists in the country.

These examples illustrate how organizations around the globe use ROI as an important tool. The ROI methodology is a global issue that is being tackled in all types of cultures and settings.

Paradigm Shift

The ROI methodology underscores the need for human capital functions to shift from an activity-based process to a results-based process. As depicted in table 8-1, a paradigm shift in recent years has produced a dramatic effect on human capital policy and practice. Organizations have moved from providing HR programs based on activity to focusing on bottom-line results. This shift is evident from the beginning to the end of the process. The activity-based approach characterized by the left side of table 8-1 describes many traditional HR functions in years past (unfortunately, some are still operating this way). These HR managers were satisfied offering all types of programs to any audience without much attempt to connect these programs to the organization or to measure any success, and certainly there was little or no communication or involvement with senior HR managers. Today's results-based approach is needed to ensure that programs begin with the end in mind, with a clear, specific business alignment. The attention and focus must be on accountability throughout the process as all stakeholders are brought into the equation. A measurement of success must exist, and that success must be communicated to a variety of groups with the results summarized in an overall scorecard. The shift has often occurred because of the forces described in chapter 5. Some progressive HR departments have recognized the need for ROI and have been persistent in making progress on this issue.

Basis for Acceptance

There are good reasons why return on investment has gained acceptance. Although the viewpoints and explanations may vary, some things are clear.

Table 8-1. Paradigm shift in human capital policy and practices.

Activity Based	Results Based
Characterized by:	**Characterized by:**
☐ no business need for the HR program	☐ HR program linked to specific business needs
☐ no assessment of performance issues	☐ assessment of performance effectiveness
☐ no specific measurable objectives	☐ specific objectives for behavior and business impact
☐ no effort to prepare HR program participants to achieve results	☐ results expectations communicated to HR participants
☐ no effort to prepare the work environment to support implementation	☐ environment prepared to support implementation
☐ no efforts to build partnerships with key managers	☐ partnerships established with key managers and clients
☐ no measurement of results or cost-benefit analysis	☐ measurement of results and cost-benefit analysis
☐ planning and reporting is input-focused	☐ planning and reporting is output-focused

Human capital budgets continue to increase annually by organization, industry, and country. Many organizations and countries see human capital as an investment instead of a cost. Consequently, senior managers are willing to invest because they can anticipate a payoff for their investments. As expenditures grow, accountability becomes a critical issue. A growing budget creates a larger target for internal critics, often prompting the development of an ROI process.

Organizations have recently seen an increase in ROI applications because of the growing interest in improvement programs, such as total quality management, continuous process improvement, and Six Sigma, particularly in North America, Europe, and Asia. Unfortunately, many of these change efforts were unsuccessful and just passing fads. Today, organizations evaluate processes and outputs not previously measured, monitored, or reported. This focus places increased pressure on the human capital function to develop measures of program success by using ROI.

Restructuring and reengineering initiatives and the threat of outsourcing have caused HR executives to focus on bottom-line issues. Many processes have been reengineered to align programs more closely with business needs to obtain maximum efficiencies in the cycle. These change processes have brought increased attention to evaluation issues and have resulted in measuring the contribution of specific HR programs including ROI.

ROI is a familiar term and concept for business managers, particularly those with business administration and management degrees. These executives apply the ROI process to the purchase of equipment, building a new facility, or buying a new company. Consequently, they understand and appreciate ROI and are pleased to see the methodology applied to human capital.

ROI is now receiving increased interest in the executive suite. Top executives watch with frustration as their human capital budgets continue to grow without the appropriate accountability measures. For years, HR managers convinced top executives that human capital could not be measured, at least not as a monetary contribution. Many executives are now aware that it can and is being measured. Subsequently, they are demanding the same accountability from their human capital functions.

ROI Is Here to Stay

One thing is certain in the ROI debate: It is not a fad. The concept of ROI has been used for centuries. The seventy-fifth anniversary issue of *Harvard Business Review* (HBR) traced the tools used to measure results in organizations.[3] In early issues of HBR, during the 1920s, ROI was the emerging tool used to place a value on the payoff of investments. As long as there is a need for accountability of expenditures and the concept of an investment payoff is desired, ROI will be used to evaluate major investments in human capital improvement.

Today, hundreds of organizations routinely develop ROI calculations for human capital programs. The status of ROI has grown significantly and the rate of implementation has been phenomenal. The number of organizations and individuals involved with the process underscores the magnitude of ROI implementation. Table 8-2 presents a summary of the current status. With this much evidence of the growing interest, the ROI process is now becoming a standard tool for HR program evaluation.[4]

THE CHALLENGES OF DEVELOPING A CREDIBLE ROI PROCESS

Although much progress has been made, the ROI process is not without its share of problems and concerns. The mere presence of ROI creates a dilemma for many organizations. When the concept is implemented, the management team usually anxiously awaits results only to be disappointed when they are not readily available. For an ROI process to be useful, it must balance many issues such as feasibility, simplicity, credibility, and reliability. More specifi-

Table 8-2. Summary of current ROI status.

- The ROI methodology has been refined over a 30-year period.
- Over 2,000 private-sector organizations have formally implemented the ROI methodology.
- Over 200 governmental units have implemented the ROI methodology.
- Approximately 5,000 studies are developed each year using the ROI methodology.
- A hundred case studies are published on the ROI methodology.
- Over 2,000 individuals have been certified to implement the ROI methodology in their organizations.
- The ROI methodology has been implemented in 40 countries.
- Fifteen books have been developed to support the process, two have won awards.
- A 600-member professional network has been formed to share information.
- The ROI methodology can be implemented for 4–5 percent of the HR budget.

cally, three major audiences must be pleased with the ROI process to accept and use it:

1. HR practitioners who design, develop, and implement programs
2. Senior managers, sponsors, and clients who initiate and support programs
3. Researchers and evaluators who need a credible process

HR Practitioners

For years, HR practitioners have assumed that ROI could not be measured with human capital projects. When they examined a typical process, they found long formulas, complicated equations, and complex models that made the ROI process appear confusing. With this perceived complexity, HR managers could only imagine the tremendous efforts required for data collection and analysis, and more important, the increased cost in making the process work. Because of these concerns, HR practitioners look for a simple and understandable process, with steps and strategies that are easily implemented. Also, they need a process that will not take excessive time to implement or consume undue precious staff time. Finally, practitioners need a process that is not cost prohibitive. With competition for financial resources, HR practitioners need a process that will require only a small portion of the HR budget. In summary, from the perspective of the HR practitioner, the ROI process must be user-friendly, time effective, and cost efficient.

Senior Managers/Sponsors/Clients

Managers who must approve HR budgets, request HR programs, or live with the results of programs, have a strong interest in the development of ROI in human capital projects. They want a process that provides quantifiable results, using a method similar to the formula applied to other types of investments. Senior managers want to have it all come down to an ROI calculation reflected as a percentage. They also want a process that is simple and easy to understand. The assumptions used in the calculations must be conservative, the methodology used in the process should be credible and reflect their point of reference, background, and level of understanding. Senior executives do not want, or need, a string of formulas, charts, and complicated models. Instead, they need a process that they can explain to others, if necessary. More important, they need a process with which they can identify, one that is sound and realistic enough to earn their confidence.

Researchers and Evaluators

Researchers and evaluators will only support a process that measures up to close examination. They usually insist that models, formulas, assumptions, and theories are sound and based on commonly accepted practices. They also want a process that produces accurate values and consistent outcomes. If estimates are necessary, researchers want a process that provides the most accuracy within the constraints of the situation, recognizing that adjustments need to be made when there is uncertainty in the process. The challenge is to develop acceptable requirements for an ROI process that will satisfy researchers and, at the same time, please practitioners and senior managers. Sound impossible? Maybe not.

Criteria for an Effective ROI Process

To satisfy the needs of the three critical groups described above, the ROI process must meet several requirements. Eleven essential criteria for an effective ROI process follow.

1. The process must be *simple,* void of complex formulas, lengthy equations, and complicated methodologies. Most ROI attempts have failed because of this requirement. In an attempt to obtain statistical perfection and use too many theories, some ROI models have become too complex. Consequently, they have not been implemented.

2. The process must be *economical* and easily implemented. It should become a routine part of the human capital function without requiring significant additional resources. Sampling for ROI calculations

and early planning for ROI can result in progress without adding new staff.

3. The assumptions, methodology, and techniques must be *credible*. Logical, methodical steps are needed to earn the respect of practitioners, senior managers, and researchers. This requires a practical approach for the process.

4. From a research perspective, the process must be *theoretically sound* and based on generally accepted practices. Unfortunately, this requirement can lead to an extensive, complicated process. Ideally, the process must strike a balance between maintaining a practical and sensible approach *and* a sound and theoretical basis for the process. This is perhaps one of the greatest challenges to those who have developed models for the ROI process.

5. The process must *account for other factors* that have influenced output variables. To gain accuracy and build credibility it is necessary to isolate the influence of the HR program; this is one of the most overlooked issues. The ROI process should pinpoint the contribution of the program when compared to the other influences.

6. The process must be appropriate with a *variety of HR programs*. Some models apply to only a small number of programs such as sales or productivity training. Ideally, the process must be applicable to all types of programs such as career development, organization development, and major change initiatives.

7. The process must have the *flexibility* to be applied on a preprogram basis as well as a postprogram basis. In some situations, an estimate of the ROI is required before the actual program is developed. Ideally, the process should be made to adjust to a range of potential time frames.

8. The process must be *applicable with all types of data,* including hard data, which are typically represented as output, quality, costs, and time; and soft data, which include job satisfaction, engagement, customer satisfaction, grievances, and complaints.

9. The process must *include the costs of the program*. The ultimate level of evaluation is to compare the benefits with costs. Although the term ROI is sometimes used loosely to express any benefit of a program, an acceptable ROI formula must include costs. Omitting or underestimating costs will only destroy the credibility of the ROI values.

10. The actual calculation must use an *acceptable ROI formula*. This is often the benefits/cost ratio (BCR) or the ROI calculation expressed

as a percent. These formulas compare the actual expenditure for the program with the monetary benefits derived from the program. While other financial terms can be substituted, it is important to use a standard financial calculation in the ROI process.

11. Finally, the process must have a successful *track record* in a variety of applications. In far too many situations, models are created but never successfully applied. An effective ROI process should withstand the wear and tear of implementation and should achieve the expected success.

Considered essential, an ROI methodology should meet the vast majority, if not all, of the criteria. The bad news is that most ROI processes do not meet these criteria; the good news is that the process presented in this book meets *all* of them.

ROI APPLICATIONS FOR HUMAN CAPITAL AREAS

Impact studies have been conducted in every human capital area. As expected, more progress has been made in some areas than others.[5] For example, productivity improvement and gainsharing programs organized by human resources have shown tremendous success with the use of ROI. Reward systems and safety programs often show impact with ROI without much difficulty. In the learning and development area, many applications have shown increasing success. Other areas have not faired so well. For a variety of reasons, ROI progress has not been made in recruiting, compliance, diversity, and career management, but the need and interest is still there. Table 8-3 provides a summary of the progress and issues with ROI applications in the various human capital areas.

The use of ROI occurs in all the areas listed in table 8-3 with increased efforts to improve accountability. Perhaps no groupings receive more criticism and calls for accountability than those labeled "soft." For example, career management, management succession, leadership development, and business coaching have been subjected to ROI accountability. ROI studies on leadership development are one of the most published areas in the last five years. Not because executives do not believe in leadership development, but because they need some sense of the contribution when a leadership development program is implemented from a vast array of possibilities.[6] To be successful with leadership ROI studies, program designers, and implementers have to shift their thinking from "attempting to place a monetary value on leadership" to "placing a monetary value on the outcomes of the leadership development

Table 8-3. ROI applications in human capital.

HR Function	Relative Use of ROI	Typical Programs for ROI Calculation	Comments
• Recruitment & Selection	Low	• Special Recruitment Programs; Employee Testing; New Employee Orientation/ On-Boarding.	• Difficult to capture benefits and convert them to monetary values.
• Learning and Development	Moderate	• Sales Training; Supervisory Training; Leadership Development; E-Learning	• Much progress has been made. More improvement is needed.
• Career Management	Low	• Dual Career Path; Cooperative Education; Succession Planning	• Difficult to convert to monetary values. Intangibles are huge.
• Organization Development	Moderate	• Performance Improvement Projects	• Consulting projects should be easy to measure.
• Compensation	Moderate	• Skill-Based Pay; Competency Based Pay; Incentives; Bonuses	• Difficult to apply to traditional compensation programs. Alternative reward systems show more promise.
• Employee Benefits	Moderate	• Wellness/Fitness Programs; Child Care Programs; New Benefits	• New benefits should be subjected to ROI calculations.
• Fair Employment/ Diversity	Low	• Sexual Harassment Prevention; Diversity Programs; Discrimination Complaints	• Difficult to convert to monetary benefits. Usually justified based on regulatory or compliance needs.
• Labor Relations	Low	• Labor Management Cooperation Program; Grievance Reduction	• Programs usually justified with nonmonetary benefits.
• Safety and Health	High	• Accident Prevention Programs; Loss Control Program; Stress Management	• New programs should be subjected to ROI calculations.
• Employee Relations	Moderate	• Absenteeism Control Program; Turnover Reduction Program	• New programs should be subjected to ROI calculations.
• Productivity/ Quality Improvement	High	• Gainsharing; Productivity Enhancement; Six Sigma	• Virtually every program should have an ROI calculation.

(continues)

Table 8-3. (Continued).

HR Function	Relative Use of ROI	Typical Programs for ROI Calculation	Comments
• Employee Involvement	Moderate	• Suggestion Systems; Empowerment Programs	• New programs should be subjected to ROI calculations.
• Performance Improvement	High	• Performance projects linked to business unit performance	• Easy to take to ROI.
• Change Management	Moderate	• Transportation; Reinvention	• Usually long-term benefits, many intangibles.

effort." This requires program owners to seek the consequences of using new leadership behaviors and competencies.

The experience with IBM underscores this important shift. IBM is making strides in showing the contribution of leadership development and they base their approach on three important principles:

1. The executives must own leadership development and demand accountability. This assures that leadership is supported from the top down and has active involvement throughout the process. Part of the involvement is to expect results and ensure that the results are there.

2. They invest in processes not products. Sometimes it is difficult to capture the value of an off-the-shelf program that may not be aligned with the organization's interests, needs, values, or business metrics. The leadership at IBM instead focuses on the specific processes they need.

3. They measure what matters. Probably the most important issue at IBM is that they are moving away from activity analysis (canning programs, projects, hours, people) to measuring investments and comparing them with the connection to superior business results.[7]

At Nortel Networks the ROI methodology is used to show the impact of business coaching. Taking on one of its more strategic and critical programs, the Leadership Edge, the researchers show the actual connection between business coaching and the monetary impact.[8] The key to ensuring that coaching assignments deliver the desired results is to ensure the initial engagement focuses on business outcome. Too often, coaching assignments focus on behavior changes and ignore the consequences of those changes. In the initial engagement, the coach must address the "so what?" with specific measures. The person being coached must articulate the impact of behavior changes within his or her sphere of work and influence. When this is accomplished, it is much easier to track the actual consequences of the business coaching process, collecting the six types of data presented in chapter 5.

Specific Measures

An important issue that often surfaces when considering ROI applications is the understanding of specific measures that are often driven by specific HR programs. While there are no standard answers, table 8-4 represents an attempt to summarize the typical payoff measures for specific human capital programs. The measures are quite broad for some programs. For example, a reward systems project can pay off in a variety of measures such as improved productivity, enhanced sales and revenues, improved quality, cycle-time reduction, or even direct cost savings. Essentially, it should drive the measure that the reward is designed to influence. In other programs, the influenced measures are quite narrow. For example, in labor management cooperation programs, the payoffs are typically in reduced grievances, less work stoppages, and improved employee satisfaction. Orientation programs typically pay off in measures of early turnover (turnover in the first ninety days of employment), initial job performance, and productivity.

The table also illustrates the vast number of applications of this methodology and the even larger set of measures that can be driven or influenced. In most of these situations it becomes a reasonable task to assign monetary values to these measures as the benefits are compared to the monetary value of a particular program to develop the ROI. Table 8-5 on pages 162–163 presents this data from the perspective of matching the payoff measures to specific human capital initiatives, listing the measures in the organization that are usually influenced with specific HR initiatives. The measures that are influenced depend on the objectives and the design of the program or project.

A word of caution is needed. Presenting specific measures linked to a program may give the impression that these are the only measures influenced. In practice, a particular HR program can have a variety of outcomes and that can make the ROI process difficult. Tables 8-4 and 8-5 show the most likely measures that arise out of the studies that the author has reviewed. In the course of a decade, the author has been involved with over five hundred of these studies, and there are some common threads among particular projects and programs.

The good news is that human capital programs and projects are driving

Table 8-4. Typical measures in ROI applications.

ROI APPLICATIONS

Program/Project	Key Impact Measurements
Absenteeism control/reduction	Absenteeism, customer satisfaction, job satisfaction
Business coaching	Productivity/output, quality, time savings, efficiency, costs, employee satisfaction, customer satisfaction
Career development/career management	Turnover, promotions, recruiting expense, employee satisfaction
Communications	Errors, stress, conflicts, productivity, employee satisfaction
Compensation plans	Costs, productivity, quality, employee satisfaction
Compliance programs	Penalties/fines, charges, settlements, losses
Diversity	Turnover, absenteeism, complaints, charges, settlements, losses
E-Learning	Cost savings, productivity improvement, quality improvement, cycle times, error reductions, employee satisfaction
Employee benefits plans	Costs, time savings, employee satisfaction
Employee relations program	Turnover, absenteeism, employee satisfaction, engagement
Gainsharing plans	Production costs, productivity, turnover
Labor-Management cooperation programs	Work stoppage, grievances, absenteeism, employee satisfaction
Leadership development	Productivity/output, quality, efficiency, cost/time savings, employee satisfaction, engagement
Marketing and advertising	Sales, market share, customer loyalty, cost of sales, wallet share, customer satisfaction
Meeting planning	Sales, productivity/output, quality, time savings, employee satisfaction, customer satisfaction
Orientation, On-Boarding (revised)	Early turnover, training time, productivity
Personal productivity/time management	Time savings, productivity, stress reduction, employee satisfaction
Project management	Time savings, quality improvement, budgets
Recruiting source (new)	Costs, yield, early turnover
Retention management	Turnover, engagement, employee satisfaction
Safety incentive plan	Accident frequency rates, accident severity rates, first aid treatments
Selection tool (new)	Early turnover, training time, productivity
Self-directed teams	Productivity/output, quality, customer satisfaction, turnover, absenteeism, employee satisfaction
Sexual harassment prevention	Complaints, turnover, employee satisfaction
Six Sigma	Defects, rework, response time, cycle time, costs

Skill-Based pay	Labor costs, turnover, absenteeism
Strategy/Policy	Productivity/output, sales, market share, customer service, quality/service levels, cycle times, cost savings, employee satisfaction
Stress management	Medical costs, turnover, absenteeism, job satisfaction
Technical training (job-related)	Productivity, sales, quality, time, costs, customer service, turnover, absenteeism, employee satisfaction
Technology implementation	Cycle times, error rates, productivity, efficiency, customer satisfaction
Wellness/Fitness	Turnover, medical costs, accidents, absenteeism

business measures. The monetary value is based on what is being changed in the various business units, divisions, regions, and individual workplaces. These are the measures that matter to senior executives. The difficulty often comes in ensuring that the connection to the program exists. This is accomplished through a variety of techniques to isolate the effects of the program on the particular business measures and was discussed in chapter 5.

Specific Case Studies

The impressive success of ROI has been widely documented in the literature. Over one hundred case studies have been published in books, trade magazines, and journals. The American Society for Training and Development has published four casebooks on ROI studies; the Society for Human Resource Management has published two. These published case studies usually follow the ROI methodology described in chapter 5 and this chapter. Table 8-6 on page 164 lists a small sample of the studies published along with the appropriate references. The ROI methodology is one of the most documented and validated processes developed for and applied to the area of human capital.

ROI STANDARDS

For any process to be credible, it must have standards. Studies must be consistent as they are developed from one application to another within an organization and also across organizations. The ROI methodology described in this chapter has been developed and refined around conservative standards known as Guiding Principles (presented as table 5-4 in chapter 5). The principles provide conservative adjustments so that if an error exists in the study, it is discounted (or removed from the analysis) as a monetary benefit. Also, when comparing costs to specific benefits, the costs are fully loaded to include all costs, both direct and indirect. These principles serve to increase the credibility, but more importantly, they obtain buy-in with senior management staff who often view the results of the programs.

Table 8-5. Measures linked to human capital programs.

Human Capital Project/Program	Absenteeism	Accident rates	Budgets	Charges	Complaints	Conflicts	Cost savings	Customer loyalty	Customer satisfaction	Cycle times	Defects	Efficiency	Employee satisfaction
Absenteeism Control/Reduction	✓								✓				
Business Coaching							✓		✓			✓	✓
Career Development/Management													✓
Communications					✓								✓
Compensation Plans							✓						✓
Compliance				✓									
Diversity	✓			✓	✓								
E-Learning							✓			✓			✓
Employee Benefits Plans							✓						✓
Employee Relations	✓												✓
Gainsharing Plans							✓						
Labor-Management Cooperation	✓												✓
Leadership Development							✓					✓	✓
Marketing and Advertising							✓	✓	✓				
Meeting Planning									✓				✓
Orientation, On-Boarding (revised)													
Personal Productivity/Time Management													✓
Project Management			✓										
Recruiting Source (new)							✓						
Retention Management													✓
Safety Incentive Plan		✓											
Selection Tool (new)													
Self-Directed Teams	✓								✓				✓
Sexual Harassment Prevention					✓								✓
Six Sigma							✓			✓	✓		
Skill-Based Pay	✓						✓						
Strategy/Policy							✓		✓	✓			✓
Stress Management	✓						✓						
Technical Training (job-related)	✓						✓		✓				✓
Technology Implementation									✓	✓		✓	
Wellness/Fitness	✓	✓					✓						

Engagement	Error reductions	First Aid treatments	Grievances	Job performance	Job satisfaction	Losses	Market share	Penalties/Fines	Productivity/output	Promotions	Quality improvement	Recruiting expense	Rework	Sales	Settlements	Stress reduction	Time savings	Training time	Turnover	Wallet share	Work stoppage	Yield
					✓																	
									✓		✓						✓					
										✓		✓							✓			
	✓								✓							✓						
									✓		✓											
				✓			✓								✓							
				✓											✓				✓			
	✓								✓		✓											
																	✓					
✓																			✓			
									✓										✓			
		✓																				✓
✓									✓		✓						✓					
							✓							✓						✓		
									✓		✓			✓			✓					
									✓									✓	✓			
									✓							✓	✓					
											✓						✓					
																			✓			
✓																			✓			
		✓																				
									✓									✓	✓			
									✓		✓								✓			
																			✓			
													✓				✓					
																			✓			
							✓		✓		✓			✓								
			✓			✓													✓			
									✓		✓			✓			✓		✓			
	✓								✓													
																			✓			

Table 8-6. Sample of published ROI studies.

Measuring the ROI:	Key Impact Measures:	ROI
Performance Management (Restaurant Chain)	A variety of measures, such as productivity, quality, time, costs, turnover, and absenteeism	298%[1]
Process Improvement Team (Apple Computer)	Productivity and labor efficiency	182%[1]
Skill-Based Pay (Construction Materials Firm)	Labor costs, turnover, absenteeism	805%[2]
Sexual Harassment Prevention (Healthcare Chain)	Complaints, turnover, absenteeism, job satisfaction	1052%[2]
Safety Incentive Plan (Steel Company)	Accident frequency rate, accident severity rates	379%[2]
Diversity (Nextel Communications)	Retention, employee satisfaction	163%[6]
Retention Improvement (Financial Services)	Turnover, staffing levels, employee satisfaction	258%[3]
Absenteeism Control/Reduction Program (Major City)	Absenteeism, customer satisfaction	882%[2]
Stress Management Program (Electric Utility)	Medical costs, turnover, absenteeism	320%[2]
Executive Leadership Development (Financial)	Team projects, individual projects, retention	62%[2]
E-Learning (Petroleum)	Sales	206%[2]
Internal Graduate Degree Program (Federal Agency)	Retention, individual graduate projects	153%[4]
Executive Coaching (Hotel Chain)	Several measures, including retention, productivity, cost control, and customer satisfaction	221%[5]
Competency Development (Veterans Health Administration)	Time savings, improve work quality, faster response	159%[4]
First-Level Leadership Development (Auto Rental Company)	Various measures—at least two per manager	105%[7]

References
1. Patricia P. Phillips, ed., *In Action: Measuring Return on Investment*, Vol. 3 (Alexandria, VA: American Society for Training and Development, 2001).
2. Jack J. Phillips, Ron D. Stone, Patricia P. Phillips, *The Human Resources Scorecard: Measuring Return on Investment* (Woburn: MA: Butterworth-Heinemann, 2001).
3. Patricia P. Phillips, ed., *In Action: Retaining Your Best Employees* (Alexandria, VA: American Society for Training and Development, 2002).
4. Patricia P. Phillips, ed., *In Action: Measuring ROI in the Public Sector* (Alexandria, VA: American Society for Training and Development, 2002).
5. Darelyn J. Mitch, ed., *In Action: Measuring Return on Investment*, Vol. 4 (Alexandria, VA: American Society for Training and Development, 2005).
6. Lynn Schmidt, *In Action: Implementing Training Scorecards* (Alexandria, VA: American Society for Training and Development, 2003).
7. Jack J. Phillips and Lynn Schmidt, *The Leadership Scorecard* (Woburn, MA: Butterworth-Heinemann, 2004).

ROI BEST PRACTICES

With the evolution of the ROI methodology and its various applications, best practices have surfaced.

An explanation of these best practices follows:

1. *The ROI methodology is implemented as a process-improvement tool, not a performance-evaluation tool.* HR staff acceptance is critical for the implementation of this process. No individual or group is willing to create a tool that will ultimately be used to evaluate his or her individual performance. Consequently, many organizations recognize that ROI is a process-improvement tool and communicate this position early. The ROI methodology shows not only the success of a particular HR project, program, or solution, but also provides detailed information about how the project can be revised to increase value. Barriers and enablers to success are always identified.

2. *The ROI methodology generates a microlevel scorecard with six types of data.* The data represents a scorecard of performance, representing both qualitative and quantitative data, often taken at different time frames and from various sources. The methodology generates a balanced, microlevel view of success for that particular program.

3. *ROI methodology data are being integrated to create a macrolevel scorecard for the human capital function.* As more and more studies are conducted, data are rolled up to create a macrolevel scorecard, showing the value of the human capital function. As shown in figure 8-2, the individual microlevel scorecard evaluation data are integrated into the overall macrolevel scorecard. This approach requires similar data collection tools and measures across projects, using technology to create the HR macrolevel scorecard. In essence, as each HR program is evaluated and selected, data are integrated. Additional information on developing an HR scorecard is presented in chapter 10.

4. *ROI impact studies are conducted selectively, usually involving 5 to 10 percent of all HR projects, programs, and solutions.* Usually, the HR programs that are targeted for business impact and ROI analysis are those that are strategically focused, expensive, high profile, controversial, and certainly those that have generated management's interest. This does not mean that other HR programs are not evaluated. It is recommended that all programs be evaluated for

Figure 8-2. Microlevel scorecard to macrolevel scorecard.

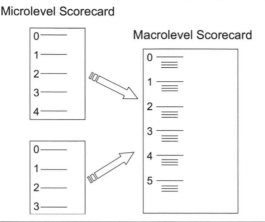

reaction and the vast majority for learning, but only a few select programs are taken to higher levels. More important, those involving the actual ROI calculation are evaluated at all five levels.

5. *ROI evaluation targets are developed, showing the percent of programs evaluated at each level.* Organizations target the desired number of programs to evaluate at each level, expressed as a percent. Figure 8-3 shows a typical profile of a best-practice organization, targeting a percent of programs at each level. Target levels are developed reflecting the resources available and the feasibility of evaluation at each level. Targets usually begin at 100 percent of programs at the first level (reaction) and include 5 to 10 percent of programs at the fifth level (ROI).

6. *A variety of data collection methods are used in ROI analysis.* ROI evaluation is not restricted to a particular type of data collection

Figure 8-3. ROI evaluation targets.

RECOMMENDED TARGETS	
Evaluation Level	Target*
Level 1 – Reaction	100%
Level 2 – Learning	60%
Level 3 – Application	30%
Level 4 – Business Impact	10%
Level 5 – ROI	5%

*Percent of programs evaluated at that level

method such as monitoring business data. Instead, questionnaires, built-in action plans, focus groups, and observations are used in developing the complete profile of six types of data in the ROI methodology.

7. *For a specific ROI evaluation, the effects of HR are isolated from other factors.* Although isolating the effects of HR is a difficult issue, best-practice organizations realize that to make a business linkage to a specific HR effort, there must be some method in place to show the direct contribution of the HR program. Using a variety of techniques ranging from control group analysis to expert estimation, best-practice organizations tackle this difficult issue with each impact study. Some argue that this is too difficult or impossible. In reality, it *must* be done for executives to understand the relative contribution of HR. Otherwise, there is a temptation to slash the budgets of major HR programs because there is no clear connection between the program and the business value.

8. *Business impact data are converted to monetary values.* These days, it may not be enough to show the actual outcome from an HR program expressed in numbers such as quality improvement, cycle-time reduction, turnover reduction, or enhancement in customer loyalty or job satisfaction. The actual value in monetary terms is needed. Best-practice organizations tackle this with a full array of approaches to develop the monetary value. This is absolutely essential because an ROI calculation compares the monetary value with the cost of the HR program.

9. *The ROI methodology is implemented for about 3 to 5 percent of the HR budget.* One of the common fears of ROI implementation is the excessive cost in both time and direct funds. Best-practice firms report that they can implement the ROI methodology for roughly 3 to 5 percent of the total direct HR development budget, using targets set in figure 8-3.

By using a variety of cost savings approaches, cost and time commitments are kept to a minimum. Some of the most common cost savings approaches are:

❑ Plan for evaluation early in the process.
❑ Build evaluation into the HR process.
❑ Share the responsibilities for evaluation.
❑ Require participants to conduct major steps.
❑ Use short-cut methods for major steps.
❑ Use sampling to select the most appropriate HR programs for ROI analysis.

- ❑ Use estimates in the collection and analysis of data.
- ❑ Develop internal capability to implement the ROI process.
- ❑ Utilize Web-based software to reduce time.
- ❑ Streamline the reporting process.

When implementing ROI, many organizations have migrated from a very low level of investment (around 1 percent or less) to the desired level by a process of gradual budget enhancements. These enhancements sometimes come directly from the cost savings generated from the use of the ROI methodology.

10. *ROI forecasting is implemented routinely.* Senior executives sometimes ask for a forecast of ROI before a human capital project is developed and implemented. Consequently, ROI forecasting is used routinely in best practice organizations to enhance the decision-making process. Recognizing the shortcomings of forecasting, conservative adjustments are made and steps taken to ensure that the best expert inputs are secured to develop the forecast.

11. *The ROI methodology is used as a tool to strengthen/improve the human capital process.* One of the important payoffs of the use of ROI over a period of time is that it transforms the role of HR in the organization. The ROI methodology focuses increased attention on alignment with business needs, improves the efficiency of design, development, and implementation, and enhances the value of human capital in the organization. More important, it builds respect, support, and commitment from a variety of groups, including senior executives and major program sponsors.

It is important to understand that the implementation of the ROI methodology is a gradual, deliberate, and planned approach to change the perceptions of these important groups. IBM's practice with this process is outlined in figure 8-4. As the figure illustrates, certain types of measures are required for all programs, others are reserved for particular types, but selected initiatives, and only a few are actually taken to the ROI level. The key issue is that these represent a variety of data important to the key groups in the organization—the sponsors, clients, and key supporters.[9]

Collectively, these best practices are evolving as hundreds of organizations use ROI each year. This underscores the progress in the use and application of ROI.

Figure 8-4. Gradual implementation in IBM.

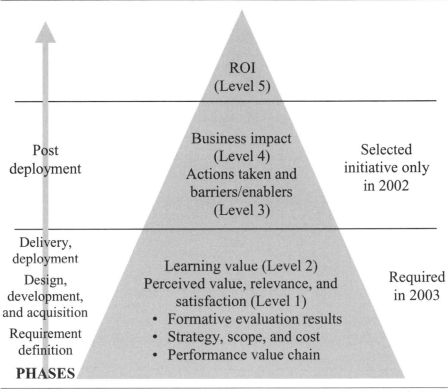

ROI
(Level 5)

Post
deployment

Business impact
(Level 4)
Actions taken and
barriers/enablers
(Level 3)

Selected
initiative only
in 2002

Delivery,
deployment

Design,
development,
and acquisition

Requirement
definition

PHASES

Learning value (Level 2)
Perceived value, relevance, and
satisfaction (Level 1)
• Formative evaluation results
• Strategy, scope, and cost
• Performance value chain

Required
in 2003

Source: IBM. From Stephen Gates, "Linking People Measures to Strategy," *Research Report R-1342-03-RR* (New York: The Conference Board, 2003), p. 11.

BARRIERS TO ROI IMPLEMENTATION

Although progress has been made in the implementation of ROI, significant barriers inhibit the implementation of the concept. Some of these barriers were briefly presented in chapter 5 as disadvantages. Many of these are realistic, while others are based on false perceptions.

Costs and Time

The ROI process adds cost and time to the evaluation process of programs, although the additional amount is usually not excessive. It is possible that this barrier stops many ROI implementations early in the process. A comprehensive ROI process can be implemented within most human capital budgets (because it represents about 3 to 5 percent of the total HR department budget). The additional investment in ROI can perhaps be offset by the additional results achieved from these programs and the elimination of unproductive or unprofitable programs.

Lack of Skills and Orientation for Human Resources Staff

Many human resources staff members do not understand ROI, nor do they have the basic skills necessary to apply the process within their scope of responsibilities. Measurement and evaluation is generally not a prerequisite for their job. The typical HR program focuses more on reaction and satisfaction than on results. HR staff members attempt to measure results by measuring reaction to the program. Consequently, a tremendous barrier to implementation is the change needed for the overall orientation, attitude, and skills of the HR staff.

Faulty Needs Assessment

Many of the current HR programs do not adequately analyze and assess need. Some of these programs have been implemented for the wrong reasons: at management's request or in an effort to chase a popular fad or trend in the industry. If the program is not needed, or is not aligned with the business, the benefits from the program will be minimal. An ROI calculation for an unnecessary program will likely yield a negative value. This is a realistic barrier for many applications.

Fear

Fear prevents HR departments from pursuing ROI, whether it is a fear of failure or fear of the unknown. Analysts, developers, consultants, and program administrators may be apprehensive about the consequence of a negative ROI. Lack of results may expose weaknesses or deficiencies in design or execution. They fear that the results will be used against them as a performance-evaluation tool, not understanding that it can work in their favor as a process-improvement tool. Also, the ROI process stirs up the traditional fear of change. This fear, often based on unrealistic assumptions and a lack of knowledge of the process, becomes a realistic barrier to many ROI implementations.

Planning and Discipline

A successful ROI implementation requires planning and a disciplined approach to keep the process on track. Implementation schedules, evaluation targets, ROI analysis plans, measurement and evaluation policies, and follow-up schedules are required. The HR staff may not have enough discipline and determination to stay on course. This becomes a barrier, particularly when there are no immediate pressures to measure the ROI in human capital. If the current senior management group does not require ROI, the HR staff may not allocate time for planning and coordination. Other pressures and priorities also often eat into the time necessary for ROI implementation. Only carefully planned implementation will be successful.

False Assumptions

Many HR staff members have false assumptions about the ROI process, which keeps them from attempting ROI. Typical assumptions are as follows:

- ❑ The impact of an HR program cannot be accurately calculated.
- ❑ Managers do not want to see the results of human capital projects expressed in monetary values.
- ❑ If the CEO does not ask for the ROI, he or she is not expecting it.
- ❑ "I have a professional, competent HR staff. Therefore, I do not have to justify the effectiveness of our HR programs."
- ❑ The human capital function is a complex, but necessary part of the business. Therefore, it should not be subjected to an accountability process.

These false assumptions form real barriers that impede the progress of ROI implementation.

BENEFITS OF ROI

Although the benefits of adopting the ROI process may appear to be obvious, several distinct and important benefits can be derived from the implementation of ROI in an organization. A few of these were briefly summarized in chapter 5 as advantages.

Measuring Contribution

Routine use of the ROI methodology is the most accurate, credible, and widely used process to show the impact of an HR program or project. The ROI will determine if the benefits of an HR program or project, expressed in monetary values, have outweighed the costs. It will show the contribution to the organization and reveal if it was, indeed, an acceptable investment.

Setting Priorities

Calculating ROI in various areas with different programs and projects will determine which HR programs contribute the most to the organization, allowing priorities to be established. Successful HR programs can be expanded into other areas—if the same need is there—ahead of other HR programs; inefficient programs can be redesigned and redeployed. Ineffective programs can be discontinued.

Focusing on Results

The ROI methodology is a results-based process that focuses on the results of all HR programs, even for those not targeted for an ROI calculation. The process requires analysts, facilitators, consultants, participants, and support groups to concentrate on measurable objectives, that is, what the program is attempting to accomplish. Thus, this methodology has the added benefit of improving the effectiveness of all programs.

Earning the Respect of Senior Executives and Sponsors

Developing ROI information is one of the best ways to earn the respect of the senior management team and the sponsor (key stakeholder). Senior executives have a never-ending desire to see ROI. They appreciate the efforts to connect human capital to business impact and show the actual monetary value. It increases their comfort level with human capital investment and makes their decisions much easier. Sponsors who support, approve, or initiate human capital programs see the use of ROI as a breath of fresh air.

Altering Management Perceptions of Human Capital

The ROI methodology, when applied consistently and comprehensively, can convince the management group that human capital is an investment and not an expense. Armed with the data, they recognize the value of human capital and build confidence about their decisions to invest in it. Key managers will see HR programs as making a viable contribution to their objectives, thus increasing the respect for the function. This is an important step in building a partnership with management and increasing management support.

These key benefits, inherent with almost any type of process improvement, make the use of the ROI methodology an attractive challenge for the human capital function.

SUMMARY

This chapter presents the microlevel analysis to show the contribution of human capital programs. At this level, the analysis focuses on the contribution of a specific program, project, initiative, or solution in the human capital arena. The process described is the ROI methodology, which has been developed and refined over a twenty-year period and has been applied to a variety of human capital areas. In the last decade, thousands of individual studies have been developed, showing the contribution of specific programs. These impact studies provide decision makers with the data needed to determine specific contributions and give insight into which programs, projects, or solutions are worthy of additional investment. Together, with the macrolevel of analysis presented in chapter 7, ROI impact studies provide some overwhelming evidence of the value of human capital in organizations today.

NOTES

1   Jack J. Phillips and Cyndi Gaudet, *HRD Trends Worldwide*, 2nd ed. (Woburn, Mass.: Butterworth-Heinemann, 2005) (forthcoming).

2   Jack J. Phillips, "The Evaluation of a Cooperative Education Program," *Journal of Cooperative Education*, Spring 1976.

3   D. Sibbet and the staff of *HBR*, "75 Years of Management Ideas and Practice 1922–1997: A Supplement to the *Harvard Business Review*," *Harvard Business Review*, September–October 1997.

4   Jack J. Phillips and Cyndi Gaudet, *HRD Trends Worldwide*, 2nd ed. (Woburn, Mass.: Butterworth-Heinemann, 2005) (forthcoming).

5   Jack J. Phillips and Patricia P. Phillips, *Proving the Value of HR: When and How to Calculate the ROI* (Alexandria, Va.: Society of Human Resource Management, 2005).

6   Jack J. Phillips and Lynn Schmidt, *The Leadership Scorecard* (Woburn, Mass.: Butterworth-Heinemann, 2004).

7   Douglas A. Ready and Jay A. Conger, "Why Leadership Development Efforts Fail," *MIT Sloan Management Review*, Spring 2003, pp. 83–88.

8   Darelyn J. Mitch (ed.) and Jack J. Phillips (series ed.), *In Action: Coaching for Extraordinary Results* (Alexandria, Va.: American Society for Training and Development, 2002).

9   Stephen Bates, "Linking People Measures to Strategy," *Research Report R-1342-03-RR* (New York: The Conference Board, 2003).

PART THREE

WHAT CAN WE MEASURE?

The Current State of the Art

CHAPTER 9

Current Human
Capital Measures

When considering human capital investment levels, it is necessary to determine the specific human capital measures to monitor. These measures provide insight into the status and health of the human capital function. They signal when additional investment is needed and they serve as the baseline for measuring the progress and payoff of investing in a specific program or project. The first step to determine the measures needed is to examine those currently in use. The most common set of measures monitored by leading organizations is presented in table 9-1. This list represents measures cited in over a dozen current studies on human capital measurement.

Some of the measures presented in this chapter evolved from the beginnings of "personnel administration" to what is today known as human resources or human capital management. They are measures that were tracked during the field's infancy, such as absenteeism and turnover, and are still tracked today. Although these measures have existed for some time, they are still important for understanding the nature, scope, and progress of human capital. The measures represent a balance of old-economy and new-economy organizations. Several measures are industry specific. For example, safety and health measurements may be an important issue where employees are routinely at risk for accidents, injuries, and illnesses. Service and white-collar businesses, such as financial services and software companies, would not necessarily list these measures as a priority. They include other measures, however, that are critical to developing and emerging industries, such as innovation, leadership, and competencies.

This chapter briefly explores each measure category in terms of how it is developed and a few of the issues surrounding it. This discussion is based on the assumption that anything can be measured, regardless of how subjec-

177

Table 9-1. Common human capital measures.

1. Innovation and Creativity • Innovation • Creativity	7. Productivity • Unit productivity • Gross productivity
2. Employee Attitudes • Employee satisfaction • Organizational commitment • Employee engagement	8. Workforce Profile • Demographics 9. Job Creation and Recruitment • Job growth
3. Workforce Stability • Turnover and termination • Tenure and longevity	• Recruitment sourcing and effectiveness • Recruiting efficiency
4. Employee Capability • Experience • Learning • Knowledge • Competencies • Educational level	10. Compensation and Benefits • Compensation • Employee benefits • Variable compensation • Employee ownership 11. Compliance and Safety
5. Human Capital Investment • HR department investment • Total HC investment • Investment by category	• Complaints and grievances • Charges and litigation • Health and safety 12. Employee Relations
6. Leadership • 360° feedback • Leadership inventories • Leadership perception	• Absenteeism and tardiness • Work/life balance

tive or soft it may be. The challenge is to increase the accuracy of the measurement, ensuring validity and reliability of the measurement process.

INNOVATION

For most organizations, innovation is a critical issue. Because innovation comes from employee creativity, it is a human capital issue. Just how important is innovation? Let's put it in perspective. If it were not for the intellectual curiosity of employees—thinking things through, trying out new ideas, and taking wild guesses in all R&D labs across the country—the United States would have half the economy it does today. In a recent report on R&D, the American Association for the Advancement of Science estimates that as much as 50 percent of U.S. economic growth during the half century since the Fortune 500 came into existence has been due to advances in technology.[1]

After a few years of retrenchment and cost cutting, senior executives across a variety of industries share the conviction that innovation—the ability to define and create new products and services and quickly bring them to market—is an increasingly important source of competitive advantage. Executives are setting aggressive performance goals for their innovation and product-development organizations, targeting 20 to 30 percent improvements in such areas as time-to-market, development costs, product cost, and customer value.[2]

But a vast disconnect lies between hope and reality. A recent survey of fifty companies conducted by Booz Allen Hamilton shows that companies are only marginally satisfied that their R&D departments are delivering their full potential. Worse, executives say that only half of the improvement efforts they launch end up meeting expectations.

Several waves of improvements in innovation and product development have already substantially enhanced companies' ability to deliver differentiated, higher-quality products to market faster and more efficiently. However, the degree of success achieved has varied greatly among companies and even among units within individual companies. The differences in success stem from the difficulty of managing change in the complex processes and organizations associated with innovation and product development.

Some companies have managed to assemble an integrated "innovation chain" that is truly global and allows them to outflank competitors that innovate using knowledge in a single cluster. They have been able to implement a *process* for innovating that transcends local clusters and national boundaries, becoming "meta-national innovators." This strategy of using localized pockets of technology, market intelligence, and capabilities has provided a powerful new source of competitive advantage: more, higher-value innovation at lower cost.[3]

Innovation is both easy and difficult to measure. It is easy to measure outcomes in areas such as new products, new processes, improved products and processes, copyrights, patents, inventions, and employee suggestions. Many companies track these items. These can be documented to reflect the innovative profile of an organization. Unfortunately, it is difficult to compare these data with previous data or benchmarking with other organizations because these measures are typically unique to the organization.

Perhaps the most obvious measure is tracking the patents that are not only used internally but are licensed for others to use through a patent and license exchange. For example, IBM has been granted more patents than any other company in the world—over 25,000 U.S. patents. IBM licensing of patents and technology generates several billion dollars in profits each year. Microsoft filed about 3,000 patents in 2004—an increase of nearly 50 percent over filings in their last fiscal year. While IBM and Microsoft are at the top of the list, most organizations in the new economy monitor trademarks, patents, and copyrights as important measures of the innovative talent of employees.

It is helpful to remember that the development of patents comes from the inventive spirit of employees. The good news is that employees do not have to be scientists or engineers to be inventive. Even though invention is sometimes thought of only in the context of technology, computing, materials, energy, and so on, it is interdisciplinary and therefore can be extracted from any technological realm and applied to problems in any area.[4]

Through the years, inventors have been viewed as "nerds," with much of their inventiveness being explained by their particular personality makeup. This is because history is laced with well-known inventors possessing unusual personalities. The fact is that inventors are usually ordinary people possessing extraordinary imaginations. Many current organizations, regardless of their focus, are placing resources to encourage employees' creativity, which can lead to significant technological advantages over the competition. To spark this ingenuity, organizations consider innovation a major human capital issue, monitor it appropriately, and take actions to enhance it.

CREATIVITY

Creativity, often considered the precursor to innovation, refers to the creative experience, actions, and input of organizations. It may be more difficult to measure the creative spirit of employees. An employee suggestion system, a long-time measure of the creative processes of the organization, flourishes today in many firms and is easily measured. Employees are rewarded for their suggestions if they are approved and implemented. Tracking the suggestion rates and comparing them with other organizations is an important bench-marking item for creative capability. Other measures, such as the number of new ideas, comments, or complaints can be monitored and measured in some way. Formal feedback systems often contain creative suggestions that can lead to improved processes.

Some organizations actually measure the creative capability of employees using inventories and instruments often distributed in meetings and training sessions. In other organizations, statements about employee creativity are included in the annual employee feedback survey. Using scaled ratings, employees either agree or disagree with the statements. Comparing actual scores of groups of employees over a period of time reflects the degree to which employees perceive that creativity in the workplace is improving. Having consistent and comparable measures is still a challenge. Still other organizations monitor the number, duration, and participation rate for creativity training programs. The last decade has witnessed a proliferation of creativity tools, programs, and activity.

EMPLOYEE ATTITUDES

Employee Satisfaction

An important item monitored by most organizations is employee job satisfaction. Using feedback surveys, executives monitor the degree to which employees are satisfied with their employer, policies, the work environment, supervision and leadership, the actual work itself, as well as other factors. Sometimes a composite rating is developed to reflect an overall satisfaction value or index for the organization, division, department, or region.

While job satisfaction has always been an important issue in employee relations, in recent years it has taken on a new dimension because of the linkage of job satisfaction to other measures. A classical relationship with job satisfaction is in the attraction and retention of employees. Firms with excellent job satisfaction ratings often attract potential employees. It becomes a subtle, but important, recruiting tool. "Employers of Choice" and "Best Places to Work," for example, often have high job satisfaction ratings. This relationship between job satisfaction and employee retention has attracted increased emphasis in recent years because turnover and retention are critical issues. Figure 9-1 illustrates the classical relationship between job satisfaction and employee turnover. These relationships are now easily developed using human capital management systems with modules to calculate the correlation between the turnover rates and the job satisfaction scores for the various job groups, divisions, and departments.

Job satisfaction has taken on new dimensions in connection with customer service. Dozens of applied research projects are beginning to show a high correlation between job satisfaction scores and customer satisfaction scores. Intuitively, this seems obvious. A more satisfied employee is likely to provide more productive, friendly, and appropriate customer service. Likewise, a disgruntled employee will provide poor service. As illustrated in chapter 7, employee attitudes (job satisfaction) relate to customer impression (customer satisfaction), which relates to revenue growth (profits). Thus, if employee attitudes improve, revenue will increase. These links, often referred to as a service-profit-chain, create a promising way to identify important relationships between attitudes and profits in an organization.

Organizational Commitment

In recent years, organizational commitment (OC) measures have complemented or replaced job satisfaction measures. Organizational commitment

Figure 9-1. Linkage of job satisfaction and employee turnover.

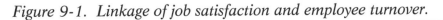

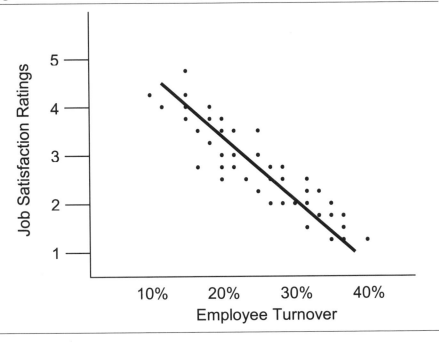

measures go beyond employee satisfaction to include the extent to which the employees identify with organizational goals, mission, philosophy, value, policies, and practices. The concept of involvement and becoming committed to the organization is a key issue. Organizational commitment more closely correlates with productivity and other performance improvement measures, while job satisfaction usually does not. Organizational commitment is often measured in the same way as job satisfaction, using attitude surveys and a five- or seven-point scale taken directly from employees. As organizational commitment scores improve (taken on a standard index), a corresponding improvement in productivity should exist.

Employee Engagement

A different twist to the organizational commitment measure is the measure that reflects employee engagement. This involves tackling issues that indicate the extent to which employees are actively engaged in the organization in a variety of ways. Engagement is included in the "Great Place to Work" (GPTW) research. The GPTW survey includes several employee engagement measures. Consider the case of Royal Bank of Scotland Group (RBS). With more than 115,000 employees, RBS considers measuring the effectiveness of its investment in people and its impact on business performance to be a strategic imperative and consequently has been building, validating, and introducing a human capital model that demonstrably links people strategies to performance.[5]

RBS moved beyond monitoring employee satisfaction and commitment to measuring whether employees actively improve business results, using an employee engagement model to assess employees' likelihood of contributing to the bank's profits. As figure 9-2 shows, this model links the separate HR information in a consistent way, which is then linked to key business indicators. The outputs enable the business to understand how to influence the bank's results through its people.

In order to test and validate the model, the HR research and measurement team of RBS reviewed all the survey instruments actually used in their activities (joiner, leaver, "pulse," employee opinion), along with the HR data available in its HRMS database. The HR team decided to put the employee engagement model into practice in the processing and customer contact centers. In these functions, productivity measures are very important, as these affect customer service. Using the amount of work processed as a throughput measure, they found that productivity increased in tandem with engagement levels. The team was also able to establish a link between increasing engagement and decreasing staff turnover.

Hundreds of organizations now use engagement data—not only reflecting the extent to which employees are engaged and connected with productivity and turnover—but also as selection criteria in the competition for the "Best Companies to Work For" in *Fortune* magazine (see chapter 6).

WORKFORCE STABILITY

Turnover and Termination

One of the greatest threats to intellectual capital drain is the unwanted departure of employees with high levels of expertise and knowledge. The survival of some firms depends on low turnover rates for critical job groups. Few measures have attracted so much attention as employee turnover. Fueled in part by low unemployment rates in North America and industrialized countries, retention has become a strategic issue. The cost of turnover, detailed in chapter 2, is staggering. The good news is that many firms have made important strides in maintaining low turnover even in high turnover industries such as retail, hotel, and restaurant groups.

Figure 9-2. Human capital model at Royal Bank of Scotland Group.

Outputs
- Informed business decisions
- Predictive analysis
- Integrated HR data

Engagement

- Work/life balance and physical environment
- Work itself
- Leadership
- Recognition
- Relationships
- Total reward
- Product brands and reputation
- Performance and development

Staff Segmentation
Tenure
Seniority
Geography/location
Gender
Age
RBS*elect* preference

Business/HR Data
Turnover
Productivity
Absence
Reward profile

Identify main drivers to business issues (engagement, turnover, leadership, etc.)
Allows business to prioritize activities
Identifies opportunities and threats to engagement levels
Action plans

HR management information

Joiner survey

Leader survey

Turndown survey

"Pulse" survey

Employee opinion survey

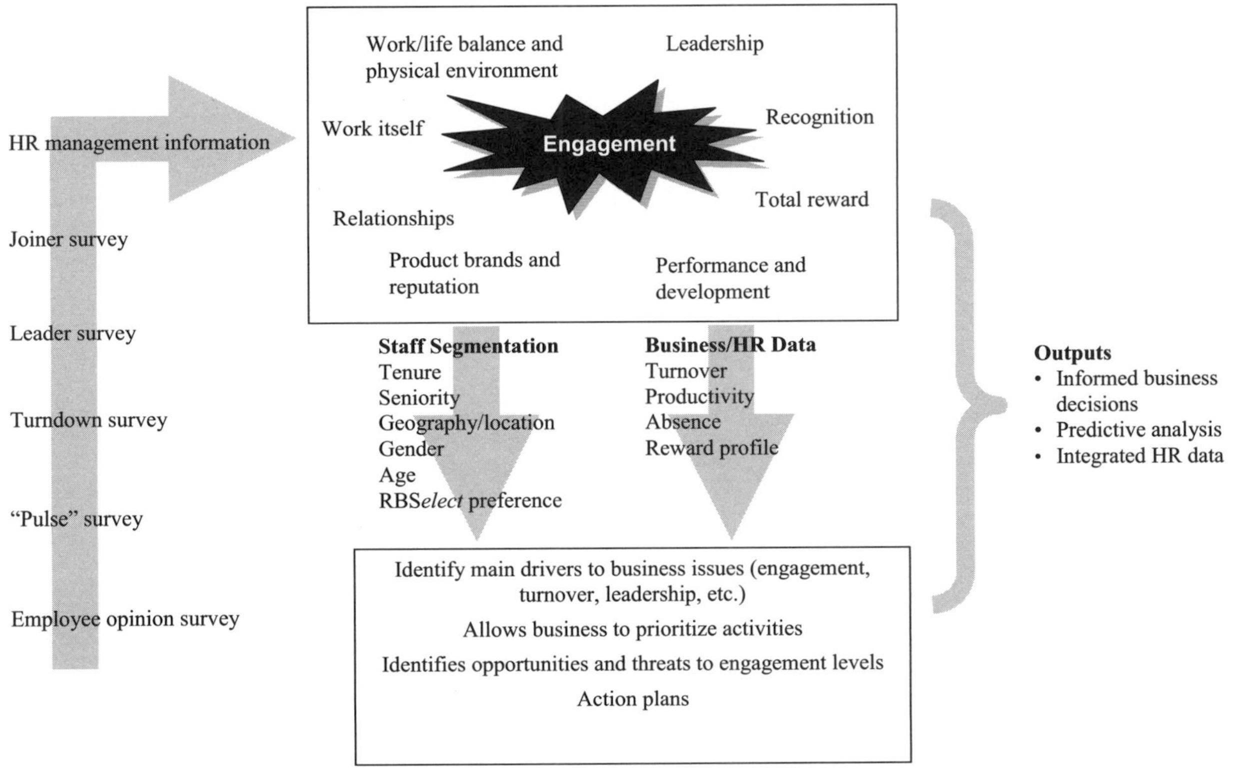

Source: Royal Bank of Scotland Group and Stephen Gates, "Linking People Measures to Strategy," *Research Report R-1342-03-RR* (New York: The Conference Board, 2003), p. 20.

Turnover is defined as the number of employees leaving in a month divided by the average number of employees in the month. This is a standard turnover rate that includes all individuals leaving. A more useful measure would be involuntary turnover, which refers to those employees who initiate their departure from the organization. It is defined as the number of employees who voluntarily leave during the month, divided by the average number of employees during the month (or number at midpoint). At first glance, this appears to be the most appropriate definition; however, a question often arises as to whether the departure was truly voluntary. Could it be that the employee is pressured into resigning? Did not adequate processes exist to salvage this individual? A more appropriate measure would be to include only turnover considered to be avoidable, usually referring to the employees who voluntarily leave or those whose departure could have been prevented. For example, if an employee is terminated for poor performance in the first six months of employment, something went wrong that could have prevented the turnover. This calculation requires the analysis of turnovers that could have been avoided in some way. Although administratively more difficult, it may be more powerful in terms of preventing unnecessary termination of employees.

A critical time in an employee's tenure with an organization is usually within the first few days, weeks, or months of employment. It is usually during this period that mismatches are identified and frustrations intensify. An employee may decide to leave if other opportunities are available. This early turnover is often the result of improper selection systems, ineffective orientation, and inadequate socialization processes to adapt employees to the organization. To understand this issue completely, an early turnover measure should be developed. This is sometimes referred to as the "churn" rate. This measure is defined as the number of employees leaving in the first sixty days of employment divided by the number of new employees hired in the same period. This period of time could vary from a shorter time frame (thirty days) to a longer one (ninety days) for professional and technical employees. Monitoring and understanding this specific rate provides an excellent opportunity to keep costs down and lower the impact of disruptions.

Specific turnover reduction and retention strategies now command much of the attention and focus of HR managers and senior staff members. Not only is turnover compared to historical rates but it is often compared to best-practice firms. The solutions are varied and opportunities are tremendous. Impact studies showing the effect of turnover reduction sometimes generate ROI values in the 1,000 percent range.[6] This is a significant area of continued focus and development and is on every human capital measurement list.

Tenure and Longevity

Along with employee turnover comes the focus on employee tenure and longevity. Tenure is the length of employee service in the current organization usually monitored for certain job groups. To a certain extent, tenure mirrors the turnover data discussed above. The average length of service is often critical as many organizations seek stability and loyalty in a workforce. It is important where expertise is critical to the success of the organization. High tenure usually translates into low turnover, which may have a tremendous impact on operating cost. Low tenure indicates instability, high turnover, and can be very disruptive for the business.

In recent years, the concept of employee loyalty has eroded significantly. Gone are the days in which employees worked for long periods of time with one employer. Instead, employees often leave after a matter of months or years, sometimes for a better opportunity, thanks in part to job growth, low unemployment rates, and higher job mobility. The challenge for executives is to keep employee loyalty at the target level, creating the desire for employees to contribute their expertise over a longer period of time.

EMPLOYEE CAPABILITY

Experience

Experience is an important measure in any organization, yet it is particularly important in organizations where the services are complex, technology is critical, and the job requires a tremendous amount of expertise. Experience can be monitored using experience levels within functions, departments, or jobs. For example, it may be helpful to track the average length of experience in the sales force, the engineering team, or the IT department. Also, it may be helpful to measure experience by job category, such as the average years of service for sales representatives, software designers, scientists, or financial analysts. Some organizations measure relevant experience in previous organizations. Recognizing the high mobility in certain professions and fields, experience in other organizations may be just as valuable as experience within the current organization, adding to the depth of understanding of capability.

An experienced workforce has a history with the expertise to handle a variety of situations. Experienced employees can develop new approaches, new processes, and even new products, based on their experience. On the downside, experienced individuals frequently cost the organization more in terms of salaries, bonuses, and benefits. Also, experienced employees are often in demand and may leave the organization when offered new opportunities with higher pay.

Inexperience rears its ugly head with the employee's inability to perform certain tasks and respond to certain issues. This sometimes leads to frustration on the part of management, as well as internal or external customers, or the employees themselves. On the upside, inexperienced individuals are often more open to new ideas and may be more flexible. Because employees usually join an organization at the entry level, lower salaries are often involved when compared to the more experienced employees. Also, if the new hires are not successful in the organization, they can be replaced with less cost.

Some organizations focus on building an environment to capitalize on enhancing work experience. Expertise is developed quickly so that an employee will have five years' experience instead of one year of experience repeated five times. By using rotational assignments, work teams, and a variety of processes, knowledge and skills transfer from the experienced to the inexperienced and are shared throughout the organization. Experienced employees are placed in roles of training, coaching, and mentoring others across the organization—with the focus on retaining the expertise.

Finally, a rich experience base is often the foundation for the culture and history of the organization. Stories abound throughout organizations about highly experienced people with extraordinary capabilities. Individuals who work for the same organization for forty-five years create cultures and legacies. Many executives are proud of their long-term, highly experienced employees and often profile them in publications and on Web sites, propagating their stories of "how things used to be."

Knowledge

As this book has emphasized, knowledge is a critical issue in the human capital arena. Attempting to measure knowledge overlaps with the measurement of other issues such as innovation, experience, learning, and competencies. However, it may be helpful to list some of the measures that are being monitored to reflect the value and intensity of knowledge in an organization.

The first measure is the actual level of intensity of knowledge. This can be calculated as a percent of revenues spent on research and development or sales from patents pending and awarded and various trademarks. Another approach is to measure the percentage of knowledge workers compared to other employees in the organization. Still another approach is to understand the amount of money spent on knowledge versus physical assets. The comparison of all expenses in these two categories reveals the intensity of knowledge spending at the present time, compared to historical and even future projections.

Second, an important measure gaining some interest is the value added per dollar of employee costs. This was originally developed by Professor Ante Pulic of the University of Graz in Austria. This measure reflects the concentration of knowledge workers in an organization. The calculation is based on totaling all of the revenues and subtracting nonemployee inputs, which is all purchased expenses, excluding expenses for payroll and benefits. This produces a measure of value added. This measure is then divided by the payroll and benefits costs, which Professor Pulic uses as a proxy for human capital. Thus, the ratio of value added divided by human capital, reflects how much of the added value has been created by one monetary unit invested in employees. This is what Pulic refers to as the "value added human capital coefficient."[7]

Third, the market-to-book ratio divides a company's market value by the book value of its assets (physical, financial, and goodwill). This attempts to explain why the large proportion of the market value is allocated to the intangibles, part of which represents the intellectual capital or knowledge in the organization.

Fourth, a measure that is taking on some interest is called Tobin's q—a statistic invented by Nobel Prize winning economist James Tobin. It is the ratio of a company's market value to the replacement value of its assets. It is developed by adding depreciation back into book value; as q moves above 1, the market seems to place increasing value on a company's intangibles.

These are only four of the measures that reflect the extent of knowledge in the organization. Others are being developed, as was stressed in chapter 6. In the future, additional measures from both the financial community and human capital professionals will be developed and, perhaps, some will become standard.

Learning

Learning is another important ingredient to build the experience base and drive success. Many executives strive to create learning organizations where many opportunities are available for employees to learn new skills, tasks, and processes necessary to become competitive leaders.[8] Some organizations attempt to measure learning by the investment in formal learning programs and processes, measured by the number of hours involved in learning or the number of programs offered. While the numbers are important as a reflection of the commitment to learning, they do not represent results. Other measures are needed.

Measures of learning are easily developed at the microlevel (for an individual learning program) but are often difficult and vague at the macrolevel (for all learning programs). A learning measurement at the microlevel is a measure of new skills and knowledge in formal learning activities. For example, as employees attend learning programs, a learning measure may be an objective measurement such as testing, simulation, or performance demonstration. Sometimes informal processes such as self-assessment, team assessment, and facilitator assessment are used. Some organizations measure the amount of learning across programs with informal techniques, using consistent rating scales and integrating data to develop a learning assessment for the entire organization (at the macrolevel).

In other situations, it is important for employees to have a certain body of knowledge in critical jobs, and the challenge is to develop meaningful ways to measure the knowledge. An example will emphasize the possibilities. In a large pharmaceutical firm, it is important for sales representatives to have immediate recall of a vast amount of information on each prescription drug they sell. The sales representative has little time to discuss products with physicians—about three to five minutes. In this time frame, the representative must have total recall on the chemical content of the drug, research studies validating the drug, typical symptoms for the use of the drug, important side effects, and the marketing strategies for the drug. To ensure that all sales representatives have instant recall of all of this information, the company has implemented a knowledge-assessment process. Each sales representative takes an exam on each product line every six months using a test with a predetermined cut-off score. If the representative scores poorly, he or she will be allowed to try again after preparing for the next exam. After the second try, the individual is reassigned to a sales support position if the score is unsatisfactory.

The important issue in this example is that knowledge is critical to success on the job and learning is obtained from a variety of sources—not just formal learning programs but through research bulletins, product bulletins, learning-on-demand modules, videos, and a variety of other channels. Although this may be an unusual case, it underscores the importance of building knowledge in an organization where knowledge capital is king.

Measures of learning will continue to be a challenge at the macrolevel as executives continue to explore ways in which a learning organization can be measured in terms of outcomes not inputs. Additional detail on measuring learning as part of a scorecard is included in chapter 10.

Competencies

Organizations are interested in developing key competencies in particular areas such as the core mission, key product lines, and proprietary processes. Core competencies are often identified and implemented in critical job groups. Competencies are measured with self-assessments from the individual employee as well as supervisor assessments. In some cases, other inputs may be necessary to measure competencies. This moves the process beyond simply learning new skills, processes, or knowledge to using the combination of skill, knowledge, and behavior on the job to develop an acceptable level of competence to meet competitive challenges.

In recent years, a quantitative process has been used to place a value on competencies. This concept—usually labeled analysis—shows the value of improving competencies of employees. Ratings are taken to measure the competencies on the job prior to specific HR solutions aimed at increasing those competencies. Postprogram ratings are also taken. Improvements in competencies are analyzed and a monetary value is placed on the improvement, based on the salaries of the individuals. For example, if an individual improved his or her competencies by 10 percent and there has been no subsequent compensation adjustment to reflect the improvement, then that employee, theoretically, is worth 10 percent more to the organization. If that employee's salary is $50,000, a value of $5,000 has been added. When these values are compared to the cost of the program, the actual return on investment can be developed. Although this process is helpful to understand the impact of competencies and their potential value, it has some shortcomings in terms of ignoring what employees actually accomplish while using their competencies. Even with its shortcomings, this process is a tool for placing value on competencies and is used in many organizations.[9]

Educational Level

In the knowledge economy, education is critical and many organizations track educational levels as an important human capital measure. This measure is usually the number of years of formal college and university education, where an average of four equates to a bachelor's level of attainment. In technology and research-based organizations, education is vital for certain job groups. Other organizations may track precollege educational levels and the percent of employees with a high school diploma or equivalent accomplishment.

Tracking educational levels is important relative to specific goals and desired levels. High levels are not always desired. For example, higher educational levels are necessary in a technology firm, such as Microsoft, but are not required in a retail store chain, such as Wal-Mart. Each company should establish a target and measure the educational level against that target. If the educational level is too high, there may be increased turnover because of the perceived overqualification. The employee may leave when another opportunity opens up.

Unfortunately, the quality of the credentials to determine a particular level of education has deteriorated. Even the standards for a high school diploma, or the equivalent certificate, are not necessarily the same standards as a few years ago. At the college level, some credentials are not quite as genuine or as rigorous as others, or as they were in the past. The educational landscape is covered with opportunities to obtain degrees and diplomas from unaccredited, unqualified, and inferior sources. Some are fraudulent. Still another quality issue is the explosive use of distance education to obtain degrees. Some educators argue that quality has deteriorated for the sake of convenience.

HUMAN CAPITAL INVESTMENT LEVELS

Human Resources Department Investment

The actual monetary investment in the human resources department is another important measure. This investment value reflects the extent to which the organization is willing to invest in the staff who spend most of their time analyzing, coordinating, developing, and implementing programs to improve human capital. In theory, the larger the HR department expense, the more productive the organization. This relationship was developed in one major study where the HR investment (divided by operating expense) had a significant correlation with gross productivity (revenue per employee) and profitability (operating income per employee). This study was presented in chapter 7 as the Phillips/Saratoga Studies.

Total Human Capital Investment

The total human capital investment is the human resources department expenditures plus all the employee compensation and benefits. Essentially, this defines the cost of acquiring, developing, motivating, compensating, and maintaining employees in the organization. Although the investment in an individual employee includes the additional costs of equipment, travel expenses, and office space, the most appropriate measure is just the measure involved in human capital. This is an important measure and one that reflects commitment to this important issue.

To provide more insight into the human capital investment by various categories, it may be helpful to calculate the human capital investment by HR function: recruiting and selection, orientation learning and development, compensation and benefits, fair employment and compliance, employee and labor relations, and support services. When compared to other organizations, these measures may provide insight into the relative allocation as well as provide information about additional allocations that may be needed. Chapter 3 provided a detailed listing of the measurement categories.

LEADERSHIP

Leadership is perhaps the most difficult measure to tackle. Leadership can (and usually does) make the difference in the success or failure of an organization. Without the appropriate leadership throughout the organization, resources can be misapplied or wasted and opportunities missed. Obviously, the ultimate measure of leadership is the overall success of the organization. Whenever overall measures of success have been achieved or surpassed, they are always attributed to great leadership—perhaps rightfully so. Attempting to use that kind of success as the only measure of leadership is a cop-out in terms of human capital accountability. Other measures must be in place to develop systemwide monitoring of the quality of leaders and leadership in the organization.

360° Feedback

Measuring leadership can be achieved in many different ways. Perhaps the most common way is the 360° feedback. Here, a prescribed set of leadership behaviors desired in the organization is assessed by various sources to provide a composite of the overall leadership capability. The sources often come from the immediate manager of the leader, a colleague in the same area, the employees under the direct influence of the leader, internal or external customers, and a self-assessment. Combined, these assessments form a circle of influence (360°).

The measure is basically an observation of behavior captured in a survey, often reported electronically. This 360° feedback has been growing rapidly in the United States, Europe, and Asia as an important way to capture overall leadership behavior change. Since behavior change usually has consequences measured as business impact, leadership improvement should connect to the business in some way. Leadership development programs aimed at improving leadership behavior and driving business improvement often have high payoff with ROI values in the range of 500 percent to 1,000 percent.[10] This is primarily because of the multiplicative effect as leaders are developed and a change of behavior influences important measures in the leader's team. The ROI Methodology, which was used to develop these studies, was described in chapter 8.

Leadership Inventories

Another way to measure leadership is to require the management team to participate in a variety of leadership inventories, assessing predetermined leadership competency statements. The inventories reflect the extent to which a particular leadership style or approach is in place. These inventories, while popular in the 1970s and 1980s, are often being replaced by the 360° feedback process described earlier.

Leadership Perception

Another way to capture the quality of leadership is from the perception of employees. In some organizations employees rate the quality of leadership using several dimensions. Top executives are the typical focal point for this evaluation, along with the employees' immediate manager. The measure is usually taken along with an annual feedback survey in the form of direct statements about the leader; the respondent agrees or disagrees using a five-point scale. This is an attempt to measure the extent to which the followers in a particular situation perceive the quality, success, and appropriateness of leadership behavior as it is being practiced.

PRODUCTIVITY

Unit Productivity

Another important measure of human capital is productivity. Productivity is output measured per employee, per hour, or on some other basis. For manufacturing organizations, a productivity measure is average production per employee. Individual productivity, showing the number of output items per employee, for example, is important to monitor within the organization. It is helpful to compare the values with previous time frames as well as across similar divisions or units. It may be difficult to benchmark with other organizations because of the uniqueness of the measure. In service organizations, and those in different businesses, other measures are needed in place of the unit productivity.

Gross Productivity

One of the most common measures for gross productivity is revenue per employee. Other options would be income per employee and earnings per employee. Benchmarking services such as the Saratoga Institute have developed and used these measures for years.[11] These types of measures are more meaningful for companies in the same business and in the same industry.

WORKFORCE PROFILE

The profile of the workforce is necessary for understanding who is employed and who should be employed, as well as the nature and scope of their backgrounds. These are traditional measures that often tell much about an organization and are sometimes the foundation for the contributions to the workforce. Demographic measures present the organization's profile in categories needed such as fair employment practices, diversity, and culture. A variety of demographics are critical (or at least very important) to an organization:

❑ Tenure—the length of service of departing employees (or tenure of remaining employees)
❑ Age breakdown of employees (or age of remaining employees)
❑ Gender of departing employees (or gender of remaining employees)
❑ Race and ethnic background of departing employees (or diversity mix of remaining employees)
❑ Educational levels of departing employees (or education of remaining employees)
❑ Family status (married, single, single head of household, with children) of departing employees (or family status of remaining employees)

These breakdowns are necessary to determine how the workforce is changing and where the turnover rates are the highest. The measures in parentheses are the retention countermeasures reflecting the status of remaining employees. Together, they provide useful tools for analyzing particular issues, understanding the causes, and ultimately developing solutions.

   Tenure and education level are covered as separate issues in this chapter because of their importance in human capital. Gender is important in the diversity mix to ensure that the male/female ratio reflects not only the local labor market, but the desired mix to achieve diversity goals and integrate with markets and customers. Continued emphasis on upward mobility of women becomes a significant tracking measure for organizations attempting to increase the female percentages.

   The race and ethnic mix of employees is another critical issue to organizations. The concept of diversity has taken on new meaning where the emphasis is not so much on meeting certain rules and regulations, but on tapping into the value of having a diverse workforce. Many studies show that a diverse ethnic mix can actually create a more productive, flexible, and responsive organization.[12]

   Family status is particularly important for understanding the causes of turnover. For example, high levels of turnover for single mothers may indicate child care issues that need to be addressed. While much of family status data is actually collected for benefit plans, it is important to understand the changing nature of the demographic profile.

   One of the most telling variables in the demographic category is the age of the workforce. This measure can be meaningful when compared to others in the same industry or in the dominant profession represented by the particular organization. For many mature organizations, the average age continues to rise. However, newer organizations, particularly those in the high-tech industry, have extremely young workforces. Measures on the extreme side of either age range can signal problems. A workforce that is getting older (for example an average age of fifty-five) may be more expensive in terms of salaries (higher salaries because of their tenure), represent a higher healthcare cost, be less flexible and versatile in skills, and may not be capable of taking on new challenges and changes in the workforce. A fast-changing growth organization, adapting to new and improved technologies, will often desire a young workforce because of employees' recent educational accomplishments, recent work experiences, and eagerness to learn new technologies and skills. A younger workforce is typically more attuned to the skill-acquisition mode than an older one.

   Organizations in mature industries may desire an older workforce, where experience with personal interactions is emphasized. Also, in some service industries, an older workforce, particularly people in their second or third job after retirement, may be available at a lower pay rate. For example, many of the retail store organizations and fast food industries recognize that an older workforce has some unique advantages. For example, the turnover rate in the older workforce is usually lower; an older workforce tends to have less unplanned and unexpected absenteeism.

When tracking age in a workforce, it is helpful to track by particular job categories. For example, an older workforce may be suitable in certain support staff positions; a young workforce may be preferable for jobs requiring creativity and innovation. Thus, tracking workforce age by job category allows the organization to strategically plan human capital acquisition.

JOB CREATION AND RECRUITMENT

Productivity Versus Job Growth

One of the more interesting human capital measures is *job creation*; it is one of the criteria *Fortune* magazine uses to select organizations for the "Best Companies to Work For" list. From an employee perspective, job creation offers future opportunities and challenges. It may help employers prevent unwanted turnover. From a public policy perspective, job creation and growth are essential. Job growth can help community development, boosting a company's image. However, job growth for the sake of job growth can breed inefficiencies and bureaucracies.

Wall Street often rewards employers when they are more productive and can trim jobs—just the announcement that jobs are slashed often sends stock prices up. Wall Street is interested in earnings and profits, and minimizing the number of employees can often increase profits, at least in the short term. For example, consider the announcement of layoffs at Nortel Networks, a manufacturer of telecommunications equipment. When Nortel announced 3,500 job cuts—about 10 percent of its workforce—to reduce costs and boost productivity, investors welcomed the news with a 4 percent increase in share price on the same day.[13]

Importance of Job Creation and Job Growth

There is a difference between job creation and job growth—both simple human capital measures. Job creation is the development of new jobs in the organization; job growth is the net gain in jobs, recognizing that some jobs are eliminated, automated, or outsourced. From the perspective of employment stability, employment opportunities, and attracting employees to an organization, job growth is very important. Creating new jobs, particularly those with higher skills and higher pay is an excellent employee relations and human capital strategy. However, as indicated above, job growth must also focus on productivity. Profitable job growth is the key.

Job growth is also important from the aspect of being a good corporate citizen and a champion in the communities. This is one of the selling points for Wal-Mart as they describe their job growth and the effect of the payroll in the community. Job growth increases tax base; all politicians love employers who add to the number of jobs, particularly those in the higher skill category. It is the prospect of new jobs that often attracts the attention of community and economic development specialists, offering employers incentives for locating to or expanding in a particular area. These new jobs add value to the community, but only if they pay well and produce great corporate citizens.

Probably the most notable reward for job growth comes from the incentives of building new plants. For example, a phenomenon has emerged in the United States where local community governments provide exorbitant incentives for automobile manufacturing companies to locate a plant in their community. The most notable example is the situation in Alabama. The state now claims four major plants (Mercedes, Toyota, Honda, and Hyundai) employing 33,800 directly and another 96,200 indirectly. For the most part, the industry was lured to Alabama by a variety of incentives.[14]

Job growth can actually reduce employee turnover. Growth often reduces uncertainty, offers new challenges, and provides advancement opportunities for the existing workforce. These are often the issues that help attract and retain employees. Thus, operational stability, which has an impact on operational profits, can be enhanced with job growth.

In recent years, much emphasis has been placed on career management. These programs are designed to help individuals grow and develop in the organization as new jobs are added, enhancing both job satisfaction and engagement—two important measures in the human capital area.

Outsourcing is the reverse of job creation. It is a subject that has become an important issue in recent years—both politically and economically—and was explored in chapter 1. Outsourcing has played an essential role in most of today's successful businesses. At the organizational level, outsourcing represents a basic structure of businesses—away from the model designed for the industrial age—to one more appropriate for today's information age. Dozens of studies show that outsourcing can reduce costs, improve productivity, allow more focus on core parts of the organization, improve the quality of processes, products, and services, and free-up capital for investment in other parts of the business.[15]

In the United States, a trend has evolved where jobs are outsourced to lower-paying subcontractors. Theoretically, this reduces the expense an organization incurs to get a particular job done. This has created a problem for some organizations in which the employees of subcontractors demand the same wages and benefits as the previous job holders. Some subcontractor employee groups have organized and attempted to negotiate contracts to obtain the same compensation levels. If the same level is provided, the primary rationale for outsourcing is negated.

Another politically sensitive issue is outsourcing jobs to other countries, often referred to as off-shoring. While off-shoring takes place in a variety of countries, the focus is currently on India. Highly skilled, technical jobs, particularly in the software industry, are being outsourced to other countries—particularly India—because a job can be completed there for one third of the rates in the United States. Some firms are targets of criticism because of their outsourcing practices and are often ridiculed in the press, criticized on Web sites, and profiled on the nightly news. Some economists believe that off-shoring is only the market system adjusting to a global economy. Others see it as a drain on national productivity. Regardless of the position, this is an important issue that must be considered in its entirety.

In summary, job creation and job growth are important human capital measures, but only if job growth comes with the proper efficiency, profitability, and value for the community.

Recruitment Sourcing and Effectiveness

Recruitment sourcing is an important measure directly related to the quality and quantity of candidates and, ultimately, to the success of employees and their stability and longevity. Monitoring recruitment sources enables HR to track candidates to the original person, place, ad, or Web site. Sometimes the recruiting channel, such as job fairs, ads, Web sites, or recruiters is important. Some recruiting sources are more effective than others and tracking the sources and connecting them to subsequent outcomes is important. The recruiting source or channel can be connected to the hire ratio—the percentage of candidates actually employed through the channel. For example, some recruiting sources attract people who are always seeking new jobs. While this may be a way to get bodies in the door, it may not be a good source for a long-term employee. For example, Cisco Systems prefers not to hire employees who are actively looking for a job and have a desire to be employed there.

When tracking a source, reflection on the effectiveness of the sources is important. Using the hire ratio—the percentage of the candidates flowing through a source divided by those being hired—the organization can measure how well the source provides appropriate, qualified candidates. Perhaps a more important measure is to compare the turnover in the first year (or months) of employment by recruiting source. This is usually called the churn rate. In some industries, where turnover is high, this period may be the first ninety days of employment. The turnover/recruiting source relationship reflects the stability of the recruiting source. A source that generates a high termination rate may not be the appropriate source to use in the future. Conversely, a source that generates long-term stable employees becomes a preferred channel. The quality of the new candidates from a specific recruiting source is another consideration. Quality is usually a subjective measure taken directly from the candidate's immediate manager. Surveys administered thirty to sixty days after employment will usually pinpoint quality issues.

All of the efforts on recruiting sources and the effectiveness of recruiting must be developed within the context of the organization's affirmative action plans and appropriate compliance initiatives and regulations.

Recruitment Efficiency

Another recruitment measure is to analyze the efficiency of the process, usually expressed as the time it takes to fill the job. Beginning from the point where the request for a new employee is submitted and ending when the candidate is actually on the job, the average time to recruit—or average time to fill jobs—is an important issue. There may be some intermediate time measures such as time to offer and time to complete the selection processes. In organizations where job growth is necessary or there is high turnover, time to recruit is an important consideration. The faster the response, the better—as long as quality is there. Thus, recruitment efficiency would have to be mitigated by the quality and stability of the individual selected through the process.

COMPENSATION AND BENEFITS

Compensation and benefits expenditures probably attract more attention than any other set of measures. Compensation costs are huge and always rising. Increases in base salary often outstrip the producer price index, while employee benefits costs continue to grow with exploding healthcare costs. All of this keeps the focus on this important area and suggests several major measurement categories.

Compensation

Compensation is a critical measure and should be reported in several ways:

❑ Total compensation for all employees. This includes direct and variable wages and salaries. Deferred compensation may be included, unless it is considered an employee benefit.

❑ Compensation cost per employee. This measures the average salary cost per employee and is usually developed by job group.

❑ Total compensation as a percent of operating expenses. This is important when comparing compensation in one organization in an industry to another. Also, it is helpful to see how the compensation expenses change relative to the overall operating costs.

❑ Total compensation as a percent of revenue. This number shows how much of revenue is going to employee wages and salaries.

❑ Total compensation as a percent of the human capital investment. In the context of understanding human capital, this may be the most important measure overall—how much of the human capital is going into actual pay. As reported in an earlier chapter, the total human capital investment is the total compensation plus total benefits plus total HR function expenses.

Regardless of the measures, the important point is to monitor and compare them, identify trends, make adjustments, and take action when compensation costs are out of line.

Employee Benefits

No single compensation-related measure has attracted more attention in the last decade than the cost of employee benefits. The first measure to consider is the total employee benefit cost, both to the organization and the employee. In good economic times, the employee benefits often mushroom as companies provide additional benefits to retain critical employees. In recent years, these perks became excessive by almost any standard and have been scaled back. Rising healthcare costs, which continue to increase in almost every country, have also contributed to the increased cost of benefits.

The second measure is employee benefits as a percent of actual payroll. This standard measure (the average in the United States is about 38 percent) is a routine benchmarking statistic. Additional reporting may include employee benefits costs on a per-employee basis as a percent of human capital or as a percent of revenue.

Another area is to compare the portion of the employee benefits costs that are borne by the employer and those by the employee. As healthcare costs increase, the employee is being required to absorb a larger part of that cost.

Too often, even the most beautifully conceived benefits package will fail to pay off in better recruiting and retention because candidates and employees do not recognize the true value of the benefits. Without understanding the details, they assume that all plans are alike. Some companies, especially those offering expensive packages, may be throwing money down the drain. To ensure that employee benefits are optimized, there must be a communications program. Employees must first know the full details and value of their packages, particularly compared to others in the industry. Then, the satisfaction level must be measured, capturing employee satisfaction with benefits. Routine data taken as part of the annual feedback survey can provide helpful insight into the role, value, and respect for employee benefits.

Variable Compensation

The last two decades have witnessed increased focus on variable compensation or pay-for-performance plans. In an attempt to focus on accountability and achieve important goals to secure results, executives use money as a motivator, that is, as a reward for achieving important objectives. Specific measures include the percent of employees on variable pay plans, the type of variable pay plans, and the variable pay as a percent of total pay. Some executives believe in having high levels of variable pay, particularly in a sales-oriented environment. Others prefer a low percentage of variable pay, often reflecting large bureaucratic organizations.

The role of variable pay can be influential in organizations. Linking pay to performance is a way many organizations have achieved excellent success and sustained performance over a period of time. Consider this example reported by Watson Wyatt Consulting.[16] A major retailer had experienced excellent performance over several years. During that time, a system of rewards and accountability had been in place, with a heavy emphasis on variable pay. The company offered stock options and other stock incentives deep in the organization to the level of assistant store manager. A stock purchase plan was available to all employees with a 15 percent discount. It had been communicated widely and had a high participation rate. A very aggressive annual incentive plan had been installed with payouts of 100 percent, 150 percent, and 200 percent of target bonus opportunities. On top of this, the company continued to weed out below-average performers while the high-performing employees were targeted for significant salary increases and special stock option grants. Stock ownership was strongly encouraged and, as a result, the senior management team and the board of directors owned a large portion of the company stock. The company's compensation philosophy offered modest base salaries combined with cash- and stock-incentive opportunities that allowed actual pay to be well above the seventy-fifth percentile. Top management had the same compensation program as the rest of the company. The result was outstanding corporate performance.

Employee Ownership

Employee ownership has always been an important consideration in the human capital area. Many advocates of this practice have suggested that higher levels of employee ownership often lead to improved organizational success measured in profitability or productivity. While the research has not always reflected this relationship, there are some encouraging signals. The Human Capital Index presented in chapter 7 shows that companies with a high percentage of stock ownership at the employee level, combined with a high level of stock owned by senior managers, and a high level of employees eligible for stock plan programs are worth 3.5 percent more on the market. Thus, stock ownership is one of the easiest ways to link pay to performance.[17] There is also some significant consideration that the higher levels of employee ownership correlate to higher levels of satisfaction and, consequently, higher levels of retention.

Different types of employee ownership positions are possible, ranging from a company being totally owned by employees to employees participating in a 401(k) plan with company stock. The American Cast Iron Pipe Company (ACIPCO), a Birmingham, Alabama-based organization, has a 100-year history, is nonunion, and completely owned by the 3,000 people it employs nationwide. The original founder of ACIPCO, John Eagan, bequeathed the company to employees in a special trust he had established prior to his death. The employees share the profits through bonuses and four elected employees serve as voting members on the ACIPCO board of directors. ACIPCO has been successful with very low employee turnover and listed in the top 10 of *Fortune* magazine's 100 Best Companies to Work For.

Some employees have the option to own the company through an employee stock ownership program (ESOP). In essence, employees usually buy the company from the owners and the company is employee-owned. In other situations, employees acquire stock in several ways: through the company's

401(k) plan, a stock purchase plan, a reward for tenure, performance, or position, or in exchange for concessions in wages and benefits. Through the 401(k) plan, employees are provided an option to invest in stock through payroll deduction, on a tax-deferred basis. The company usually matches the contribution at a 50 percent level. This plan has made some employees in successful companies quite wealthy. Stock purchase plans allow employees to purchase stock through payroll deduction either at a discount or with no fees. This is not a tax-deferred plan, but often a way for employees to accumulate additional stock. Some employees are provided stock options, which is basically an option to buy the stock at a later date at a price fixed at the time the option is granted. For a company where the stock price is increasing, stock options can be a tremendous income windfall for employees. Long-term employees of some organizations, such as Microsoft and General Electric, literally become wealthy through stock options. Finally, as companies undergo serious difficulties and must reduce benefits and wages of employees—such as the difficulties facing the airline industry in 2004—wage concessions are sought and company stock is provided to employees in exchange.

Specific measures should be developed, showing ownership by various types of plans and changes in the ownership profile. Total numbers and percentages are appropriate. There is a negative side of employee ownership. If the stock declines, employees lose much of their investment. With employees having a significant amount of their investment in company stock, this not only reduces their savings, but also lowers morale. During an economic slump, when a company must have employees who are highly engaged and motivated, a significant stock price reduction can have the opposite effect. In extreme cases where the company goes into bankruptcy, huge employee ownership blocks can spell disaster for employees and their families who not only face a job loss but a loss of their personal investments.

FAIR EMPLOYMENT, COMPLIANCE, AND SAFETY

Areas that often reflect employee dissatisfaction—and the legal issues that may surround it—include fair employment, safety, and compliance. In these categories, measures are tracked that reflect activity, concern, action, and consequences.

Complaints and Grievances

Employee dissatisfaction may appear in many ways and is usually accompanied by dire consequences. A dissatisfied employee is seldom motivated to

perform above the minimum level. Dissatisfied employees vent their frustrations and anxieties, usually to other employees. At a certain level of dissatisfaction, there is a loss of morale and efficiency and the organization ceases to be
as successful as it could be. This is an important area to monitor routinely and
take action quickly when data indicate problem areas.

Employee complaints can be monitored both internally and externally.
When there is a formal complaint process, such as an employee concerns program in a nuclear power operating company, the number of complaints is
monitored. Complaints are filed when something is perceived to be unfair,
inappropriate, or perhaps illegal. The actual number must be evaluated based
on the purpose and scope of the complaint process. Complaints can be too
low (managers are discouraging complaints) or too high (out of control).
Employee complaints may be informally reported on a variety of feedback
mechanisms. In some cases, complaints are lodged anonymously, through
mechanisms particularly created for collecting complaints.

Similar measures are taken for grievances, which require more formal
processes for complaint resolution. In union organizations, grievances are
typically filed and resolved in a four-step process. Nonunion grievance systems mirror the unionized grievance process and similar monitoring would be
available there. The number of grievances and the percent resolved at different
levels are often important data.

Charges and Litigation

Another complaint measure is from employees who feel that they have been
victims of discrimination. These formal complaints represent potentially explosive issues that must be resolved—internally at first, and later with an
agency, if the complaint is elevated to that level. For most organizations, the
more formal version of discrimination complaints is an EEOC charge. Other
charges, such as improper time keeping and overtime are filed under the Fair
Labor Standards Act and unfair labor practices filed under the National Labor
Relations Act provide opportunities for tracking and monitoring.

Formal charges, either through the EEOC, Fair Labor Standards Act,
National Labor Relations Act, or other agencies, represent serious issues that
can be devastating for an organization. Not only do they take up precious time
and energy, they lower morale, and can be a public relations nightmare for
organizations. Thus, monitoring the charges and tracking their resolution—
even the time and steps it took to resolve—provides a more complete profile
of this activity. Also, it is helpful to track litigation status and costs.

All complaints should be monitored in some way. Recording the type, resolution percentage, and cost per complaint is a possibility. Monitoring these items allows comparisons with trends and benchmarks from other organizations.

Health and Safety

For some industries, the health and safety of employees is a critical issue. Depending on the type of organization, health and safety measures could be as simple as first-aid treatment, a minor slip or fall, or a worker's compensation claim in a service industry. In heavy manufacturing firms, as many as twelve measures are possible, including first-aid treatments, worker's compensation claims, accident frequency rates, accident severity rates, OSHA incidents, OSHA fines, OSHA inspections, near misses, and several others. When safety is a concern, it is important to monitor these measures and compare them with history and benchmarking data.

EMPLOYEE RELATIONS

The virtual catch-all category of employee relations covers the "other issues not covered in the previous areas." While many of the measures relate to employee relations, two important employee relations groups of measures are covered in this category. The first one is absenteeism, which plagues many organizations and hampers productivity efforts. It is one of the most visible signs of employee withdrawal, often reflecting employee dissatisfaction or problem employees. The second area that is becoming an important issue involves the fragile balance between work and personal lives.

Absenteeism and Tardiness

Employee absence, tardiness, or partial absences can be very disruptive and costly for organizations. These measures represent pesky issues that are difficult to address and measure. Appropriate record-keeping systems must be in place to monitor the data accurately (the occurrence and sometimes the reason). The most important measure is the percent of unplanned and unexpected absenteeism. These types of absences can cause operational instability, customer service problems, and, in some cases, can be the ultimate demise of organizations when absenteeism cannot be controlled. In critical jobs, absenteeism can shut down stores, restaurants, plants, branches, even cancel flights. Monitoring this measure and using it to drive improvement allows for comparisons with trends, expectations, and benchmarks.

Work/Life Balance

In the last decade, few areas within HR have received more attention than work/life balance. Increased technology has left employees constantly plugged into cell phones designed for 24/7 contact and e-mail that can be accessed anywhere on laptops with Wi-Fi connections. Cell phones, pagers, voice mail, and a myriad of other "conveniences" keep everyone engaged. It is in this kind of environment that some of the best innovations have been created and outstanding performances have been logged. However, this environment may leave employees struggling with the issue of separating their work lives from their personal lives. This is a dilemma for employers as well—they want their employees informed, up-to-date, motivated, challenged, and engaged in their work. Yet, they realize that excessive focus on work leads to burnout, stress problems, and ultimately withdrawal, in the form of absenteeism and turnover. In some cases it leads to severe medical problems.

Excessive overtime can indicate work/life imbalances. Organizations monitor this issue in several ways. The amount of time an individual devotes to the job, particularly for professional employees, is an important measure. Even though employees may be exempt from overtime pay, organizations implement ways to compensate them for working long hours or providing conveniences to hold them with the extra hours. For example, Microsoft and QUALCOMM provide child care and dinners to employees who work late hours. Those employees are encouraged to invite their family members to join them for dinner.

Monitoring healthcare claims for stress-related counseling and emotional issues is another way to determine if imbalances are creating a problem. Monitoring the use of the employee assistance program where employees seek help with this issue is another measure.

Monitoring programs geared to help the work/life balance is important. These include such programs as flexible work schedules, job sharing, and telecommuting. Reporting the percent of employees involved in flexible scheduling is a typical measure. Although these arrangements may cause unique management issues, they are excellent ways for employees to attend to issues that require work schedules outside the normal 9-to-5 schedule. Other efforts include offering a special assistance program for child care in the evenings, on-site daycare, and assistance with elderly parents. All of these programs are an attempt to help employees deal with a variety of personal issues, even on work time, so their work/life balance is improved.

Employee feedback on the work/life balance is also helpful. Through feedback mechanisms and annual attitude surveys, employees provide input on the progress made with work/life balance issues and the organization's willingness to support programs. Employees need to see genuine support from top executives. For example, Baxter International, an $8.9 billion company with 51,000 employees has a significant focus on work/life issues. The CEO, Harry Kraemer, Jr., sets the example for the staff by taking time off to spend with his children and help out with many of the family chores. He encourages employees to adjust their schedules to fit their needs, for example, starting later in the morning so they can get the kids off to school or working one day a week from home. By doing this, the CEO concludes that Baxter can attract and retain top-notch people. Also, the company receives more quality work time from employees because they are less distracted while at the office.[18] This is an area that is still evolving and additional measures will be needed in the future.

SUMMARY

This chapter explored the most common measures considered important in the human capital monitoring mix. These measures, while sometimes difficult to capture, reflect the potential success and challenges in today's organizations. They are measures that can make a difference in the growth, development, and sustainability of an organization.

Some of the measures reflect time-tested, traditional measures of human capital; others reflect new economy issues; still others are specific to a certain industry or represent fundamental measures that have existed for some time. In any case, they are important measures and should be evaluated in some way. They are areas that if measured can guide actions that create opportunities and solve problems.

NOTES

1   Stuart F. Brown, "Scientific Americans," *Fortune*, Sept 20, 2004, p. 175.

2   Alexander Kandybin and Martin Kihn, "Raising Your Return on Innovation Investment," *Strategy + Business*, Issue 35, 2004.

3   José Santos, Yves Doz, and Peter Williamson, "Is Your Innovation Process Global?" *MIT Sloan Management Review*, Summer 2004, p. 31.

4   Evan I. Schwartz, *Juice: The Creative Fuel That Drives World-Class Inventors* (Boston: Harvard Business School Press, 2004).

5   Stephen Bates, "Linking People Measures to Strategy," *Research Report R-1342-03-RR* (New York: The Conference Board, 2003).

6   Jack J. Phillips and Adele O. Connell, *Managing Employee Turnover* (Woburn, Mass.: Butterworth-Heinemann, 2003).

7   Thomas A. Stewart, *The Wealth of Knowledge: Intellectual Capital in the 21st Century Organization* (New York: Currency Books, 2001).

8   Cliff Purington, Chris Butler, and Sarah Fister, *Built to Learn: The Inside Story of How Rockwell Collins Became a True Learning Organization* (New York: AMACOM, 2004).

9   Wayne Casio, *Costing Human Resources*, 4th ed. (Cincinatti, Ohio: Southwestern Publishing, 2000).

10   Jack J. Phillips and Lynn Schmidt, *The Leadership Scorecard* (Woburn, Mass.: Butterworth-Heinemann, 2004).

11   Jac Fitz-enz, *The ROI of Human Capital* (New York: AMACOM, 2001).

12   Edward E. Hubbard, *The Diversity Scorecard* (Woburn, Mass.: Butterworth-Heinemann, 2003).

13   Mark Heinzl, "Nortel Network Announces Job Cuts," *Wall Street Journal,* Aug 20, 2004.

14   Micheline Maynard, *The End of Detroit* (New York: Currency Doubleday, 2003).

15   Michael F. Corbett, *The Outsourcing Revolution: Why It Makes Sense and How to Do It Right* (Chicago: Dearborn Trade Publishing, 2004).

16   Bruce N. Pfau and Ira T. Kay, *The Human Capital Edge: 21 People Management Practices Your Company Must Implement (or Avoid) to Maximize Shareholder Value* (New York: McGraw-Hill, 2002).

17   Ibid.

18   M. Arndt, "How Does Harry Do It?" *BusinessWeek*, July 22, 2002, pp. 66–67.

PART FOUR

WHAT IS THE EXECUTIVE'S ROLE?

Why and How Top Management Should Be Involved

CHAPTER 10

Creating and Using the Human Capital Scorecard

Scorecards have become the predominant method used by organizations to ensure that appropriate measures are tracked and improvement occurs. Top executives must take an active role in developing an appropriate human capital scorecard and must ensure that critical measures are tracked and monitored routinely; otherwise, the scorecard measures may be dominated by items that are not meaningful or strategically focused. Executives must also ensure that specific actions are taken to correct situations where measures are less than optimal. Using the ROI methodology presented in chapters 5 and 8, executives should take part in examining the payoff of investments in human capital projects.

This chapter outlines the issues involved in creating a human capital scorecard. Although the human capital metrics process may take on different names, *scorecard* is a term that particularly resonates with the human resources community. This chapter explores the development of these scorecards and the role of top executives in ensuring their proper implementation. The chapter presents available possibilities and offers nine scorecard options, highlighting the various issues, advantages, and disadvantages. It ends with a description of how the scorecard process can drive value in an organization. Proactively using the scorecard measures can alleviate future problems or correct minor problems as they appear. The most critical issue for executives is to use scorecards to drive performance.

PROGRESS AND OPPORTUNITY

The previous chapter presented measurements that are currently being monitored in best-practice organizations. Data are collected from a variety of studies illustrating what is possible and what is being achieved in these organizations. Unfortunately, many organizations have not made enough progress, even though an ongoing mandate for this type of measurement exists.

The Current Status

A variety of studies highlight the status of metrics and scorecard development in organizations. Some of the most interesting information comes from a survey conducted by the Corporate Leadership Council of the Corporate Executive Board. In this survey of HR metrics, the majority of the 138 companies involved (80%) have yet to deliver the metrics needed.[1] Only 8 percent have extensive use of the data in advising business leaders on workforce management issues. These statistics need to be reversed.

Another major study on this issue was conducted by Deloitte & Touche. (Deloitte & Touche has the largest human resources consulting practice in the United Kingdom, with over 800 consultants in human capital management.) The study primarily involved organizations in the United Kingdom and identified impediments to progress in implementing scorecards. Fifty-two percent of survey respondents indicated the lack of time and resources as the number one barrier to making progress with scorecards; other priorities tended to get in the way. Forty-one percent listed the second reason as not recognizing measurement as a priority for the business; they failed to see the business need for evaluating success. As the third reason, forty-seven percent indicated the lack of clarity as to what the benefits for the business would be. Finally, the lack of clarity as to what exactly should be measured was reported by thirty-one percent. Human capital professionals find these figures disturbing. So much has been written about human capital and so many tools are available to assist in the development and use of human capital scorecards, it seems these reasons are mere excuses for not taking accountability seriously. Unfortunately, many HR managers see human capital measurement as resource intensive, but, more important, they are unclear both in terms of what should be measured and how these results should be used. These reasons support the conclusion that human capital professionals must use targeted approaches that can deliver clearly defined, measurable benefits.[2]

The Mandate

Although progress has been slow and legitimate barriers for progress exist, the mandate is clearly present. Organizations *must* show the value of scorecards. The Corporate Leadership Council survey described previously shows that the pressure is on. In 37 percent of organizations, CEOs, COOs, and CFOs, the top three individuals in any major organization, are applying pressure to deliver and enhance HR data and capabilities.

This kind of pressure will undoubtedly increase. At the same time, organizations recognize the need to build a human capital scorecard. In the Deloitte & Touche study, organizations were asked about the rationale for building a more comprehensive scorecard and the benefits that can be derived. Figure 10-1 shows the major responses. Here, almost 50 percent of the respondents desire an important scorecard so that human capital can be measured in a recognized way. Over 40 percent indicate that the human capital scorecard forms a basis for performance management/reward systems and allows the organization to specify how to increase human capital investment. Still almost 40 percent see the value in justifying the investment in human capital and over 30 percent track changes in the value of human capital. Clearly, there is not only pressure to measure human capital, but major rationale for accomplishing it.[3]

METRIC FUNDAMENTALS

When determining the type of measurement system to use, it is helpful to review metric fundamentals. The first important issue is to identify what

Figure 10-1. Rationale for building a human capital scorecard.

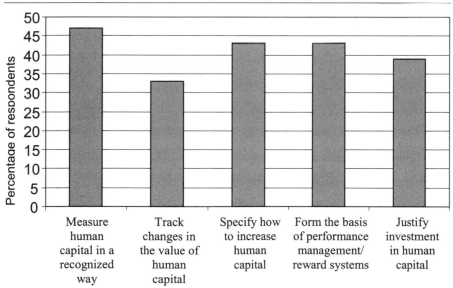

Source: Adapted from Brett Walsh, *Measuring Human Capital Value* (London: Deloitte & Touche, 2002).

makes an effective measure. Table 10-1 shows some of the criteria of an effective measure. These are critical issues that should be explored when examining any type of measure.

These criteria serve as a screening checklist as measures are considered, developed, and ultimately added to the scorecard list. In addition to meeting criteria, the factual basis of the measure should be stressed. In essence, the measure should be subjected to a fact-based analysis, a level of analysis never applied to decisions about human capital before, even when these decisions involve huge sums of money. It is helpful to distinguish between the various "types" of facts. As shown below, the basis for facts range from common sense to what employees "say" to actual data:

❑ *No Facts.* Common sense tells us that employees will be more productive if they have a stake in the profits of the business.

Table 10-1. Criteria for effective measures.

Criterion: Effective measures are . . .	Definition: The extent to which a measure . . .
Important	Connects to strategically important business objectives rather than to what is easy to measure.
Complete	Adequately tracks the entire phenomenon rather than only a part of the phenomenon.
Timely	Tracks at the right time rather than being held to an arbitrary date.
Visible	Is visible, public, openly known, and tracked by those affected by it rather than collected privately for management's eyes only.
Controllable	Tracks outcomes created by those affected by it, who have a clear line of sight from the measure to the results.
Cost-effective	Is efficient to track by using existing data or data easy to monitor rather than requiring a new layer of procedures.
Interpretable	Creates data that are easy to make sense of and translate to employee actions.
Simplicity	Simple to understand from each stakeholder's perspective.
Specific	Is clearly defined so people quickly understand and relate to the measure.
Collectable	Can be collected in a way where the effort required is proportionate to the resulting usefulness of the measure.
Team-based	Will have value with a team of individuals and not just an individual judgment.
Credible	Provides information that is valid and credible in the eyes of management.

Source: Adapted from Steve Kerr, "On the Folly of Hoping for A While Rewarding B," *Academy of Management Journal,* vol. 18 (1995): 769–783; and Andrew Mayo, *Measuring Human Capital* (London: The Institute of Chartered Accountants, June 2003).

❏ *Unreliable Facts*. Employees say they are more likely to stay if they are offered profit sharing.

❏ *Irrelevant Facts*. We have benchmarked three world-class companies with variable pay plans: a bank, a hotel chain, and a defense contractor. All reported good results.

❏ *Fact-Based*. Lower employee turnover in call centers is reducing operational costs.[4]

Interest in Scorecards

In recent years, there has been much interest in developing documents that reflect appropriate measures in an organization. Scorecards, such as those originally used in sporting events, provide a variety of measures for top executives. In Kaplan and Norton's landmark book, *The Balanced Scorecard* (1996), the concept was brought to the attention of organizations. Kaplan and Norton suggested that data be organized in four categories: process, operational, financial, and growth.[5]

But what exactly is a scorecard? The *American Heritage Dictionary* defines a scorecard from two perspectives:

1. A printed program or card enabling a spectator to identify players and record the progress of a game or competition
2. A small card used to record one's own performance in sports such as golf[6]

Scorecards come in a variety of types, whether it is Kaplan and Norton's balanced scorecard, the scored set in the president's management agenda using the traffic light grading system (green for success, yellow for mixed results, red for unsatisfactory), or some other kind. Regardless of the type, top executives place great emphasis on the concept of scorecards. In some organizations, the scorecard concept has filtered down to various functional business units and each part of the business has been required to develop scorecards. A growing number of HR executives have developed the scorecard to reflect the human capital segment of the business.

The scorecard approach is appealing because it provides a quick comparison of key measures and examines the status of human capital in the organization. As a management tool, scorecards can be very important to shape the direction of human capital investment and improve or maintain performance of the organization through the implementation of preventive programs.

Interest in scorecards has been phenomenal, particularly the Kaplan and

Norton balanced scorecard. The Deloitte survey reports that 32 percent of organizations used the balanced scorecard methodology; 46 percent of those said this was effective for them.

Other similar terms are also used such as HR benchmarking, HR metrics, HR reports, HR information systems, HR dashboards, and HR human capital reports. This chapter will use the term scorecard to denote a range of possibilities for presenting data in a meaningful, organized way and representing performance from a variety of perspectives, using qualitative and quantitative data. More important, the data from a scorecard can help organizations understand problems and opportunities and can be used for both diagnostic and prescriptive possibilities.

Selecting the Measures That Matter

Executive input is critical when it comes to selecting the measures to be included in the human capital scorecard. There are a variety of options and categories. The remainder of this chapter will cover a variety of approaches that can bring together the concepts and concerns discussed earlier in the chapter.

When building the scorecard, it is helpful to start with the organization's strategy. Rather than search for an illusive "best list" of human capital measures, some professionals prefer to know more about how they can implement a metrics project or convince managers and others to endorse the creation and use of people measures. The starting point of any measurement project is to place it in the context of the company's strategic planning process. This is difficult if the HR executive is outside the upper management loop. Many HR executives are outside the strategic planning process, which adds to the challenge. Fortunately, this situation is changing; strategic planning and human resource planning are sometimes—and should be—collectively connected. Figure 10-2 shows the primary promoters of measurement metrics projects. This project developed by the Conference Board, shows that the HR director was the principle leader 56 percent of the time; the business unit leaders led 36 percent of the time. The involvement of the business unit leaders is rapidly changing. Ten years ago there would be almost no involvement. It is important for executives to be involved and take important roles in developing metrics projects. For example, Cisco Systems, the worldwide leader in networking for the Internet, listed sales in their 2004 annual report at over $22 billion and employees counted in at more than 34,000 worldwide. They have made tremendous strides in the development of a human capital scorecard.

Several of Cisco's HR professionals are collaborating cross-functionally within HR to produce a roadmap that will deliver much-needed networked

Figure 10-2. HR is the primary promoter and leader of initiatives.

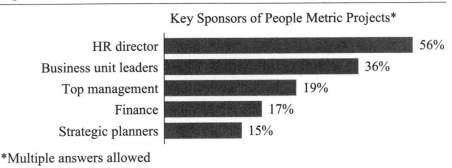

Key Sponsors of People Metric Projects*

HR director	56%
Business unit leaders	36%
Top management	19%
Finance	17%
Strategic planners	15%

*Multiple answers allowed

Source: Stephen Gates, "Linking People Measures to Strategy," *Research Report R-1342-03-RR* (New York: The Conference Board, 2003), p. 24.

intelligence. Since the members of this group understand that business continues while they chart the new map, they are also building a few temporary solutions along the way. For example, when the HR team reviewed the current state of people data, they discovered duplicated requests for numerous reports and that individuals were asking for information that already existed in other places. The need for more sharply defined human capital metrics led to the interim solution of a human capital scorecard. The first scorecard covered a number of topics, including headcount, diversity, turnover, employee satisfaction, talent and movement, span of control, expense per employee, revenue per employee, ROI on human capital, and various HR functional measures. While the scorecard is receiving wide use now, Cisco's goal is to continue developing innovative solutions for bringing intelligence to the right people. Figure 10-3 shows steps taken to develop the human capital metrics.[7]

SCORECARD OPTIONS

As previously mentioned, several scorecard options exist. This section provides nine options that represent different approaches and philosophies for scorecard development. Each has its unique advantages and disadvantages and the list is typically presented in terms of the efforts required to produce them.

Workforce Measurement Scorecard

One approach is to develop a scorecard that shows the basic workforce measures, from demographics to mobility to workforce relations. Figure 10-4 shows the chart presented by the corporate executive board in a major study.

Figure 10-3. Human capital metrics development.

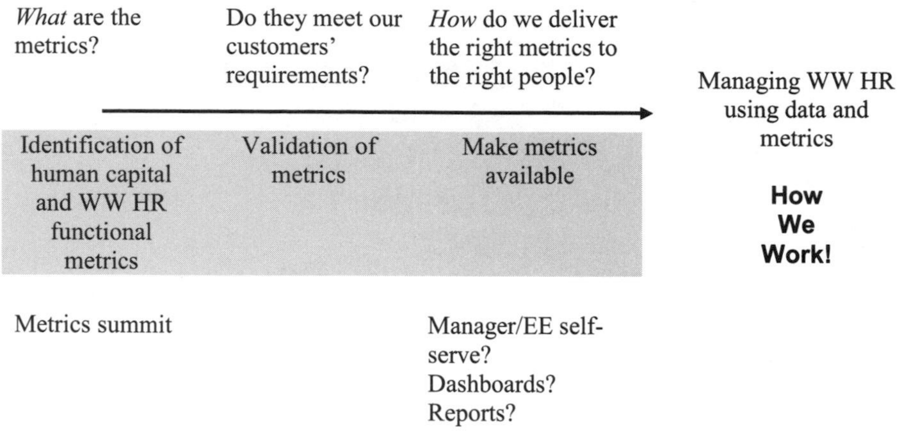

What are the metrics?	Do they meet our customers' requirements?	*How* do we deliver the right metrics to the right people?	Managing WW HR using data and metrics
Identification of human capital and WW HR functional metrics	Validation of metrics	Make metrics available	**How We Work!**
Metrics summit		Manager/EE self-serve? Dashboards? Reports?	

Source: Cisco Systems, Inc. From Stephen Gates, "Linking People Measures to Strategy," *Research Report R-1342-03-RR* (New York: The Conference Board, 2003), p. 28.

Figure 10-4. Basic workforce measures scorecard.

Category	Description
A. Demographic Profile	Describes and compares organizational segments on a range of demographic and personal attributes, e.g., age, employment status, occupational group, tenure, gender and ethnic diversity.
B. Productivity	Combines a range of "input" and "output/outcome" measures that can be examined together to gauge organizational effectiveness.
C. Availability	Measures and compares availability and absence patterns of employee segments.
D. Mobility	Monitors and compares flow of the workforce into, within, and out of the organization.
E. Performance and Development	Quantifies current and emerging skills profile of the organization and the resources devoted to organizational development.
F. Compensation and Benefits	Monitors and compares the compensation and benefits made available to reward and retain employees.
G. Workforce Relations	Measures labor relations effectiveness and costs.

Source: Adapted from *CLC Metrics: Operationalizing Integrated Human Capital Management* (Washington, D.C.: Corporate Leadership Council, 2004).

These are traditional measurement fundamentals and often reflect early developments of the scorecard.

Basic IPO Scorecard

Another approach is to examine HR from the perspective of inputs, processes, and outcomes (IPO). As shown in figure 10-5, the basic IPO scorecard shows inputs such as programs, participants, and money. These inputs are used in a variety of processes to show activity, progress, implementation, and the ultimate outcomes in simple, easy-to-connect-to measures, such as retention, productivity, and job satisfaction. This approach quickly shows the relationship of input to output, and is a simplistic approach to the process.

The Balanced Scorecard Process

Figure 10-6 shows balanced scorecard categories where human capital measures are shaped into the Kaplan and Norton categories.[8] While this process provides a little more perspective than that contained in the simplistic IPO approach, it is still sometimes awkward to implement. Not all HR issues fit into these categories and the scorecard fails to offer the kind of balance that may be needed.

The Causal Chain Scorecard

Figure 10-7 represents a more comprehensive approach, one possessing seven categories of data and reflecting the causal chain that usually takes place in human capital projects. The categories move from inputs to the financial results—ROI. These seven categories represent important measures to the

Figure 10-5. A basic IPO scorecard.

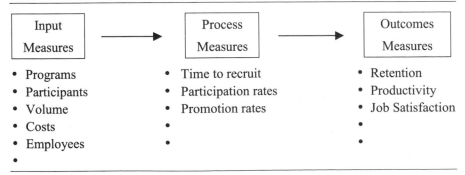

Figure 10-6. The Kaplan and Norton balanced scorecard.

Employee Learning & Growth	Internal Processes	Customer	Financial
• Number of Programs • Hours of Training	• Participation Rates • Completion Rate • Process Times	• Stakeholder Satisfaction • Reaction • Perceived Value	• Costs of Human Capital • Costs of Program • Costs of Processes • ROI

organization and include all types of data (from qualitative to quantitative) and they are taken from various perspectives.

The first category—input—shows the scope and the volume of human capital. It divides individuals into a number of categories and tracks their involvement in a variety of activities and the number of hours they spend in different programs and projects. The various costs are typically included in this category as the cost of the project or program is put into the human capital mix.

The second category focuses on costs of human capital programs. The costs are tracked by program, activity, project, and employee. The total investment in human capital is included in this category.

The third category tracks employees reactions and their degree of satisfaction. This is a critical measure where employees' feedback is obtained about specific programs, initiatives, and projects and information is gathered on issues such as their jobs, their career, and the organization. In addition, organizational commitment and engagement are often included in this category.

The fourth category tracks and monitors skills and the learning that takes place in an organization; this is done in such a way as to show an organization's capabilities. Issues related to readiness are included in this category.

The fifth category, application and implementation, measures processes in place and the degree to which HR programs and solutions are working effectively. This is similar to the Kaplan and Norton process category but can be much broader.

The sixth category considers impact, particularly impact in the organiza-

Figure 10-7. Scorecard categories organized by causal chain of impact.

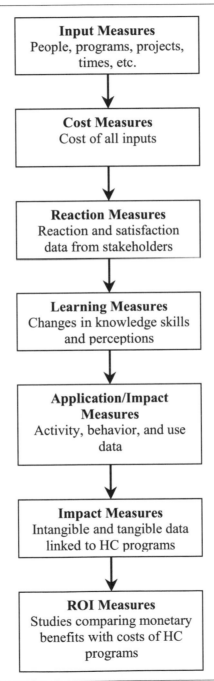

tion as a consequence of the various programs, projects, and processes. It may include things like retention, absenteeism, and even connections to the business in terms of sales, productivity, quality, and cycle time. The tangible or hard data measures are easily converted to monetary value if the organization so desires. Some measures represent intangible or soft data categories. Typically, the mechanisms do not exist (nor are they accepted) to place monetary values on these soft data categories in the organization. Therefore, the measures are purposely not converted to monetary value. However, these intangibles have an important meaning of their own and often drive many HR solutions.

The seventh and last category is financial results and contains measures to show the payoff of particular projects or programs, including ROI calculations, benefit-cost ratios, and payback period. These measures are usually developed from microlevel studies conducted to show the actual cost versus the benefits of a particular solution, as described in chapters 5 and 8.

These categories are comprehensive and reflect the variety and type of measures linked to the human capital function in an organization. These measures also reflect the data that are collected to show the impact of an HR solution, project, program, or initiative. For example, if a retention solution is implemented to improve turnover or termination rate, the success of the solution can be monitored along these seven measures. The following categories would be measured:

- ❑ *Inputs* of the number of individuals involved, the duration of the solution, and the time to develop the solution.
- ❑ *Costs* of the solution and its parts and components.
- ❑ *Reaction* from stakeholders to the solution.
- ❑ *Learning* and changes in knowledge skills and perceptions to make the solution successful.
- ❑ *Application* and implementation of the solution.
- ❑ *Impact* of turnover reduction. Intangibles connected with the process, such as an increase in job satisfaction, stress reduction, and reduced conflicts, are monitored as well.
- ❑ *Financial results* showing the cost of the solution compared to the monetary value of the turnover reduction.

When a human capital solution is implemented to drive a particular measure, a profile of success can be developed to include the seven categories of data shown in figure 10-7. In essence, a microlevel scorecard analysis can be developed around every HR solution and progress can be reported routinely. In addition, the data from the microlevel scorecard can be integrated into the macrolevel scorecard. For example, the reaction to an HR program can be monitored as reaction and satisfaction data. A single measure such as relevance or importance can be reported in a macrolevel scorecard. Thus, it is possible to have both microlevel and macrolevel scorecards. Ideally, the same types of data are developed as recommended here. The scorecards must be compatible, at least conceptually, for easy integration.

The Value-Added Scorecard

The causal chain can be structured differently to show the actual added value. Figure 10-8 shows a scorecard based on the data categories described in the causal chain, but the categories are organized according to the value added from the perspective of the senior management team. This chart shows that ROI measures usually have the highest value, followed by impact and intangible measures. Input, reaction, and cost measures have the lowest value. The placement of data in a report format underscores the value of the measures.

Human Resources Process Scorecard

The next approach is to consider the processes involved in the human resources acquisition and maintenance. This approach, shown in figure 10-9, illustrates the processes used by the human resources function in a sequence from acquiring employees to their departure from the organization. Measures are captured along the way. This scorecard clearly shows where measures are developed and can help pinpoint where problems exist in the process chain.

Human Capital Monitor

Another approach is to report the progress made in the contribution. As shown in figure 10-10, the human capital monitor, advocated by Mayo, is designed to link three areas of measures in a logical way:

1. The intrinsic worth of the human capital available together with the key processes used in the business unit to maximize it
2. The working environment and its influence of motivation, commitment, and their contribution
3. The level of the contribution itself

This approach is much more than just a list of measures about people, classified in three categories. It specifically attempts to link the capability of

Figure 10-8. Scorecard categories organized by value added.

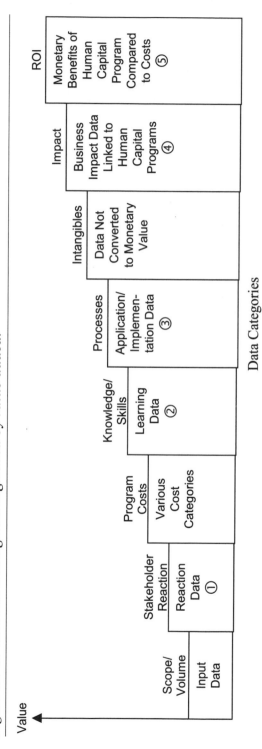

Figure 10-9. The HR process scorecard.

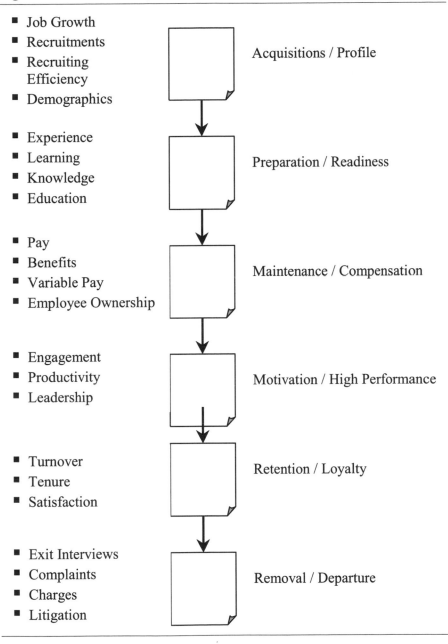

Figure 10-10. The human capital monitor.

People as assets		People motivation and commitment	People contribution to added value

"Human asset worth"
 	
= employment costs x
  individual asset multiplier
  (IAM)/1000
 	
"IAM" = a function of:
• capability
• potential
• contribution
• values alignment
 	
Maximizing human capital
 	
• acquisition - how successful
• retention   are we?
• growth   - what drives
• divestment   success?
	+	Measures
		
		– how successful are we?
		
		--- 	
		
		The work environment that drives success
		
		--- 	
		
		• work challenge
		• leadership
		• practical support
		• the workgroup
		• learning and development
		• rewards and recognition
			=	The value added to each stakeholder
				
				• financial
				• non financial
				
				• current
				• future
				
				Productivity ratios

Source: Adapted from Andrew Mayo, *Measuring Human Capital* (London: The Institute of Chartered Accountants, June 2003).

people with the contribution they make to stakeholder value. The idea is that it is created for defined groups of people.[9]

Best-Practice Scorecard

Perhaps an even more comprehensive approach would be to use the measures that represent best practices, detailed in chapter 9. These show the current and emerging measures taken from best-practice organizations; they were collected from a variety of studies aimed at understanding the trends toward measurement possibilities. This list of measures is presented here as table 10-2. It represents the most comprehensive process. Not only are the traditional measures covered, but some of the more intriguing and difficult-to-measure issues, such as innovation and leadership, are also represented.

Transactional Benchmarking

A final scorecard option is transactional benchmarking. Here, the traditional benchmarking report is replaced by a dynamic database where the users involved in a benchmarking project provide the data in real time. The transactional analysis enables the data to be sliced in a variety of ways important to the user that might not be contained in the static report. This replaces the

Table 10-2. Best-practices scorecard.

Common Human Capital Measures

1. Innovation and Creativity
   - Innovation
   - Creativity
2. Employee Attitudes
   - Employee satisfaction
   - Organizational commitment
   - Employee engagement
3. Workforce Stability
   - Turnover and termination
   - Tenure and longevity
4. Employee Capability
   - Experience
   - Learning
   - Knowledge
   - Competencies
   - Educational level
5. Human Capital Investment
   - HR department investment
   - Total HC investment
   - Investment by category
6. Leadership
   - 360° feedback
   - Leadership inventories
   - Leadership perception

7. Productivity
   - Unit productivity
   - Gross productivity
8. Workforce Profile
   - Demographics
9. Job Creation and Acquisition
   - Job growth
   - Recruitment sourcing and effectiveness
   - Recruiting efficiency
10. Compensation and Benefits
    - Compensation
    - Employee benefits
    - Variable compensation
    - Employee ownership
11. Compliance and Safety
    - Complaints and grievances
    - Charges and litigation
    - Health and safety
12. Employee Relations
    - Absenteeism and tardiness
    - Work/life balance

paper-based report with a dynamic database that instantly compares data to benchmarks.[10] As discussed earlier, there are limitations to using benchmark data: They may or may not represent the best practice or the needs of any one organization; therefore, they may not be important to the current processes.

USING THE SCORECARD

Important reasons for having a scorecard are to manage human capital effectively, optimize the status of human capital, and drive continuous improvement in the use of human capital. Because of this, continuous monitoring and action is required when necessary. The HR staff will be responsible for monitoring the data and recommending or reporting actions to keep measures where they are or to improve measures that are unacceptable. However, executives should be actively involved in the process. It is too important to delegate this responsibility entirely to the HR staff. The involvement and commitment of the senior team is essential to ensure appropriate actions are taken and those actions are monitored to check the progress being made. Figure 10-11 shows all the steps needed to drive improvement with the use of scorecards.

Select the Measures

Earlier in this chapter, specific recommendations for selecting the measures were presented. It is important for all key stakeholders to agree on the measures, so the concerns of the human resources staff and the senior executive team are balanced. After the measures are selected, the format for presentation is determined so that data are routinely, if not instantaneously, available to the management group and the HR staff.

Set the Target

For each measure on the scorecard, specific target (performance) levels need to be established for almost all measures. The first target level is the minimum acceptable level. This may be developed through operational requirements and guidelines, or perhaps even through benchmarking or industry standards. Anything below this level would be considered unacceptable. Another target could be best practice, which may be above average for the industry or a measure that is found only in best-practice organizations. Finally, targets can be set that represent stretch goals, which only an exceptional performance will deliver. These stretch goals are the measures that truly build excellence in organizations and high-performing groups, exceeding what best practice normally requires.

The typical approach is to set the levels at one of the three targets and take action whenever one of the measures falls below one of the targets, or take action when it is necessary to stay at a desired level. For example, in one organization, action is taken to move a measure to best practice. When best practice is reached, preventive action is needed to keep it at that level. Other kinds of action are needed to move it to a stretch-goal level of performance.

Monitor the Data

Scorecard data can be monitored in a variety of ways depending on the desires of the executive team and the feasibility of presentation. The old way is to send detailed paper-based reports to executives for review and analysis. Brief reports are better; scorecards are much better. In some cases, data are posted on a Web site where an executive can monitor it at will. The Web sites have drill down capability to get more detail about a particular measure and its status including trends, forecast, benchmarking comparisons, and so on.

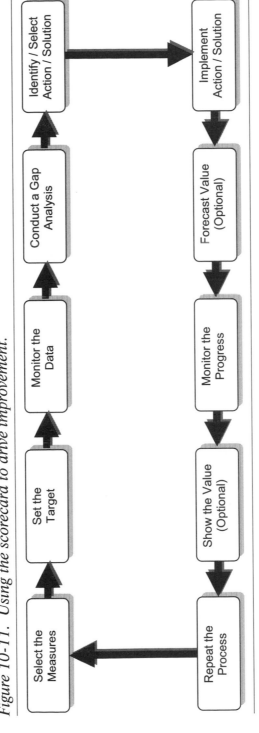

Figure 10-11. Using the scorecard to drive improvement.

Executives may receive e-mail reports highlighting particular measures, comparing those to target levels, goals, benchmarking data, or other important comparisons. These are sent with routine operational and financial data for the executive.

Still other organizations have color-coded reports where various colors represent different issues. For example, measures that are not doing so well are colored red; those that are considered to be exceptional and may even be a stretch goal are shown in green. These allow for quick review and often look like scorecards so executives can quickly see that things are okay or that there are signs of trouble.

Conduct a Gap Analysis

Perhaps one of the most difficult, yet critical, issues is to determine what is causing a gap in a specific measure. If a current measure is less than the desired target, this should be cause for concern. The challenge is to determine the cause of the gap so that appropriate, remedial actions can be taken. Collecting the appropriate data to understand the cause is important. Some causes may be obvious; others may be elusive. In some situations, both the problem and solution are equally apparent. For example, if the profile of new employees differs from the desired profile in terms of ethnic diversity and other requirements, the obvious solution is to change recruiting strategies to ensure that the proper mix is achieved. In other situations, such as an excessive termination rate for a key job group, the causes may not be obvious and a variety of diagnostic tools may be necessary to uncover the exact cause. While several diagnostic processes are available, table 10-3 shows an initial list of tools for this type of analysis.

Identify/Select Action/Solution

The HR staff is sometimes creative with their approach to the gap analysis, and this results in dozens of solutions that create unintended confusion. While

Table 10-3. Tools to analyze gaps.

Demographic analysis	Nominal group technique
Diagnostic instruments	Brainstorming
Focus groups	Cause-and-effect diagram
Probing interviews	Force-field analysis
Employee surveys	Mind mapping
Exit interviews and surveys	Affinity diagrams
	. . . and the list continues

there are specific actions to improve the situation, the challenge is to select the most feasible solution for the organization. This subject is beyond the scope of this book, but a variety of solutions are available. At this stage of analysis, it is helpful to ensure that a range of possibilities is identified and a proper one is selected.

Implement Action/Solution

This step goes hand in hand with the previous one. After the appropriate action or solution is selected, it must be implemented over a predetermined time period to tackle the problem. When attempting to implement the solution, it is important to consider resources, planning, data collection, and reporting. This may be as simple as making a minor adjustment in hiring practices or changing a communication or employee benefit, it may be as difficult as improving the scores on engagement surveys or solving a serious problem with absenteeism in the call centers.

Forecast the Value

An optional step is to forecast the value of the solution or action, including the impact and ROI. This forecast allows the team to establish priorities, work with a minimum number of solutions and actions, and focus on the solutions for the greatest forecasted return on investment. Forecasting can be difficult, challenging, and even risky. As much data as possible must be accumulated to verify the estimate and build credibility for the process. This step should be reserved only for those solutions that are considered expensive, time consuming, highly visible, or, perhaps, even controversial. Ideally, the forecast should contain an expected return on investment value. This is perhaps one of the most difficult parts of the process and is described in other publications.[11]

Monitor the Progress

Because the gap analysis is conducted only with those areas where the measures are below the target, it may be useful to outline the progress made in these areas. Progress reporting can either be conducted along with the scorecard report or in a report by itself. A progress-in-action report is often generated to complement the human capital scorecard. In Web-based human capital scorecards, actions and their progress are detailed when the executive clicks on a particular measure. The detailed information indicates what, if any, actions are in progress; the status of those actions; the estimated completion date, and if applicable, the forecasted value from the project.

Show the Value

Another optional step is the actual calculation of the impact of the solution to close the gap. This step is often skipped because it can be difficult and time consuming. However, if the solution is very expensive, has a high profile, involves a large number of employees, and perhaps is controversial, it may be beneficial to show the value of the solution. This brings the ROI methodology, described in chapters 5 and 8, into use to measure the payoff of a particular human capital project. In this context, the project or program is designed to change the measure that is out of alignment.

Repeat the Process

The process should be repeated, making any necessary adjustments in the measures, adjusting targets, monitoring the data, and following the other steps. The improvement process is continuous—the scorecard provides the data and the challenge is to manage it in a proactive way that continues to improve the status, capability, and success of human capital.

SUMMARY

This chapter focused on building an appropriate measurement and reporting system for the human capital function. Although the report may be called a scorecard, dashboard, metric report, human capital monitor, or benchmarking report, the term *scorecard* is used because of interest in the concept and term. The various issues involved in developing this scorecard were covered, along with nine options for format and content. The scorecard must be developed to meet the needs of the organization and must be driven by the senior executive team with the human resources staff providing the input, coordination, and implementation. Executive involvement is critical to success and is necessary for improvements in human capital. The chapter concluded with a recommended process to use the scorecard and drive performance improvement. The scorecard will be meaningless if it is not used in a dynamic, routine way to understand problems, develop solutions, implement those solutions, and monitor progress throughout the cycle.

NOTES

1   *CLC Metrics: Operationalizing Integrated Human Capital Management: Measurement Tools and Techniques* (Washington, D.C.: Corporate Leadership Council, 2004).

2   Brett Walsh, *Measuring Human Capital Value* (London: Deloitte & Touche, 2002).

3   Ibid.

4   Haig R. Nalbantian, Richard A. Guzzo, Dave Kieffer, and Jay Doherty, *Play to Your Strengths: Managing Your Internal Labor Markets for Lasting Competitive Advantage* (New York: McGraw-Hill, 2004).

5   Robert S. Kaplan and David P. Norton, *The Balanced Scorecard: Translating Strategy into Action* (Boston: Harvard Business School Press, 1996).

6   *The American Heritage Dictionary of the English Language,* 3rd ed. (Boston: Houghton Mifflin Company, 1992), p. 1619.

7   Stephen Bates, "Linking People Measures to Strategy," *Research Report R-1342-03-RR* (New York: The Conference Board, 2003).

8   Robert S. Kaplan and David P. Norton, *The Balanced Scorecard: Translating Strategy into Action* (Boston: Harvard Business School Press, 1996).

9   Andrew Mayo, *Measuring Human Capital: Good Practice Guideline* (London: The Institute of Chartered Accountants, June 2003).

10   *CLC Metrics: Operationalizing Integrated Human Capital Management: Measurement Tools and Techniques* (Washington, D.C.: Corporate Leadership Council, 2004).

11   Jack J. Phillips, Ron D. Stone, and Patti P. Phillips, *The Human Resources Scorecard: Measuring Return on Investment* (Woburn, Mass.: Butterworth-Heinemann, 2001).

CHAPTER 11

Executive Commitment
and Support

Lack of support for HR is a serious and universal problem. An absence of strong executive and management support will inhibit an otherwise successful human capital investment. Indeed, most human capital improvement projects have little chance of being effective without such support. The problem can be serious enough in some organizations to cause the ultimate demise of the HR function. This chapter explores commitment and support issues, detailing how both can be increased. Three key strategies are explored in more detail: building partnerships, creating a special workshop for managers, and tying bonus plans to human capital measures. The focus of this chapter is on both executives, who must provide commitment and support, and the human resources staff, who must convince managers and senior executives that they show support.

THE MANAGEMENT SUPPORT DILEMMA

As a preliminary step to improve support, it is helpful to assess the current level of support from the management group. An excellent tool for this assessment is presented in appendix A. It addresses twenty important issues that collectively measure the degree of management support for the HR function. The target group for assessment may be any management group (division, plant, corporate, or regional—the middle- or senior-level management). High scores on this instrument indicate a strong, supportive environment needing few additional efforts. Low scores indicate serious problems, signaling a need for actions to improve support. An analysis of scores is included at the end of the appendix.

Why Executives Fail to Support Human Resources

Executives and managers are reluctant to support HR for a variety of reasons. Some are valid, while others are based on misunderstandings about HR and its impact in the organization. An analysis of the current level of support will usually reveal the most common problems, which are outlined below.

❑ *No Results.* Managers are not convinced that HR programs and projects add value in terms they understand and appreciate. They do not see HR programs producing results in ways to help them reach their objectives. Managers are rarely asked, "Is this HR program working for you?" or "Is HR adding value to your department?" Human resources professionals deserve much of the blame for this situation. HR team members routinely judge the effectiveness of their function by the reactions of those engaged in the HR initiative. Managers need more evidence, such as impact and ROI data, that shows HR practices add value.

❑ *No Input.* Unfortunately, HR is often perceived as dictatorial rather than as collaborative. Managers do not support HR because they are not offered an opportunity for input into the process. They are not asked for their views on the content or focus of a program during the initial analysis or program formulation. They are rarely provided objectives that link HR to job-performance improvements or business results. Without input, managers will not develop the ownership for HR and will continue to resist its efforts.

❑ *Too Costly.* Managers perceive HR as a double cost. The direct cost for some HR programs is ultimately taken from the operating profits and charged to their department. They also see some HR programs as taking employees away from their jobs, resulting in a loss of productivity. They experience a personal cost of finding ways to get the job done while an employee is involved in the program. They must rearrange work schedules to meet deadlines, find new ways to meet service requirements, redistribute the workload, or secure a replacement. Sometimes, the method of recording time when employees are involved in HR programs reinforces this concept, since many situations result in the time being labeled "nonproductive." Unfortunately, this sends an important and sometimes negative message throughout the organization. Because the perception that HR programs represent double costs is unfounded, managers have to be shown the true cost of HR programs, they have to be persuaded of the value of HR. Changing their perceptions, however, is challenging.

❑ *No Relevance.* Managers have little reason to believe that HR programs have relevance or will help their department or work unit. They see little resemblance to work-related issues. They hear about HR activities that are unrelated to current challenges faced by the team. Managers have many requests and demands for resources. They quickly eliminate the unnecessary frills and activities. No relevance equals no need, which equals no priority and eventually leads to no support.

❑ *No Involvement.* Managers do not support HR because they are not actively involved in the process in any meaningful way. Even in some of the best organizations, the manager's role is severely restricted or limited, sometimes by design and other times by default. To build respect for the HR function, managers should have some type of active involvement in the process, ranging from reinforcing HR programs to coordinating or managing part of a program.

❑ *No Time.* Managers do not have time to support formal HR programs. They are very busy with increasing demands on their time. When establishing daily priorities, the specific actions necessary to show support for HR do not make their top priority list. Consequently, nothing happens. Managers often perceive that requests for increased support will require additional time. (In reality, many supportive actions do not require much time; it's often a matter of perception.)

❑ *Lack of Preparation.* Sometimes managers do not have the skills necessary to support HR programs. Although they may be willing to offer support, managers may not know how to provide feedback, respond to issues, guide their employees through specific problems, or help achieve results with HR programs. Specific skills are needed to provide effective reinforcement and support, just as specific skills are required for planning, budgeting, delegating, and negotiating.

❑ *Lack of Knowledge About Human Resources.* Managers are not always aware of the nature and scope of HR. They may understand that it is a legitimate function necessary to attract, develop, and maintain employees with the specific skills and knowledge required for the job. Beyond that, they are not fully aware of what HR provides for the organization. They do not fully understand the different steps involved from needs assessment to development, to implementation, and to evaluation. They see bits and pieces of the process but may not know how the process is integrated to create an effective human capital program. It is difficult for managers to support a process they do not fully understand.

❑ *No Requirements.* Finally, managers do not support HR because they are not sure what they are supposed to do. If the only request from the HR staff is to provide information or allow employees to be involved in a program, that is all they will do. The HR staff usually creates this problem because they do not "make the call"; they do not communicate directly with the operating managers to let them know what is needed and what managers must do to make the HR process work.

Collectively, these reasons for nonsupport equate to challenges for HR departments and represent opportunities for managers. If the issues are not addressed in an effective way, management support will not exist, human capital program implementation will be diminished, and consequently, results will be severely limited or nonexistent.

IMPROVING COMMITMENT AND SUPPORT

Definitions

Management's actions and perceptions significantly affect the impact and success of HR programs. This influence is critical in the workplace—beyond program development and implementation. Although HR staff members may have little direct control over some of these factors, they can exert a tremendous amount of influence on them. Table 11-1 lists the key actions needed with the management team.

Table 11-1. Comparison of key management actions.

Management Action	Target Group	Scope	Payoff
Management Commitment	Top Executives	All Programs	Very High
Management Support	Middle Managers, First-Level Supervisors	Most Programs	High
Management Reinforcement	First-Level Managers	Specific Programs	Moderate
Management Involvement	All Levels of Managers	Specific Programs	Moderate

Several of the terms in this table need additional explanation. *Management commitment, management support, management involvement, and management reinforcement* are overlapping terms and are sometimes confusing.
Management commitment usually refers to the top-management group and
includes its pledge or promise to allocate resources and support to the HR
effort. *Management support* refers to the actions of the entire management
group, which reflect their attitude toward HR programs and HR staff.

The major emphasis is on middle- and first-line management. Their supportive actions can have a tremendous impact on the success of programs.
Management involvement refers to the extent to which executives and managers are actively engaged in the HR process in addition to participating in programs. Because *management commitment, support,* and *involvement* have
similar meanings, they are often used interchangeably.

Management reinforcement refers to actions designed to reward or encourage a desired behavior. The goal is to increase the probability of the behavior change linked to an HR program.

Increasing Commitment

Commitment is necessary to secure the resources for a viable HR effort. A
self-assessment of current CEO commitment is presented in appendix B. This
exercise lists a variety of activities that reflect the degree of commitment from
top executives, particularly the CEO. Although the exercise is labeled CEO
commitment, it is also appropriate for the senior executive group. It contains
twenty-five issues important to the success of human capital management.
The issues define the extent of involvement in the process, the support provided to HR and human capital projects, and the current level of involvement
in particular programs, solutions, and human capital initiatives. It is recommended that each top executive participate in this exercise to reflect on the
current status of commitment and support for the human capital processes in
the organization. Table 11-2 shows the ten general areas of emphasis for
strong top-management commitment to human resources. These ten areas
need little additional explanation and are necessary for a successful HR effort.

Now for the big question: How can top-management's commitment increase? The amount of commitment varies with the size or nature of the organization. Quite often the extent of commitment is fixed in the organization
before the HR manager becomes involved with the function. It usually depends on how the function evolved, the top-management group's attitude and
philosophy toward HR, and how the function is administered. The key to the

Table 11-2. Example of executive commitment for human capital management.

The Ten Commitments for Executives

For strong commitment to human capital management, executives should:
1. Develop or approve a mission for human capital management.
2. Allocate the necessary funds for successful HR programs.
3. Encourage employees to participate in HR programs.
4. Become actively involved in HR programs and require others to do the same.
5. Support the HR efforts and ask other managers to do the same.
6. Position the HR function in a visible and high-level place on the organization chart.
7. Require that each HR program be evaluated in some way.
8. Insist that HR programs be cost effective and require supporting data.
9. Set an example for self-development, leadership, and continuous learning.
10. Create an atmosphere of open communication with the HR manager.

question of increasing commitment lies in the results. The commitment of top management usually increases when programs obtain desired results. As figure 11-1 illustrates, this is a vicious cycle because commitment is necessary to build effective HR programs from which results can be obtained. And when results are obtained, commitment increases. Nothing is more convincing to a group of top executives than programs with measurable results they can understand. When a program is proposed, additional funding may be based solely on the results the program is expected to produce.

In addition to providing results, several actions or strategies can help increase commitment. Commitment is increased when managers are actively involved in HR programs and projects. This involvement, which can occur in almost every phase of the HR process, reflects a strong cooperative management effort to use human resources effectively.

A highly professional and competent HR staff can help improve commitment. While the achievement of excellence is the goal of many professional groups, it should be a mandate for the HR department. The HR staff must be perceived as professional in all actions including welcoming criticism, adjusting to the changing needs of the organization, maintaining productive relationships with other staff, and setting an example for others to follow.

Top executives are more inclined to provide additional funds to an HR staff that understands the business and are willing to help the business reach its goals. A comprehensive knowledge of the organization, including opera-

Figure 11-1. The results commitment cycle.

tions and finance, is a key ingredient in building respect and credibility with the management group.

The HR department must communicate needs to top management and help them to understand that HR is an integral part of the organization. When top management understands the results-based process, they will usually respond with additional commitment.

The senior HR executive should be in a visible role, preferably alongside key executives, helping to solve operational problems and address strategic issues. Top executives want staff members who are involved, with a hands-on philosophy and a desire to be "where the action is." Top management will usually support those who meet this challenge.

The HR department should avoid being narrowly focused. Human resources programs should not be confined to those mandated by regulations, laws, or organizational necessities. The HR staff must be perceived as problem solvers or performance enhancers. A progressive HR staff should be versatile, flexible, and resourceful, and utilized in a variety of situations to help make a contribution to organizational success.

Finally, the HR department must have a practical approach to the design, development, and implementation of new human capital projects. An approach that focuses on theories and philosophical ideas may be perceived as not contributing to the organization.

Increasing Management Support

Middle- and first-level managers are important to HR program success. Before discussing the techniques to improve support for programs, it is appropriate to present the concept of ideal management support. Ideal support occurs when a manager reacts in the following ways to an HR program:

❑ Volunteers personal services or resources to assist with HR programs
❑ Encourages employees to participate in programs
❑ Outlines expectations to direct reports about the HR program, detailing the objectives of the program
❑ Reinforces the HR program in a variety of ways
❑ Helps determine the results achieved from the HR program
❑ Recognizes employees who participate in, or achieve success with, the HR program
❑ Provides unsolicited positive comments about the success of HR programs

This level of support for a program represents utopia for the HR staff. Support is necessary before and after the program is implemented. Effective actions prior to a program can significantly influence the success of the program.

The degree to which managers support programs is based on the value they place on human capital and the success of specific HR programs. To improve management support, the HR staff must routinely show the results achieved from programs, help managers assume more responsibility for HR, explore ways to increase the level of involvement, and teach them about the value of human capital. One key strategy for accomplishing this is a special workshop for managers, described later in this chapter.

Improving Reinforcement

The importance of management reinforcement as an integral part of the HR process cannot be overstated. Too often participants—the key stakeholders involved in programs—have roadblocks to utilizing an HR program successfully. Faced with these obstacles, even some of the best participants fail to be involved with or make the program succeed. In fact, regardless of how well the program is designed, unless it is reinforced, most of the effectiveness is lost. This reinforcement should come from the immediate manager of the participant.

The reason for this problem lies in the nature of HR programs. When faced with a new process, participants experience a frustrating period of resistance. The results are not generated and this period is difficult for sponsors. Without proper reinforcement participants may abandon the program. However, the individuals who persist are successful and often rewarded for their success.

A participant's immediate manager is the primary focus for reinforcement efforts. The manager can exert influence on the participant's behavior by providing reinforcement in the following ways:

❑ Helping the participant diagnose problems to determine if the program is needed
❑ Discussing possible alternatives for handling specific situations, acting as a coach
❑ Encouraging the participant to use the HR program
❑ Serving as a role model for the proper utilization of the program
❑ Giving positive rewards to the participant when the program is successfully implemented

Each of these activities reinforces the objectives of the HR program. In some organizations, managers are required to provide this level of reinforcement. Job expectations and job descriptions are adjusted to reflect reinforcement processes. In other organizations, reinforcement is encouraged and supported from the top executives. Managers learn how to provide reinforcement in special workshops, such as the one described later in the chapter.

Improving Management Involvement

Management involvement in human resources is not new. Organizations have practiced it successfully for many years. Management should be involved in most of the key decisions of the HR department. Although almost as many opportunities exist for management's involvement in HR as there are steps in an HR cycle, management input and active participation generally only occur in the key steps and most significant programs. The primary vehicles for obtaining management involvement are presented here.

❑ *Advisory Committees.* Many organizations develop committees to enhance key management involvement in the HR process. These committees, which act in an advisory capacity to the department, may have other names, such as councils or people systems boards. As

shown in table 11-3, committees can be developed for individual programs, specific functions, or multiple functions.

❑ *HR Task Forces.* Another potential area for management involvement
is a task force. The task force consists of a group of employees, usually management, who are charged with the responsibility for developing an HR program. Task forces are particularly useful for
programs beyond the scope of HR staff capability. Also, a task force
can considerably reduce the time required to develop a new HR program. At Vulcan Materials Company, the nation's leading producer
of construction aggregates, a group of sales managers participated in
the design of a new variable pay program for the sales team. This task
force was charged with the design and implementation of the new
program.

❑ *Managers as Experts.* Managers may provide expertise for program
design, development, or implementation. Subject matter experts
(SMEs) provide a valuable and necessary service while developing
attachment to the program. At Whirlpool, a manufacturer of major
appliances, the traditional assembly line was replaced with a work
cell arrangement. The expertise of the managers was critical to the
program's design and ultimate success. At Nextel Communications,
a wireless telecommunications company, managers participated in a
diversity awareness program designed for all employees. This participation was helpful to achieve success with the program.

❑ *Managers as Participants.* Managerial participation can range from
participating in an HR program to auditing a portion of a program
designed for their immediate employees. However, participation may

Table 11-3. Types of committees.

Responsible for:	Examples:
Individual Program	All-Inclusive Workplace Committee Account Executives' Development Committee New Employee Orientation Committee Employee Feedback Committee
Specific Function	Customer Service Committee Technical Staffing Committee Intellectual Property Committee Safety and Compliance Committee
Multi-functions	Management Development Committee Employee Benefits Committee Employer of Choice Committee Employee Retention Committee

not be feasible for all types of programs, such as specialized programs designed for only nonmanagement employees.

❑ *Program Leaders.* A powerful way to enhance management involvement is to use them in HR program leadership roles. Facilitation, coordination, and leadership build ownership. The business press is laced with examples of executive involvement in HR programs. Some executives, for example, ensure that diversity initiatives are fully implemented or that employee retention is appropriately addressed. The former CEO of General Electric, Jack Welch, made an effort to devote a specific number of days each month at GE's Management Institute. His involvement went beyond the welcome, overview, and congratulation presentation to include actually teaching part of the process. Bill Gates, Microsoft's chairman, gets involved in the executive portion of the new employee orientation. The important part is that involvement as a leader of a particular process, program, or initiative provides visibility and role modeling that is necessary to enhance overall commitment in any organization.

❑ *Involving Managers in Human Capital Measurement.* The evaluation of programs is another area in which managers can be involved. Although management is sometimes involved in assessing the ultimate outcome of HR programs, this process focuses directly on measurement at different times. Several ways in which managers may be involved in HR evaluation are to:

❑ Invite managers to participate in focus groups about HR program success.
❑ Ask managers to collect application and impact data.
❑ Review program success data with managers.
❑ Ask managers to assist with the interpretation of data.
❑ Convene managers to share overall results.
❑ Ask managers to communicate data, including ROI information.

Involving managers, and showing them how HR evaluation can work, increases commitment and support for HR and evaluation.

❑ *New Roles for Managers.* The approaches described above are primary ways to involve managers in HR programs when the focus is on achieving results. Other ways are available including changes in the role or job description for HR managers. Some organizations define new HR roles for managers in an organization. In these roles, managers:

❏ Coordinate/organize HR programs.
❏ Participate in the assessment of original need for the HR program.
❏ Facilitate HR programs and processes.
❏ Serve as subject-matter experts in the design and development of HR programs.
❏ Reinforce HR programs and their applications.
❏ Evaluate HR programs at the application and impact level.
❏ Drive actions for improvement.

Ideally, managers should assume these roles, and the HR staff should seek input and communicate results frequently.[1]

Collectively, these actions will increase support and commitment, as well as enhance input from each HR role. Table 11-4 shows the opportunities for management involvement in the various steps of the HR program design, development, implementation, and evaluation cycle. The remainder of this book describes the three most critical strategies for improving support and commitment. Other strategies are available in other resources.[2]

KEY STRATEGY: DEVELOPING PARTNERSHIPS WITH MANAGERS

Building a partnership with key managers is one of the most powerful ways to increase management involvement and support. A partnership relationship can take on several different formats and descriptions. In some organizations, the relationship is informal, loosely defined, and ill-structured. By design,

Table 11-4. Manager involvement opportunities.

Steps in the HR Results-Based Process	Opportunity for Manager Involvement	Most Appropriate Strategy
Conduct Analysis	High	Task Force
Development Measurement/ Evaluation System	Moderate	Advisory Committee
Establish Program Objectives	High	Advisory Committee
Develop HR Program	Moderate	Task Force
Implement HR Program	High	Program Leader
Monitor HR Costs	Low	Expert Input
Collect/Analyze Data	Moderate	Expert Input
Interpret Data/Draw Conclusions	High	Expert Input
Communicate Results	Moderate	Manager as Participant

these organizations do not want to develop the relationship to a formal level but continue to refine it informally. In other organizations, the process is formalized to the extent that specific activities are planned with targeted individuals, all for the purpose of improving relationships. The quality of the relationship is discussed and assessments are typically taken to gauge progress. Still, in other situations, the process is very formal, where individuals are discretely identified for relationship improvement and a written plan is developed for each individual. Sometimes a contract is developed with a particular manager. Assessments are routinely taken, and progress is reported formally. Although these three levels of formality are distinct, an HR department can move through all these different levels as the partnering process matures and achieves success.

For relationship building to be effective, the HR staff must take the initiative to organize, plan, and measure the progress. The staff must want to develop the relationship. Rarely will key managers approach the HR staff to nurture these relationships. In some organizations, key managers do not want to develop relationships because of the concern about the time it may take to work through these issues. They may see no need for the relationship and may consider it a waste of time. This requires the HR staff to properly assess the situation, plan the strategies, and take appropriate actions, routinely and consistently, to ensure that the process is working.

For this process to be effective, the executive/manager responsible for HR must take the lead and involve others as appropriate and necessary. The direction must come from the top. Although this responsibility cannot be delegated, it can involve many other members of the HR staff, if not all. Two critical issues are involved: the first, and perhaps most important, deals with the specific steps necessary to develop a partner relationship; second, a set of principles must be followed when building and nurturing the relationship.[3]

Steps to Develop a Partner Relationship

Several steps are suggested to develop an effective partnership:

❑ *Assess the current status of partnership relationships.* The first course of action is to determine the current condition. Table 11-5 shows some of the key issues involved in determining current status. It is recommended that this instrument be completed by key HR staff members to determine present partnering status and use it to plan specific issues and activities. In essence, this instrument provides information for planning and provides an opportunity to determine progress in the future. A total score of twenty or less on the table 11-5 assessment indicates that a partnership is nonexistent and the potential for partnership development is weak. If the score is in the twenty-one to fifty range, several problems exist with the partnership or anticipated partnership. Some progress can be made, but it will be difficult. If the score falls in the fifty-one to sixty range, the partnership is working effectively or has great potential for working. A score of sixty-one or better reflects an outstanding partnership relationship or a great potential for one. By providing the appropriate up-front attention, it may be possible to assess the potential before spending a significant amount of time on the relationship.

❑ *Identify key individuals for a partnership relationship.* Building a partnership works best when it clearly focuses on a few individuals. Too many individual targets could dilute the effort.

❑ *Learn the business.* An effective partnership relationship cannot be developed unless the HR staff member understands the operational and strategic issues of the organization. It is absolutely essential for this understanding to be developed!

❑ *Consider a written plan.* The process is often more focused when it is written with specific details for each manager. A written plan enhances commitment.

❑ *Offer assistance to solve problems.* The HR staff supports managers and provides assistance to solve, or prevent, problems. Managers are usually seeking help with problems.

❑ *Show results of programs.* When results are achieved, quick communication with partners is important to demonstrate to them how a program achieved success. In addition, the results achieved from other programs, where partners may not be directly involved, should be communicated to these key managers.

❑ *Publicize partners' accomplishments and successes.* At every opportunity, give proper credit to the accomplishments of the partner. The HR staff should not take credit for successes.

❑ *Ask the partner to review the needs analysis.* Whenever a needs analysis is requested or undertaken as part of the development of a new HR program, the partner should review the information and confirm, or add to, the analysis. This, of course, assumes the partner is knowledgeable about the issues in the analysis.

❑ *Have the partner serve on an advisory committee.* A helpful approach to provide guidance and direction to the HR staff or a particular pro-

Table 11-5. Assessment of partnership.

Assessment of Partnership Potential for Success

Scale
1 = strongly disagree
2 = disagree
3 = neither agree nor disagree
4 = agree
5 = strongly agree

	Circle One
1. Choice of partners (Is this a strategically valuable partner for HR?)	1 2 3 4 5
2. Willingness to become a partner (Does this party desire to become your partner?)	1 2 3 4 5
3. Trust (Is there an adequate level of trust or the possibility of achieving it?)	1 2 3 4 5
4. Character and ethics (Does this partner operate in an ethical manner?)	1 2 3 4 5
5. Strategic intent (Are the long-term aspirations of both partners compatible?)	1 2 3 4 5
6. Culture fit (Do the partners come from compatible cultures?)	1 2 3 4 5
7. Common goals and interests (Are the goals and interests of the partners shared fairly equally?)	1 2 3 4 5
8. Information sharing (Can both partners freely share information?)	1 2 3 4 5
9. Risks shared fairly (Are the risks to both partners fairly equal?)	1 2 3 4 5
10. Rewards shared fairly (Are the rewards and potential gains for both partners fairly equal?)	1 2 3 4 5
11. Resources adequately matched (Do both partners have adequate resources to support the relationship?)	1 2 3 4 5
12. Duration mutually agreed upon as long term (Do the partners agree on a long-term partnership?)	1 2 3 4 5
13. Commitment to partnership by both (Is there a fairly broad level of commitment by both partners?)	1 2 3 4 5
14. Value given and received (Do both partners have similar perceptions of the value of what the other brings to the partnership?)	1 2 3 4 5
15. Rules, policies, and measures (Do these key issues reinforce the desired partnership behavior?)	1 2 3 4 5

Total Score: _____

Source: Adapted from John L. Mariotti, *The Power of Partnership* (Cambridge: Blackwell Publishers, 1996).

gram is to establish an advisory committee. If appropriate and feasible, the partner should be invited to serve on the committee.

❑ *Shift responsibility to partner.* Although the success of HR programs rests with stakeholders who have major responsibilities, the primary responsibility for HR must lie with the management group. When it is appropriate and feasible, some responsibility should be transferred to the partner, if the partner is prepared for the responsibility.

❑ *Invite input from the partner about key plans and programs.* Routinely, partners should be asked to provide information on issues such as analysis, program design, use of new technology, program roll out, and follow-up evaluation.

❑ *Ask partner to review program objectives, content, and implementation.* As a routine activity, these managers should review objectives, content, and planned implementation for each new program or major redesign.

❑ *Invite partner to coordinate a program or portion of a program.* If appropriate, the partner should be asked to help organize, coordinate, or implement a part of a program. It is important to do this without "dumping" work on the partner, to be sensitive to the partner's other tasks and priorities.

❑ *Review progress and replan strategy.* Periodically the partnership process should be reviewed to check progress, adjust, and replan the strategy. Continuous process improvement should be the focus.

Key Principles

As the specific steps listed above are undertaken, it is important to preserve the nature and quality of the relationship with a partner. Several essential principles serve as an operating framework to develop, nurture, and refine this critical relationship. Table 11-6 lists key principles that should be integrated into each step.

KEY STRATEGY:
MANAGER WORKSHOP ON HUMAN CAPITAL MANAGEMENT

Another effective approach to secure increased management involvement and support for human resources is to conduct a workshop for managers. Varying in duration from one-half day to two days, this practical workshop, "The Manager's Role in Human Capital Management," shapes critical skills and alters perceptions about human capital. Managers leave the workshop with an

Table 11-6. Key principles when developing a partnership relationship.

Partnering Principles

1. Be patient and persistent throughout the process.
2. Follow a win-win philosophy for both parties.
3. Confront problems and conflicts quickly.
4. Share information regularly and purposefully.
5. Always be honest and display the utmost integrity in all the transactions.
6. Maintain high standards of professionalism in each interaction.
7. Give credit and recognition to the partner routinely.
8. Take every opportunity to explain, inform, and educate.
9. Involve partners in as many activities as appropriate and feasible.
10. Eventually, ensure that a balance of power and influence is realized between the two parties.

improved perception of the impact of human capital and a clearer understanding of their roles in the HR programs. More important, they often have a renewed commitment to make HR work in their organization. This is the most critical workshop offered by the human resource staff.

Because of the importance of this topic in management development, this workshop should be required for all managers unless they have previously demonstrated strong support for the HR function. It is essential for senior executives to encourage and support this workshop and, in some cases, take an active role in conducting it. To tailor the workshop to specific organizational needs, a brief needs assessment may be necessary to determine the specific focus and areas of emphasis in the workshop.

Workshop Issues

While the target audience for this workshop is usually middle-level managers, the group may vary with different organizations. In some organizations, the target may be first-level managers; in others, the target may be second-level managers. Three important questions help determine the proper audience:

1. Which group has the most direct influence on the HR function?
2. Which management group is causing serious problems with its lack of support?
3. Which group must understand more about human capital so they can influence HR program success?

The answers to these questions often point to the middle-level managers.

Ideally, this workshop should be conducted early in the management development process before nonsupportive habits are developed. When implementation is planned throughout the organization, it is best to start with higher-level managers and work down in the organization. If possible, a version of the program should be part of a traditional management training program provided to new team leaders when they are promoted into managerial positions.

Checklists, exercises, case studies, and skill practices are all helpful in this workshop to illustrate and reinforce concepts. As with any management training program, active involvement is essential. Case studies help illustrate the problems of lack of support for HR. The material used in this workshop must be practical and easy to understand by the management group. It must be free of typical HR jargon. It should be targeted to the specific needs of managers and presented from the perspective of the manager. "Nice to know" topics should be avoided.

Because of its importance, the most effective facilitators, who have credibility with the management team, must conduct this program. Sometimes external consultants, who enjoy an excellent reputation in the HR field, are used in the workshop.

Workshop Content

The program can be developed in separate modules focusing on a particular issue related to support and commitment (or lack of it). Five modules are recommended.

1. *The Importance of Human Capital.* After completing this module, managers should perceive human capital management as a critical issue in the organization and be able to describe how specific HR programs and projects contribute to strategic and operational objectives. With this module, managers become convinced that HR is a mainstream responsibility that is gaining in importance and influence in the organization. Data from the organization is presented to show the full scope of human capital. The strategy or strategies used to set the investment level is explained following the options in part one of this book. Tangible evidence of top management commitment is presented in a form of memos, directives, and policies signed by the CEO or other appropriate top executives. The presence of top executives is better.

2. *The Impact of Human Capital Programs.* After completing this module, managers will be able to understand the impact of human capital from a top-level view (macro) and identify the steps to measure the impact of specific HR programs on important output variables (micro). Reports and studies are presented, showing the impact of HR programs, using measures such as productivity, quality, cost, cycle times, and customer satisfaction. If internal reports are not available, success stories or case studies from other organizations can be utilized. This module is essentially a summary of chapters 6 and 7, tailored to the organization with customized data.

3. *Humans Resources Programs and Processes.* After completing this module, managers should be able to describe the HR function in their organization and understand each critical step of the HR cycle. Managers usually will not support activities or processes that they do not fully understand. During this module, managers are made aware of the effort that goes into developing an HR program and their role in each step of the process. A short case, illustrating all the steps, is usually included in this module.

4. *Responsibility for Human Resources.* After completing this module, managers should be able to list their specific responsibilities for human resources. Defining who is responsible for formal HR programs is important to the success of the process. The human capital scorecard, developed in chapter 10, is presented and discussed, highlighting manager responsibilities for specific measures. Managers see how they can influence HR program results and the degree of responsibility they must assume in the future. A case study is utilized to illustrate the consequences when responsibilities are neglected or when there is failure to follow-up by managers.

An exercise in this module reveals the perceptions of support offered by managers when compared to the level of support perceived by their direct reports. Data from a follow-up study is presented to show the profile of manager behavior after a participant is involved in a formal HR program. The same profile of behavior is collected from the managers and compared to the input from participants. Table 11-7 shows the two sets of actual data from a follow-up on a leadership development program at Nortel Networks designed for first-level team leaders (participants). There is a marked difference in manager behavior as perceived by the participant who was involved in the program and the manager's own perception of actual support

Table 11-7. The contrast of perceptions of management support for leadership development.

Participant responses concerning manager support:

My manager told me to forget what I've learned; it doesn't work here	12%
My manager said to be very careful about using the material; it may not work here	22%
My manager said nothing	53%
My manager said that I should (could) try to use what I've learned	8%
My manager said that he/she expects me to use this material	5%
My manager coached and supported me through the application of the material	0%

Manager responses concerning his/her support:

I told him/her to forget what was learned; it won't work here	0%
I told him/her to be very careful about using the material; it may not work here	0%
I said nothing	4%
I told him/her to try (consider trying) to use what was learned	11%
I said that I expected him/her to use the material	36%
I coached and supported him/her through the application of the material	49%

provided. These differences are typical. This exercise emphasizes several key points:

❑ Manager support is not as effective and helpful as managers typically perceive it to be.
❑ Participants usually perceive manager support as being ineffective.
❑ Management support is an extremely important issue in the success of HR programs.

5. *Active Involvement.* One of the most important ways to enhance manager support for HR is to get them actively involved in the process. After completing this module, managers will commit to one or more ways of active involvement in the future. Table 11-8 shows twelve ways that one company involved management. The information in the table was presented to managers in the workshop with a request for them to commit to at least one area of involvement. After these areas are fully explained and discussed, each manager is asked to select one or more ways in which he or she will be involved in HR in the future. A commitment to sign up for at least one involvement role is required. If used properly, these commitments are a rich source of input and assistance from the management group.

Table 11-8. Management involvement in human resources.

The following are areas for present and future involvement in the human resources education process. Please check your areas of planned involvement.

	In Your Area	Outside Your Area
Provide input on a needs analysis	☐	☐
Serve on an HR Advisory Committee	☐	☐
Provide input on a program design	☐	☐
Serve as a subject-matter expert	☐	☐
Serve on a task force to develop HR program	☐	☐
Volunteer to evaluate an HR program	☐	☐
Assist in the selection of an outsource supplier	☐	☐
Participate in a program designed for your staff	☐	☐
Provide reinforcement to your employees involved in an HR program	☐	☐
Coordinate an HR program	☐	☐
Assist in program evaluation or follow-up	☐	☐
Coordinate a portion of an HR program	☐	☐

Workshop Features

Although the workshop format and presentation may vary, here are some common variations:

- ❏ The program is held off-site to take participants away from job pressures and distractions. This can help them to focus directly on the workshop material without interruption.
- ❏ Prework is required. Having participants complete the survey in appendix A and read cases in advance can be helpful.
- ❏ Cross-functional groups are used so that participants see the perspectives of HR from different areas in the organization.
- ❏ The workshop is an excellent opportunity to present impact studies or other data that show the business results from HR.
- ❏ Reference materials are provided. Several books may be appropriate for the workshop and a reading list is usually provided. Although the books may not be read completely or even referenced regularly, managers feel some comfort that the material is there, if needed.

Top Management Participation

Top management should be involved in this workshop. However, it is the challenge of the senior human resources manager to convince top executives to support it. Three approaches should be considered:

1. Discuss and illustrate the consequences of inadequate management support for human capital. The statistics in wasted time and money are staggering.
2. Show how current support is lacking. A recent evaluation of an HR program will often reveal the barriers to successful implementation. Lack of management support is often the primary reason, which brings the issue close to home.
3. Demonstrate how money can be saved and results can be achieved by having managers more involved in the HR process.

The endorsement of the top management group is important. In some organizations, top managers attend the program to explore first hand what is involved and what they must do to make the workshop successful and improve their support for, and involvement with, human capital management. At a minimum, top management should support the program by signing memos describing the program or by approving policy statements for required participation.

Impact of the Workshop

The success from this workshop should appear in a variety of forms because many of the barriers to implementing successful HR programs are caused by a lack of management support. There should be increases in supportive actions, measured in follow-up surveys, where the extent and level of management support is collected. The individual manager commitments for active involvement are tangible evidence of success, since the involvement can be measured by the follow through on the preplanned actions. Also, participation in all HR programs should improve, where participation is voluntary. When managers fully understand the HR process and their role in it, they have a "renewed" determination to make it work. Manager perception toward HR should be more positive as measured on a postprogram assessment, using the same instrument as the preprogram assessment—appendix A.

KEY STRATEGY:
TYING BONUS PLANS WITH HUMAN CAPITAL MEASURES

The best way to get a manager's attention on an issue is to link compensation to it. Therefore, an effective third strategy is to link manager bonuses to human capital measures. While managers might not agree with the construction of the metrics or the measures as targets, managers will become more aware of the company's people goals. Survey data from the Conference Board suggests that putting human capital measures in bonus plans correlates with successful links between business strategies and certain people measures.[4] This is still a minority practice, with only 39 percent of firms rewarding managers systematically based on human capital measures, as shown in figure 11-2.

A primary difficulty in getting managers to buy-in to human capital measures is their relatively minor participation in the selection of measures, which is the situation at most companies. Few managers understand the measures well enough to improve on their own performance. However, if managers could negotiate how measures are set within their bonus plans, they might be more willing to accept them. The workshop described earlier and concrete action plans might help both generate greater acceptance among managers and give HR more confidence in the ability of managers to use the measures.

There is some reason to be optimistic. Only 15 percent of managers think that human capital measures in bonus plans make no difference in the way managers allocate human capital investments and manage their employees, as shown in figure 11-3.

Business leaders at American Express have long had a significant incentive to take people measures seriously. Up to 25 percent of their annual bonus depends on an employee-satisfaction level scored through the annual em-

Figure 11-2. Embedding metrics in bonus plans.

Are human capital measures included in bonus plans?

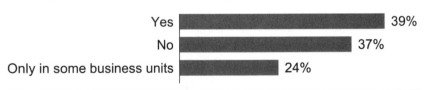

Source: Research Report R-1342-03-RR (New York: The Conference Board, 2003), p. 26.

Figure 11-3. Impact of human capital measures in bonus plans.

Will managers decide differently about human capital investments when people metrics are in their bonus plans?

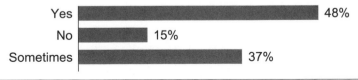

Source: Research Report R-1342-03-RR (New York: The Conference Board, 2003), p. 26.

ployee survey. Bonus scores were calculated using an algorithm that rewarded not only high overall scores, but also year-over-year improvement and lack of disparity between scores for males and females and majority and minority groups.[5]

These measures were refined when the algorithm was further developed to reward year-over-year improvements in units scoring in the bottom 10 percent of the distribution. In addition, the bonus weighting for the survey score was reduced to 15 percent. This was done to allow retention measures to be included at a 10 percent weighting. The company's retention measures and standards focus on high-performing managers and customer-facing employees (for example, customer service, sales). The HR functions are currently working on a variety of other talent measures that may eventually be included in the bonus calculation.

Of course, the entire effort will be seen as window dressing if the weighting assigned to these measures is not significant enough to focus managers' attention. Ideally, human capital measures should be audited both internally and externally so managers do not manipulate the results. If creative accounting is possible with well-established financial control measures, then there is an even greater risk that managers could alter results with innovative people measures.

SUMMARY

This chapter explored the critical influence of the management group on the success of human capital management and the HR function. It is impossible for an HR program to be successful without the positive and supportive influence of the management group. The target groups for action include the top managers who must demonstrate their commitment to HR through resource allocation. Middle managers, who support HR in a variety of ways, are ideal targets for partnership relationships with the HR staff. First- and second-level managers must support and reinforce the objectives of the HR programs. Without this reinforcement, programs will not be as successful as they should be. This chapter outlined a variety of strategies to work effectively with all of these groups, with specific emphasis on three key strategies: developing partnerships, conducting a special workshop for managers, and tying bonus plans to human capital measures. These critical strategies should have a very high payoff of increased commitment and support.

NOTES

1 Chip R. Bell and Heather Shea, *Dance Lessons: Six Steps to Great Partnerships in Business & Life* (San Francisco: Berrett-Koehler Publishers, 1998).

2   Dana G. Robinson and James C. Robinson, *Strategic Business Partner: A Critical Role for Human Resource Professionals* (San Francisco: Berrett-Koehler Publishers, 2005).

3   Sarah Gerdes, *Navigating the Partnership Maze: Creating Alliances that Work* (New York: McGraw-Hill, 2003).

4   Stephen Bates, "Linking People Measures to Strategy," *Research Report R-1342-03-RR* (New York: The Conference Board, 2003).

5   Ibid.

———————————————◄O►———————————————

A P P E N D I X   A

Self-Test: How Results-Based Are Your Human Resources Programs?

A SURVEY FOR MANAGERS AND EXECUTIVES

Select the response that best describes the situation in your organization and circle the letter preceding the response.

1. Performance measurements have been developed and are used to determine the effectiveness of:
   A. All human resources (HR) functions
   B. Approximately half of the HR functions
   C. At least one HR function
2. Major organizational decisions:
   A. Are usually made with input from the HR function
   B. Are usually made without input from the HR function
   C. Are always made with input from the HR function
3. The return on investment in HR is measured primarily by:
   A. Intuition and perception by senior executives
   B. Observations by management and reactions from participants and users
   C. Improvements in productivity, costs, time, quality, and so on.
4. The concern for the method of evaluation in the design and implementation of HR programs occurs:
   A. Before a program is developed

This survey is adapted from previous versions developed by the author and published in several publications.

B. After a program is implemented

C. After a program is developed but before it's implemented

5. New HR programming, without some formal method of measurement and evaluation, is:

A. Never implemented

B. Regularly implemented

C. Occasionally implemented

6. The costs of specific HR programs are:

A. Estimated when the programs are implemented

B. Never calculated

C. Continuously reported

7. The costs of absenteeism and turnover:

A. Are routinely calculated and monitored

B. Have been occasionally calculated to identify problem areas

C. Have not been determined

8. Benefit/cost comparisons of HR programs are:

A. Never developed

B. Occasionally developed

C. Frequently developed

9. In an economic downturn, the HR function will:

A. Be retained at the same staffing level, unless the downturn is lengthy

B. Be the first to have its staff reduced

C. Go untouched in staff reductions and possibly be increased

10. The cost of current or proposed employee benefits are:

A. Regularly calculated and compared with national, industry, and local data

B. Occasionally estimated when there is concern about operating expenses

C. Not calculated, except for required quarterly and annual reports

11. The chief executive officer (CEO) interfaces with the senior HR officer:

A. Infrequently; it is a delegated responsibility

B. Occasionally, when there is a pressing need

C. Frequently, to know what's going on and to provide support

12. On the organizational chart, the top HR officer:

A. Reports directly to the CEO

B. Is more than two levels removed from the CEO

C. Is two levels below the CEO

13. Management involvement in implementing HR programs is:

A. Limited to a few programs in its area of expertise

B. Nil; only HR specialists are involved in implementing programs

C. Significant; most of the programs are implemented through management

14. The HR staff involvement in measurement and evaluation consists of:
   A. No specific responsibilities in measurement and evaluation with no formal training in evaluation methods
   B. Partial responsibilities for measurement and evaluation, with some formal training in evaluation methods
   C. Complete responsibilities for measurement and evaluation; even when some are devoted full time to the efforts, all staff members have been trained in evaluation methods

15. Human Resources Development (HRD) efforts consist of:
   A. A full array of courses designed to meet individual's needs
   B. Usually one-shot, seminar-type approaches
   C. A variety of education and training programs implemented to improve or change the organization

16. When an employee participates in an HR program, his or her supervisor usually:
   A. Asks questions about the program and encourages the use of program materials
   B. Requires use of the program material and uses positive rewards when the employee meets program objectives
   C. Makes no reference to the program

17. Variable pay programs (bonuses, incentive plans, etc.):
   A. Exist for a few key employees
   B. Are developed for all front-line employees
   C. Are developed for most employees, line, and staff

18. Productivity improvement, cost reduction, or quality improvement programs:
   A. Have not been seriously considered in the organization
   B. Are under consideration at the present time
   C. Have been implemented with good results

19. The results of HR programs are communicated:
   A. Occasionally, to members of management only
   B. Routinely, to a variety of selected target audiences
   C. As requested, to those who have a need to know

20. With the present HR organization and attitude toward results, the HR function's impact on profit:
   A. Can be estimated but probably at a significant cost
   B. Can be estimated (or is being estimated) with little additional cost
   C. Can never be assessed

SCORING AND INTERPRETATION

Scoring: Assign a numeric value to each of your responses to the questions based on the following schedule: 5 points for the most correct response, 3 points for the next most correct response and 1 point for the least correct response. Total your score and compare it with the analysis that follows.

The following schedule shows the points for each response:

POINTS	POINTS	POINTS	POINTS
1. A—5	6. A—3	11. A—1	16. A—3
B—3	B—1	B—3	B—5
C—1	C—5	C—5	C—1
2. A—3	7. A—5	12. A—5	17. A—1
B—1	B—3	B—1	B—3
C—5	C—1	C—3	C—5
3. A—1	8. A—1	13. A—3	18. A—1
B—3	B—3	B—1	B—3
C—5	C—5	C—5	C—5
4. A—5	9. A—3	14. A—1	19. A—3
B—1	B—1	B—3	B—5
C—3	C—5	C—5	C—1
5. A—5	10. A—5	15. A—3	20. A—3
B—1	B—3	B—1	B—5
C—3	C—1	C—5	C—1

Rationale: Explanations for responses are given below.

1. Performance measurements should be developed for all HR functions. When that is not feasible, at least a few key measures should be in place in each function; otherwise, a function may be perceived to be unimportant or not a contributor.

2. *Major* organizational decisions should always involve input from the HR function. HR policymakers should have input into key decisions where human resources issues are involved.

3. Whenever possible, the investment in human resources should be measured by improvements in productivity, costs, time, and quality. Although other types of evaluation are important and acceptable, these measures are the ultimate proof of results.

4. The concern for the method of evaluation should occur before the program is developed. In the early stage, some consideration should be given to how the data will be collected and how the program will be evaluated. This ensures that the proper emphasis is placed on evaluation.

5. Human resources programs should never be implemented without a provision for at least some type of formal method of measurement and evaluation. Otherwise, the contribution of the program may never be known.

6. The costs of all individual HR programs should be continuously monitored. This provides management with an assessment of the financial impact of these programs at all times—not just when the program is implemented.

7. Because these important variables represent a tremendous cost for the organization, the cost of absenteeism and turnover should be routinely calculated and monitored.

8. Benefit/cost comparisons of HR programs should be conducted frequently, particularly when a significant investment is involved. Even rough estimates of payoffs versus estimated costs can be helpful in the evaluation of a program.

9. In an economic downturn, the HR function should go untouched in staff reductions or possibly increased. Ideally, the function should enhance the bottom line by improving productivity or by reducing costs that can keep the organization competitive in the downturn.

10. Because employee benefits represent a significant portion of operating expenses, they should be routinely monitored and compared with national data, industry norms, and localized data. Projected future costs of benefits should also be periodically reviewed.

11. The CEO should frequently interface with the executive responsible for human resources. It is important for the CEO to know the status of the HR function and receive input on employee satisfaction and commitment. This provides an opportunity for the CEO to communicate concerns, desires, and expectations to the HR executive. Frequent meetings are important.

12. The top HR executive should report directly to the CEO. A direct link to the top will help ensure that the HR function receives proper attention and commands the influence necessary to achieve results.

13. Management involvement in the implementation of HR programs should be significant. Management's participation in the design, development, and implementation of HR programs will help ensure its success. Managers should be partners with the HR staff.

14. The entire HR staff should have some responsibility for measurement and evaluation. Even when some individuals are devoting full time to the effort, all staff members should have a partial responsi-

bility for measurement and evaluation. Staff members should also have training in measurement and evaluation methods. This comprehensive focus on evaluation is necessary for successful implementation.

15. Human Resources Development (HRD) efforts should consist of a variety of learning and development programs implemented to increase the effectiveness of the organization. HRD involves more than just courses or short seminars. It should include a variety of instructional methods aimed at improving organizational effectiveness.

16. When an employee completes an HR program, his or her supervisor should require use of the program material and reward the employee for meeting or exceeding program objectives. This positive reinforcement will help ensure that the appropriate results are achieved.

17. Variable pay programs should be considered for most employees, both line and staff. Although usually limited to a few key line employees, these programs are appropriate for all employees. Through gainsharing plans, bonuses, and incentives, employees can see the results of their efforts and are rewarded for their achievement. This is fundamental to a results-oriented philosophy for the HR function.

18. Productivity improvement, cost reduction, or quality-improvement programs should be implemented in many locations and should achieve positive results. These programs are at the very heart of bottom-line HR contributions and have been proven successful in all types of settings. The HR function should take the lead to ensure that these programs are administered efficiently and are successful.

19. The results of HR programs should be routinely communicated to a variety of selected target audiences. Different audiences have different interests and needs, but several important audiences should receive information on the success of HR programs. While some may need only limited general information, other audiences need detailed, bottom-line results.

20. The impact of the HR function on the bottom-line contribution can be estimated with little additional cost. If measurement and evaluation is an integral part of the organization's philosophy, data collection can be built into the human resources information system. It adds a little cost but should generate data necessary to calculate program results.

Analysis of Scores

Total score should range from 20 to 100. The higher the score, the greater your organization's emphasis on achieving results with the HR function.

Score Range	Analysis of Range
81–100	This organization is truly committed to achieving results with the HR function. Additional efforts to improve measurement and evaluation for the HR function is not needed. There is little room for improvement. All HR subfunctions and programs appear to be contributing to organizational effectiveness. Management support appears to be excellent. Top management commitment is strong. This HR department is taking the lead in measurement and evaluation by showing the contribution it can make to the organization's success. Chances are, it is a vital part of an effective and successful organization.
61–80	This HR department is strong and is contributing to organizational success. The organization is usually better than average in regard to measurement and evaluation. Although the attitude toward achieving results is good, and some of the approaches to evaluation appear to be working, there is still room for improvement. Additional emphasis is needed to make this department continue to be effective.
41–60	Improvement is needed in this organization. It ranks below average with other HR departments in measurement and evaluation. The attitude toward results and the approach used in implementing HR programs are less than desirable. Evaluation methods appear to be ineffective and action is needed to improve management support and alter the philosophy of the organization. Over the long term, this department falls far short of making a significant contribution to the organization.
20–40	This organization shows little or no concern for achieving results from the HR function. The HR department appears to be ineffective and improvement is needed if the department is to survive in its current form and with its current management. Urgent attention is needed to make this department more effective in contributing to the success of the organization.

This instrument has been administered to HR managers and specialists attending local, regional, national, and international HR conferences. The typical respondent has been the individual responsible for the HR function. The instrument was administered anonymously and the respondents were provided ample time at the beginning of the meeting to complete it. Questions and answers were allowed during the administration of the instrument. To date, there have been more than 1,500 usable responses representing an average score of 62.9 with a standard deviation of 7.3.

The score can reveal much about the status of human resources in an organization and the attitude toward measurement and evaluation. A perfect score of 100 is probably unachievable and represents utopia; however, it is the ultimate goal of many HR executives and a few other key executives. On the other extreme, a score of 20 reveals an ineffective organization, at least in terms of the contribution of the HR function. The organization will probably not exist for long in its current form or with the current staff.

Although the analysis of these scores is simplistic, the message from the exercise should be obvious. Achieving results from the HR function is more than just evaluating a single program or service. It represents a comprehensive philosophy that must be integrated into the routine activities of the HR staff and supported and encouraged by top executives.

CEO Commitment Checklist

Obtaining top executive commitment is an important challenge for the HR staff, particularly as the staff attempts to change current practices to focus additional attention on results. This instrument is designed to assess the current level of CEO commitment and identify areas where additional commitment is needed. It also triggers critical areas that may be important for the executives to understand and explore. Consequently, it is recommended that top executives complete the checklist. It often opens their eyes in terms of possibilities and expectations.

Respond to the following checklist:

YES NO

____ ____ 1. Do you have a corporate policy or mission statement for the HR function?

____ ____ 2. Do you hold executives/managers accountable for the HR metrics in their areas of responsibility?

____ ____ 3. Does your organization set goals for employee participation in formal learning and development programs?

____ ____ 4. Is your involvement in HR more than written statements, policy communications, or speeches?

____ ____ 5. Did you attend an external development program in the past year?

____ ____ 6. Do you require your immediate staff to attend development programs each year?

____ ____ 7. Do you occasionally conduct a portion of an internal development program conducted for other managers?

_____ _____ 8. Do you require your managers to be involved in the HR process?

_____ _____ 9. Do you require your managers to develop a successor?

_____ _____ 10. Do you encourage operating managers to participate in formal learning and development programs?

_____ _____ 11. Do you require your management to support and reinforce HR programs?

_____ _____ 12. Do you require your top managers to have development plans?

_____ _____ 13. Is your HR manager's job an attractive and respected executive position?

_____ _____ 14. Does the HR manager report directly to you?

_____ _____ 15. Does the HR manager have access to you regularly?

_____ _____ 16. Do you frequently meet with the HR manager to review HR problems and progress?

_____ _____ 17. Do you frequently meet with the HR manager to review the effectiveness of HR programs?

_____ _____ 18. Do you require a proposal for a major new HR program?

_____ _____ 19. When business declines, do you resist cutting the HR budget?

_____ _____ 20. Do you frequently speak out in support of HR?

_____ _____ 21. Do you often suggest that HR staff help solve performance problems?

_____ _____ 22. Do you require the HR department to have a budget and cost control system?

_____ _____ 23. Is the HR department required to evaluate each program?

_____ _____ 24. Do you ask to see the results of at least the major HR programs?

_____ _____ 25. Do you encourage an ROI evaluation for major HR programs?

CEO Commitment Checklist
Interpretation of Results

Number of Yes Responses	Explanation
More than 20	Excellent top management commitment, usually tied to a very successful organization.
More than 15	Top management commitment is good, but still some room for additional emphasis.
More than 10	Adequate top management commitment, much improvement is necessary for the HR department to be effective.
Less than 10	Almost no top management commitment; HR barely exists in the organization.

Question for Discussion:

How can top management commitment for HR be improved?

_____

_____

_____

_____

_____

_____

_____

_____

Index

About the Author

Jack J. Phillips, Ph.D., is a world-renowned expert on human capital measurement and evaluation and is chairman of the ROI Institute, Inc. Through the Institute, Dr. Phillips provides consulting services for Fortune 500 companies and major organizations in forty-one countries. He conducts workshops for major conference providers throughout the world. Phillips is also the author or editor of more than thirty books and more than one hundred articles.

His expertise in human capital measurement and evaluation is based on almost thirty years of corporate experience in five industries (aerospace, textiles, metals, construction materials, and banking). Phillips has served as training and development manager at two Fortune 500 firms, senior HR officer at two firms, president of a regional bank, and management professor at a major state university.

His background in HR led Phillips to develop the ROI Methodology™—a revolutionary process that provides bottom-line figures and accountability for all types of training, performance improvement, human resources, learning, coaching, consulting, quality, and technology programs.

Phillips's most recent books include *Proving the Value of HR,* SHRM 2005; *The Leadership Scorecard*, Elsevier Butterworth-Heinemann 2004; *The Human Resources Scorecard,* Butterworth-Heinemann 2001; *The Consultant's Scorecard,* McGraw-Hill 2000; *Managing Employee Retention,* Butterworth-Heinemann, 2003; *Return on Investment in Training and Performance Improvement Programs,* Second Edition, Butterworth-Heinemann 2003; *The Project Management Scorecard,* Butterworth-Heinemann 2002; *Accountability in Human Resources Management,* Gulf Professional Publishing 1996; and *Performance Analysis and Consulting,* ASTD 2000. Phillips is series editor for ASTD's In Action casebook series and serves as series editor for Butterworth-Heinemann's Improving Human Performance series. His books have been published in twenty-five languages.

Phillips has undergraduate degrees in electrical engineering, physics, and mathematics, a master's degree in decision sciences from Georgia State University, and a Ph.D. in human resource management from the University of Alabama. In 1987 he won the Yoder-Heneman Personnel Creative Application Award from the Society for Human Resource Management.

Jack Phillips can be reached at 350 Crossbrook Drive, Chelsea, AL 35043 or by phone at (205) 678-8101, fax at (205) 678-8102, or e-mail at jack@roiinstitute.net.

Learn more about additional titles from AMACOM at
www.amacombooks.org

Designing Dynamic Organizations: A Hands-on Guide for Leaders at All Levels by Jay Galbraith, Diane Downey, and Amy Kates $29.95

Effective Succession Planning: Ensuring Leadership Continuity and Building Talent from Within, Third Edition, by William J. Rothwell $65.00

HR from the Heart: Inspiring Stories and Strategies for Building the People Side of Great Business by Libby Sartain with Martha I. Finney $24.95

How to Develop Essential HR Policies and Procedures by John H. McConnell $49.95

Outsourcing for Radical Change: A Bold Approach to Enterprise Transformation by Jane C. Linder $35.00

The 7 Hidden Reasons Employees Leave: How to Recognize the Subtle Signs and Act Before It's Too Late by Leigh Branham $24.95

The New Workforce: Five Sweeping Trends That Will Shape Your Company's Future by Harriet Hankin $27.95

The ROI of Human Capital: Measuring the Economic Value of Employee Performance by Jac Fitz-enz $29.95

**Available: At your local bookstore, online,
or by calling 800-250-5308**

Savings start at 35% on **Bulk Orders** of 5 copies or more!
Save up to 55%!
For details, contact AMACOM Special Sales
Phone: 212-903-8316. E-mail: SpecialSls@amanet.org